New Zealand and
SECOND WORLD WAR

New Zealand and the
SECOND WORLD WAR
The people, the battles and the legacy

Ian McGibbon

Hodder Moa Beckett

National Library of New Zealand Cataloguing-in-Publication Data

McGibbon, I. C. (Ian C.), 1947–
New Zealand and the Second World War / Ian McGibbon.
1st ed.
Includes bibliographical references and index.
ISBN 1-86958-954-8
1. World War, 1939-1945—New Zealand.
940.5393—dc 21

Published in 2004 by Hodder Moa Beckett Publishers Ltd
[a member of the Hodder Headline Group]
4 Whetu Place, Mairangi Bay
Auckland, New Zealand

Designed and produced by Hodder Moa Beckett Publishers Ltd
Printed by Tien Wah Press Ltd, Singapore

Front cover: Members of the 28 (Maori) Battalion in Faenza, Italy in 1945. War History Collection, Alexander Turnbull Library, F-8057-½-DA

Back cover: Soldiers leaning out of a train as they depart to serve in the Second World War. Alexander Turnbull Library, F-161218-½

Contents

Acknowledgements

I am grateful to the following publishers, literary executors or authors for permission to include extracts from their published works: Quality Publications, for the extract from Pat Kane's *A Soldier's Story* on p.20; Reed Publishing (NZ) Ltd and David Grant, *Out in the Cold*, p.30; Mrs B.L. Gray, *Spitfire Patrol*, p.34; Sir Henare Ngata, letter by Captain Parekura Tureia, from *28 Maori Battalion, 23rd National Reunion*, p.43; Allan Yeoman, *The Long Road to Freedom*, pp.43–4; Dan Ford and The Warbird's Forum (www.warbirdforum.com), Vic Bargh's recollections, p.57; Scott Rennie, Frank Rennie's *Regular Soldier*, p.60; David Higham Associates, Sir Howard Kippenberger's *Infantry Brigadier*, p.67; HarperCollins Ltd, London, *For Five Shillings A Day*, p.72; Reed Publishing (NZ) Ltd, Eve Ebett's *When the Boys Were Away*, p.91; Ngaio Press, *Up the Blue*, p.104; John Crawford, *North to Taranto*, p.105; Martin Middlebrook, *Convoy*, p.109; The Caxton Press, Denis Glover's *D-Day*, p.115; Sir Geoffrey Cox, *The Road to Trieste*, p.118; Keith Mulligan, *Kittyhawks and Coconuts*, p.123. Wilson & Horton Newspapers Ltd kindly gave permission for the publication of two cartoons by Gordon Minhinnick. I have made every effort to trace the owners of copyright and to acknowledge sources. My thanks too to the Alexander Turnbull Library, the Australian War Memorial, the Royal New Zealand Navy Museum, the RNZAF Museum, Queen Elizabeth II Army Memorial Museum and Archives New Zealand for permission to publish images in their possession.

I am indebted to the late Ian Wards for reading several of my drafts and for his encouraging comments. Professor David McIntyre, Grant Crowley, Dr Malcolm McKinnon, Dr Gavin McLean and John Crawford (the Defence Historian) also read drafts of some or all of the manuscript and made helpful suggestions. Peter Cooke and Hilary Stace provided invaluable help in the gathering of illustrations. I am indebted to Sir John White for allowing me to use photographs from his collection. John Martin also assisted by providing material relating to his father's service. Thanks too to Linda Cassells, formerly of Hodder Moa Beckett, for encouraging me to undertake the project and to the former Chief Historian Jock Phillips and his successor, Bronwyn Dalley, for their support. My employer, the Ministry for Culture and Heritage, kindly gave me the opportunity to get away from office distractions to write the book in Los Angeles. My wife Sonia's support is much appreciated.

Finally I am grateful for the help given by Jeanette Cook, who edited my text with much skill, Chris O'Brien, who drew the maps, and Jane Hingston and the team at Hodder Moa Beckett, who very efficiently saw the manuscript through the publication process.

ICM

Preface

The Second World War is the most extensive and most destructive conflict ever to engulf the world. It took the lives of 50 million people including one in every 150 New Zealanders, in some way or other affected almost everyone on the planet, and shaped the world that we have lived in ever since. In this great conflagration, which began with cavalry charging tanks and ended with the explosion of nuclear weapons over cities that opened a new era in warfare, New Zealand played a role relatively as substantial as that of any other country, though of course a nation of 1.6 million people could make but a minor impact on the course of events overall. The war of 1939 to 1945 demanded of New Zealanders their greatest national effort, and they were to be found making a contribution in almost every theatre, on the land, on the sea and in the air, as well as on the home front.

New Zealand, Australia and the United Kingdom were the longest involved of the democratic states that took part in the Second World War. They fought for all but three of the 2179 days now accepted as encompassing the Second World War from the German invasion of Poland on 1 September 1939 to the capitulation of Japan on 15 August 1945. Alongside them for this whole period were the many non-self-governing territories of the British Empire, including India, that were involved as a result of the British government's decision. New Zealand's war, like that of all the other parts of the British Commonwealth and Empire, was longer than those of both major European adversaries — Germany and Italy — but not that of Japan, if account is taken of that country's undeclared war with China dating from 1937, which would become part of the wider Pacific War from December 1941.

New Zealand's war was also global. This was because of the scope of its interests and the nature of its war effort. The war effort was developed within a security system focused on preserving the British Commonwealth and Empire, which encompasssed both the colonial territories controlled by the United Kingdom and the self-governing Dominions. This Commonwealth/Imperial framework would, after December 1941, be subsumed within a wider Allied effort led by the United States. Although unable to maintain large forces in peace time, New Zealand did possess well-motivated, self-reliant and determined men who, as the First World War experience had proved, made good soldiers. In the technical arms — the navy and the air force — the advantages of channelling such men through the British services were manifest, more especially if they were to fight in theatres close to the United Kingdom. As a result New Zealanders percolated through the Royal Navy and Royal Air Force, and were to be found everywhere those services operated.

Far from reflecting an unthinking willingness on New Zealand's part to subordinate its interests to those of the United Kingdom — as some commentators today claim — New Zealand's effort was founded in a strong sense of shared interests between the two countries. To be sure there was disagreement and dissension at times, but New Zealand kept the goal in sight and, above all, played for the team. Only by a collective effort did it see any hope of achieving its primary war aims, and that effort was necessarily led by the United Kingdom in the first two years of the war, when the essential character of New Zealand's war effort was settled.

This is a brief account of New Zealand's war. The purpose is to set New Zealand's effort within a wider context, to explain why it participated so fully in the war and in particular theatres, and to describe briefly the various activities of the armed forces and the civilians at home. The Official History of New Zealand's involvement in the Second World War, published between 1949 and 1986, took up 48 volumes; to encompass such a wide-ranging effort in one short volume has inevitably meant an attenuated coverage of the various campaigns in which New Zealanders were involved. In particular, the lack of space available has made it difficult to do justice to the New Zealanders' contribution to the Royal Navy and the Royal Air Force and to expand on their various efforts in these services. Readers wanting more detailed treatment of this and other aspects of New Zealand's war may refer to the official histories, which in many facets of the war are still the most authoritative source. Excellent histories of particular campaigns or aspects of New Zealand's involvement and biographies of participants have also been produced, and these are listed in the Bibliography. Suggestions for further reading are provided in references.

14 Mar – German troops occupy Czechoslovakia

31 Mar – UK and France offer guarantee to Poland

7 Apr – Italy invades Albania

14 Apr – New Zealand discusses defence plans with Britain and Australia in Wellington

17 May – NZ National Military Reserve established

Australian War Memorial, PO2018.002

German troops move down a road past staff cars during the invasion of Poland.

Prologue

As dawn broke on 1 September 1939, Polish soldiers stationed on their country's long frontiers with Germany came under attack.

For weeks these soldiers had lived in a state of tension amid mounting reports of German concentrations of tanks, guns and infantry on the other side of the border. Hopes of a diplomatic settlement of the crisis that had arisen between the two countries persisted, and only recently had they been ordered to dig in and throw up barbed wire entanglements.

As German troops entered Poland all illusions disappeared. Above the advancing tanks and infantry, aircraft filled the sky, squadron after squadron heading in orderly patterns towards the Polish capital, Warsaw. Before long the scream of dive-bomber sirens added to the cacophony of war. 'Case White' — a deliberate attack by Germany on its neighbour — had begun.

During the day, German radio announced that Poland had attacked Germany and that Germany was taking counter-measures. 'Evidence' of this Polish provocation had been carefully provided: during the night German special forces, disguised as Poles, had 'attacked' a German radio station, leaving the Polish-uniformed corpse of a concentration camp inmate to indicate responsibility. By the end of the day the German 'counter-attack' had taken German forces, 1.7 million strong, deep into Polish territory, and the hapless Polish forces were falling back in growing confusion in many areas.

Germany's invasion of Poland brought to a head a crisis that had beset Europe in the previous six years. But it had much deeper roots. The German-Polish war was a new round in a contest for dominance of the European continent that had begun in the previous century with the rise of Prussian power and the unification of Germany. The proclamation of the German Empire in 1871 had highlighted the emergence in central Europe of a power of growing economic and military strength. Over the next 20 years careful diplomacy alleviated the impact of this development on the balance of power. But from the early 1890s Germany embarked on a very different course, unsettling the existing framework of European security. This culminated in the outbreak, in 1914, of a war more destructive than any that had preceded it, a conflict that pitted Germany and its ally Austria-Hungary (later joined by the Ottoman Empire) against the British, French, Japanese and Russian empires, and belatedly the United States.

The outcome of this 'war to end all wars' provided the essential background to the new conflict that broke out in 1939. After four years of unprecedented bloodletting Germany and its allies had been forced into submission in 1918. Its armies had, at least in the west, been defeated in the field, its population had been brought to the brink of starvation by the Allied blockade. As revolutionary ferment wracked its cities, Kaiser Wilhelm II, the embodiment of German militarism in Western perception, had abdicated and a republic had been proclaimed with its seat at Weimar in central Germany.

At least in the eyes of the Western powers, the Great War seemed to have settled the issue of the German challenge in Europe. The peace settlement they imposed on Germany at Versailles in 1919 reinforced this impression. The Treaty of Versailles set strict limits on the military forces Germany could maintain, imposed a huge reparations bill on it as the power adjudged responsible for the war (the 'war guilt' clause), and alienated parts of German territory. It was a harsh peace — though not as harsh as that the Germans had imposed on their defeated Russian adversary in 1918.

In reality the First World War settlement rendered a renewed German challenge very likely. Few Germans were reconciled to the judgement imposed on them for what they perceived as a defensive war. Their soldiers had, they believed, bravely and successfully defended the borders of Germany for four long years and had marched home to acclaim following the armistice. Many of these soldiers were susceptible to the notion that Germany's plight derived from a 'stab in the back' by politicians in Germany itself. Brutalised by their experience, they remained at war with the society that had produced this situation.

Despite French hopes to the contrary, the limitations on Germany's power imposed by the Treaty of Versailles had not fundamentally altered its position. Some territory had been lost, but it remained essentially intact, with a large population and great industrial capacity. The means remained for a future reassertion of German power should a government emerge with the goal of reversing the verdict of Versailles.

Much depended on the ability of the Weimar Republic to consolidate its position. Although it successfully withstood numerous challenges during the 1920s, not least severe financial crises arising from the reparations burden, democracy foundered as the Great Depression battered Germany. The economic chaos of the early 1930s opened the way for challenges to the existing order from extremist groups on both left and right.

Of the right-wing groups the most significant was the National Socialist (Nazi) Party led by the Austrian-born Adolf Hitler. Ruthless, intelligent, and determined, Hitler had achieved some notoriety as an orator and leader of a failed coup in Munich in 1923. He tapped a pervasive

Adolf Hitler.

sense of grievance among Germans over the Versailles settlement, particularly the 'war guilt' clause of the treaty. His strident attacks on Jews as the root cause of Germany's problems, his fanatical opposition to communism and his vision of a Germany restored to greatness and expanding eastwards appealed to many. Nevertheless, it is unlikely that the Nazi Party would have made sufficient headway to secure power had it not been for the economic catastrophe that befell Germany in the early 1930s. Enough people now voted for the party to give credibility to Hitler's efforts to secure the chancellorship. His successful achievement of this goal in January 1933 sounded the death knell of the ailing Weimar Republic.

Hitler's personality and aims were crucial to the events leading to the outbreak of war in 1939. He had been a corporal on the Western Front during the First World War, but had emerged from the experience without the aversion to war common to many of his contemporaries. Imbued with a crude Social Darwinist belief that international relations, like nature, were no more than the survival of the fittest, he set about restoring Germany's military capacity. As a first step he instituted a programme of clandestine rearmament, building on efforts that had been proceeding even under the Weimar Republic to circumvent provisions of the Versailles Treaty. Evidence of this rearmament programme, eventually openly proclaimed in March 1935, confronted the Western democracies with a direct challenge.

London and Paris did not take up this challenge. A feeling that the Versailles settlement had been too harsh, a desire to avoid any repetition of the bloodletting of the First World War, a willingness to accept Hitler's assurances that his aims were limited, a belief that Hitler was amenable to conciliatory treatment and provided a bulwark to communism, and a sense of national demoralisation on the part of France at least — all contributed to the unwillingness of the Western powers to confront Germany at a time when it was too weak to resist. This irresolution was apparent when Hitler, in March 1936, took a major risk by sending troops into the

Adolf Hitler addresses a vast crowd of Nazi stormtroopers in the city square of Dortmund.

Australian War Memorial, 044580

Rhineland, an area that had been demilitarised under the Versailles Treaty. The failure of the Western powers to react yet again to an overt breach of the peace settlement only served to embolden him.

After successfully incorporating Austria within the Reich in March 1938, Hitler turned on Czechoslovakia, one of a number of states created in 1919 from the defeated Austro-Hungarian Empire and the only functioning democracy in central Europe. He demanded the incorporation of the large German-speaking area of that country — the Sudetenland — into the Reich. When the Czechs inevitably baulked — their main defences against Germany lay in the Sudetenland — he set in motion an invasion plan. Once again, Britain and France sought security in conciliation and concession. British Prime Minister Neville Chamberlain, after visiting Hitler, returned to London proclaiming faith in the dictator's word and 'peace in our time'. A wave of relief that war had been averted swept Europe. At a four-power conference in Munich in September 1938 — attended by Britain, France, Germany and also Italy — Czechoslovakia was dismembered. In a settlement that was later condemned as a shameful purchase of peace at the expense of a small democratic power that was not even represented at Munich, the Sudetenland was ceded to Germany.

Events soon dispelled hopes that Hitler's appetite had now been satiated. In March 1939 he ordered the occupation of the remainder of Czechoslovakia. The German troops advancing into Prague brutally exposed the bankruptcy of the conciliatory Anglo-French approach and the falsity of Hitler's claims to be concerned only with incorporating German-speaking areas within the Reich. Resolved at last to draw a line in the sand, the British and French governments announced that they would resist attacks on Belgium, Holland and Switzerland. More significantly, on 31 March they extended a unilateral guarantee of support to Poland should it be attacked (and did the same later to Greece and Romania as well). Had they enlisted the support of the Soviet Union, a powerful

deterrent to German action might have been created. But the half-hearted British diplomatic efforts in this direction during 1939 did not impress the Soviet dictator, Josef Stalin. His decision for the time being to turn away from the idea of attempting to constrain Germany by force would have a major bearing on the outbreak of the Second World War.

The guarantee to Poland assumed central importance because that country was clearly in Hitler's sights. Ominously, pressure had been mounting on Warsaw since the beginning of the year to agree to a revision of Versailles provisions that had given Poland a substantial territorial gain at Germany's expense. This was the Polish Corridor, a strip of former German land that connected Poland with the Baltic Sea near Danzig, a German city that had been placed under international administration. This arrangement left East Prussia divided from the rest of Germany. Perhaps over-confident of their ability to repel a German attack, the Poles did not bow to German demands.

Hitler did not find this Polish resistance unwelcome, so determined was he to have a war. On 22 August 1939 he pulled off a diplomatic coup, concluding a non-aggression pact with Stalin that shocked the world. Not only had two erstwhile arch-enemies come together but also their collusion had rendered war seemingly inevitable. Only the deterrent effect of the Anglo-French guarantees now stood between Hitler and his goal of subjugating Poland, for few expected the Polish armed forces, outnumbered nearly three to one, to stand up to the *Wehrmacht* for long. But Hitler discounted the guarantees. With the Soviet Union neutralised, he confidently expected the British and French to back down if he forced the issue — a fatal misperception of the reasons behind their abandonment of appeasement. Nine days after the Russo-German agreement, his troops marched into Poland. When, to Hitler's consternation, France and Britain stood by Poland as promised, Germany found itself once again at war with an Anglo-French coalition. A new round in the contest for dominance in Europe had begun.

Europe in 1939

1 Sep – Germany
invades Poland

3 Sep – New Zealand,
along with Britain
and France, declares
war on Germany

5 Sep – PM Michael Savage
tells nation 'Where Britain
goes, we go'

12 Sep – Enlistment for
a Special Force begins

A paperboy sells newspapers on 2 September 1939 with a billboard proclaiming the outbreak of war. New Zealand's declaration of war in 1939 contrasted starkly with its entry to the First World War. In 1914 King George V's declaration of war on Germany (made on the advice of the British Cabinet) had automatically committed all his territories and possessions, including the self-governing Dominions. New Zealand and the other Dominions had had a choice only as to the extent of their participation.

New Zealand Goes to War

Late in the evening of Sunday 3 September 1939 New Zealand faced its gravest crisis. For the first time, the issue of peace or war confronted its leaders — not because some power threatened to invade its territory but because of the conflict that had begun three days earlier in eastern Europe. When Britain had demanded an immediate halt to Germany's invasion and the withdrawal of its forces from Poland, the possibility of war became very real for New Zealand and all other members of the British Commonwealth of Nations.

Huddled around their short-wave radios, many New Zealanders heard a weary and resigned Chamberlain state that Berlin had ignored the British ultimatum, due to expire at 11 a.m. GMT and that in consequence Britain was now at war with Germany. None of those who listened to this statement had any illusions about what it meant for their own country, despite its distance from the scene of action. Most assumed, correctly, that their government would quickly associate New Zealand with Britain and that for the second time in quarter of a century New Zealand would be at war with Germany.

Official word of Britain's declaration of war reached Wellington eight minutes before midnight on 3 September. By this time, the government had determined New Zealand's course. In a document dated 3 September Governor-General Lord Galway proclaimed a state of war between New Zealand

17

and Germany to have existed from the time of the expiry of the British ultimatum — this was 9.30 p.m. New Zealand time.[1] Shortly before 2 a.m. on 4 September New Zealand advised London of its declaration of war.[2] New Zealand then went to war at the same moment as Britain — not twelve hours before because of the time zone difference as a later prime minister would claim.[3]

New Zealand was one of the first democratic states to enter the Second World War — alongside Britain, Australia and France. After a few days' neutrality Canada and South Africa would join them. The huge British and French empires, including India, had no choice in the matter. They were automatically involved by the declarations of war of the governments in London and Paris respectively.

New Zealanders went to war with resignation. For many, conflict had long seemed inevitable: 'We all realised a showdown was coming,' one later recalled.[4] Relief that the issue had at last been faced and that a stand would now be made against the aggressor mingled with trepidation about what lay ahead. Memories of the tragic impact of the 1914–18 war ensured that there would be no repetition of the enthusiasm that had marked New Zealand's entry to that earlier conflict.

Only a few stood against the war tide. From the very outset pacifists objected to New Zealand's involvement in the war. Within a short time, communists joined them, their initial confusion having been resolved by instructions from Moscow to oppose what was dismissed as an imperialist war. But these dissenting groups, both very small, had no impact on public opinion.

Three main influences lay behind the strong consensus supporting the government's action — a desire to stand shoulder-to-shoulder with kith and kin in the United Kingdom, a concern for New Zealand's economic and physical security, and a recognition of the implications for international order of the successive crises that preceded the German onslaught on Poland. Each on its own might have impelled New Zealand into the war; together they amounted to a powerful basis for action, and ensured almost universal acceptance of the government's decision for war.

Kith and kin

New Zealand's relationship with the United Kingdom was of paramount importance. Its roots lay in the nature of New Zealand colonisation, the flow of mainly British immigrants seeking to improve their lot that changed the character of the country in the second half of the nineteenth century. Predominantly English and Scots, they had no sense of grievance with the United Kingdom (as did many Irish immigrants to other Dominions and the United States) and they retained close ties with and affection for the 'Mother Country'. Indeed even second or third generation New Zealanders remained proud of their Britishness. They did not find it incompatible with a developing sense of national identity that left them often bemused and even slightly contemptuous of aspects of life in Britain: 'We were quietly proud to call ourselves British but at the same time feeling a bit sorry for the old fashioned state of the Britain we knew little about.'[5]

Such feelings did not, of course, apply to the indigenous population of New Zealand, the Maori. Some had resisted British colonisation, only to be defeated by a combination of imperial and colonial forces — an outcome that was followed by confiscation of land that still deeply rankled among affected tribes, especially in the Waikato and Taranaki. Sickness and demoralisation had by late in the nineteenth century reduced the Maori population to an extent that some were predicting their eventual extinction. But a revival began from the 1890s that would bring Maori numbers back up to about 90,000 in 1939 — just under six per cent of the total population. They were not exactly ignored by successive governments; but nor did they exercise much influence on national attitudes or policy.

Self-interest buttressed sentimental ties with Britain. The introduction of refrigeration in the 1880s had allowed New Zealand to compete effectively in the British market for the sale of meat and dairy products, which, with wool, became the staple of the New Zealand economy in the next century and beyond. New Zealand's

Imperial War Museum, QG2835

Ships of the Royal Navy in line ahead: HMS *Renown, Rodney, Warspite* and *Malaya*. They formed part of the British battlefleet, which was the lynchpin of imperial defence in 1939.

farmers looked to Britain as the source of their prosperity. In the late 1930s, 80 per cent of its exports went there, while British imports and capital dominated the domestic economy. Preferential trading arrangements and lack of alternative markets tightened this economic link with Britain.

Defence considerations powerfully reinforced these ties. New Zealand had developed under the shield of the Royal Navy. So strong was this navy in the early years of New Zealand's European settlement that settlers had few concerns about their external security other than perceiving the danger of hit-and-run raids if the British Empire came into conflict with some other power. This picture began to change in the 1880s. The relative strength of the Royal Navy declined as other powers, both in Europe and outside it, built up their fleets. New Zealand's increasingly fervent imperialism reflected the

insecurity that this changing strategic outlook engendered among a small population on the periphery of the Empire.

Although sometimes now depicted in negative terms as lacking independence, this approach had a more complex basis than mere subservience. New Zealanders proudly saw themselves as junior partners in a powerful entity, one they believed to be beneficial to the world. They recognised the vital importance of imperial unity. Only by standing together had Britain and its Dominions been able to surmount the challenge presented by Germany in 1914–18.

The First World War enhanced the status of the Dominions, both within the British Empire and internationally. At its conclusion they signed the Treaty of Versailles and joined the new League of Nations. The Dominions' autonomy and equality of status with

Michael Savage (centre) and WE Parry (to his right) surrounded by well-wishers on the night of the Labour Party's success in the general election in 1935.

20

Britain was proclaimed in 1926 and, five years later, formalised by the British Parliament in the Statute of Westminster. To be sure, New Zealanders had little liking for this development. Convinced that they had all the self-government they needed, they feared a weakening of the all-important imperial unity. Like Australia, New Zealand refrained from adopting the operative sections of the Statute of Westminster.

Even if it hesitated to change the forms of New Zealand's relationship with London, the New Zealand government in 1939 was not averse to altering the substance by asserting the rights of Dominion status in practice. The Labour Party that Michael Savage, an Australian by birth, had led to victory four years earlier had long since toned down much of its early anti-imperialist rhetoric. Its leading members, notably Savage, the Scots-born Deputy Prime Minister Peter Fraser and English-born Walter Nash, the Minister of Finance, acknowledged the importance to New Zealand of its close relationship with Britain. But they did not find this incompatible with expressing a firm New Zealand viewpoint internationally — or even differing with the British government in public. This approach set them apart from their predecessors, who had generally confined criticism to the privacy of imperial councils.

In aligning New Zealand with Britain, Savage's Cabinet exercised the fundamental right of a sovereign community to go to war (the clearest sign possible of equality of status with Britain). It knew that standing with Britain in 1939 held no political dangers. Indeed these would have come from any hesitance in supporting Britain, given the mood of the people. New Zealand's intention had, in any case, been signalled well in advance: 'If the Old Country is attacked we are too...,' Nash had stated in London on 16 May 1938, and he promised that New Zealand would 'assist her to the fullest extent possible'.[6] Most New Zealanders applauded such assertions. The fact that war came in September 1939 without an attack on the British Isles made no difference to their belief in the rightness of the declaration of war.

When on 5 September the ailing Savage — suffering from the cancer that would kill him early the following year — spoke to the nation by radio, he encapsulated New Zealand's war strategy in terms that struck a chord with his British-oriented audience: 'Both with gratitude for the past, and with confidence in the future, we range ourselves without fear beside Britain. Where she goes, we go, where she stands, we stand.'[7]

Strategic influences

New Zealand was propelled towards war by strategic considerations rooted in its geographical and economic circumstances and its military weakness. The country's attention was drawn towards Europe, where the security of its chief market, the basis of its economy, was threatened. The long sea route between New Zealand and that market, across the Pacific and Atlantic Oceans via the Panama Canal, also had to be protected. This demanded sufficient ships (and increasingly aircraft) and bases to command the seas in the relevant areas.

New Zealand could never hope to undertake this task on its own. Nor did it have to, for Britain had an equal interest in keeping the sea lane open. It also had the means — the Royal Navy and its bases throughout the world. Between the wars New Zealand had consistently opposed anything that appeared likely to weaken that navy's capacity to protect merchant shipping.

Paradoxically New Zealand's concern for its physical security in the Pacific also drew its attention to Europe — for the same reason. New Zealand alone could not hope to repel a full-scale invasion by a major power. It looked to British naval power, mainly concentrated in Europe, to deter such attack. But Europe was far distant — and, as New Zealanders realised, attack could come from a power located outside Europe. Increasingly, concern focused on Japan. Seventy million strong in 1937, this power cast a dark shadow over the South Pacific.

Opened to the West only in the mid-nineteenth

century, Japan had responded by embarking on a vigorous programme of modernisation. It was the first state in Asia to industrialise, and its economic development soon translated into growing military power. With this rising strength came ambitions to create a sphere of influence in the region — a development that inevitably presented a challenge to the European powers that controlled much of the region either directly or through economic means. Successful wars against China and Russia had brought Japan an incipient empire with the acquisition of Formosa (now Taiwan) and Korea.

In 1905 in the Tsushima Strait, which lies between Japan and Korea, the Japanese Navy annihilated a Russian fleet sent from the Baltic Sea to relieve Russian forces besieged in Port Arthur. This dramatic event first awakened New Zealand to growing Japanese power (until then Russia had been the bogey). Fears that Japan might become an enemy in the future began to influence defence thinking in Wellington. But for the time being Japan was a friendly power, having allied with the British Empire in 1902. As the Royal Navy increasingly concentrated in the North Sea to meet the threat to imperial naval supremacy posed by the burgeoning German fleet, Britain made clear that imperial security depended on continuing this arrangement with Japan, despite the disadvantages this caused in relations with the United States. An emerging Japanese-American rift foreshadowed future problems.

Japan joined the coalition against Germany in 1914, and a Japanese cruiser helped escort the New Zealand Expeditionary Force that departed for Europe. Japanese warships later patrolled the South Pacific on the lookout for raiders and made visits to New Zealand. Nonetheless the First World War experience only increased New Zealand's worries about Japanese intentions. The problems the Royal Navy would face if ever engaged simultaneously in both the Pacific and Europe had been amply demonstrated. Japan had also taken the opportunity to advance its interests in China and, to New Zealand's unease, moved closer to the South Pacific by

seizing the German islands north of the equator (and later retaining them as mandates of the League of Nations). Concern increased when, in 1921, the Anglo-Japanese Alliance came to an end — a development New Zealand had resisted because of the fear that it would hasten Japanese enmity at a time when the British Empire was unprepared for conflict in the Pacific. Heavily indebted to the United States because of its war effort, Britain had no choice but to bow to American pressure to end the arrangement.

The Singapore strategy

By 1920 the Japanese fleet ranked third in the world. Only Britain and the United States surpassed Japan in naval strength. New Zealand inevitably looked to the former for strategic cover, but straitened financial circumstances prevented the stationing of a British fleet in Pacific waters capable of meeting Japan's fleet. If Japan made trouble, Britain would have to send its main battlefleet from Europe to deal with it. But for the time being that fleet could not even operate in the Pacific, for the simple reason that none of its most modern battleships could dock there. Before the plan could be implemented, therefore, the necessary facilities would have to be created, and secured from pre-emptive Japanese attack. It was decided a base would be built at the strategically sited Singapore.

Political changes in Britain affected the project almost from the outset. New Zealand protested when work on it was briefly abandoned in 1924 and delayed in 1929, and tried to encourage completion by contributing £1 million towards its costs. The stop-start progress ensured that the base remained little more than a hole in the ground when the international outlook in Asia darkened in the early 1930s. Aggressive actions by Japan in China from 1931 prompted the British authorities to speed up work at Singapore. Yet although the dock facilities were formally opened in 1938, much remained to be done to make the base operative and secure from attack.

New Zealand and Australian leaders knew that a base alone, even if strongly defended, would not suffice to contain Japanese sea power. As the situation in Europe deteriorated in the 1930s, Britain's ability to send a battlefleet to Singapore began to erode. Both the number of ships that could be sent and the time they would take to reach the base — a critical issue if it were not to fall to Japanese attack before their arrival — became steadily less precise. Clearly the Royal Navy would struggle to deal with Japan if engaged with a resurgent Germany. When Italy also emerged as a potential enemy in the mid-1930s, the strategic problem facing Britain became almost insoluble.

Despite the growing uncertainties, the Singapore strategy still underpinned New Zealand's defence policy in 1939. It had little option but to rely on it. The United States had the power to counter Japan at sea but seemed virtually paralysed by isolationist sentiment. To rely on American power to counter Japanese aggression against British territory did not seem sensible. Some reassurance could nevertheless be drawn from the presence of a superior US battlefleet at San Diego from April 1939, with a major base at Pearl Harbor in the Hawaiian Islands that would lie on the flank of any Japanese move to the south. Far from encouraging American movement into the South Pacific in the late 1930s, even though the development of civil aviation routes offered a means to do this, New Zealand did the opposite. Worried about compromising Commonwealth civil aviation interests and New Zealand's sovereignty over certain islands, it resisted American encroachment into the region.

New Zealand took some steps to meet the increased potential threat that would arise from delay in implementing the Singapore strategy. It invited British and Australian representatives to Wellington in April 1939 to discuss defence plans in the South-West Pacific. They agreed to bolster the defences of Fiji and to create a line of air reconnaissance between the Cook Islands and New Guinea. Even so, the strategic requirements of a Commonwealth-focused defence policy left such measures ultimately of secondary importance to ensuring that the main Commonwealth concentration of force, inevitably in Europe, remained undefeated.

The brutal logic of New Zealand's strategy meant that its own physical security must take second priority to that of Britain. If the main British forces were defeated in Europe, New Zealand would lose its protective shield; if, on the other hand, these forces were undefeated, nothing that happened in the Pacific would be anything more than contingent, even the occupation of New Zealand.

Carl Berendsen, the government's trusted adviser on international affairs, comments on defence policy in 1938:

> *The main defence of this Dominion is not here but in Europe. Quite apart from sentiment, if Britain falls or is materially weakened nothing that can be done in this country can be of any real effect against an attack by a first-class power. We must, therefore, to the utmost extent of our means and our power, assist in British defence as the first line of New Zealand defence.*[8]

New Zealand went to war with Germany in 1939 to help preserve the only security system that it believed capable of meeting its defence requirements.[9]

New Zealand opposes appeasement

Awareness of the issues involved strongly reinforced sentiment and strategy in impelling New Zealanders towards war. Indeed, the way New Zealand had responded to international developments in the preceding three years left it little room for manoeuvre if it were to remain consistent. The stance it had taken implied a willingness to stand up and be counted and to use force if necessary to combat aggression.

Many New Zealanders favoured war because of their view of Hitler's regime. They abhorred the way the Nazis had come to power, the increasing militarism of the Nazi state, and the harsh treatment meted out to perceived enemies of the state, not least the Jews. But such negative attitudes would not alone have been enough to drive New Zealand to war. Germany's challenge to the international order provided the main impetus. Fraser made this clear two days after the declaration of war: the conflict, he declared, was 'between two diametrically opposed conceptions of international relationships, between reason and force'. Most New Zealanders accepted in September 1939 that a stand had to be taken against Germany. Some feared it had come too late to prevent what Fraser warned would be 'the triumph of violence and the trampling underfoot of all that we hold dear'.[10]

Although concerns centred on Germany, several other powers contributed to the general international crisis in the late 1930s. Indeed Japan's challenge to the existing order pre-dated the advent of the Nazi regime in Germany. In 1931, acting without orders from Tokyo, Japanese troops protecting Japanese interests in the Manchurian railway in China had taken control of the whole province. Subsequent international efforts to secure a withdrawal were unavailing. Ignoring condemnation of its actions, Japan created the puppet state of Manchukuo with the former Chinese emperor as its nominal head. The growing military domination of the Japanese government was

Japanese soldiers march through a viaduct into Nanking in December 1937.

Australian War Memorial, PO2164.001

24

reflected in further aggressive action against Chinese interests early in 1932 when Japanese troops fought Chinese near the international settlement in Shanghai. Japan's decision to withdraw from the naval limitation treaties that had underpinned Pacific security since 1921 caused further anxiety, as did reports that it was building bases in its Micronesian mandates. In 1936 Japan joined Germany in the Anti-Comintern Pact.

An incident at a bridge near Peking in July 1937 provided Japan with a pretext to launch full-scale, though undeclared, war against China. Japanese troops occupied Peking and pushed southwards against opposition weakened by internal division between the Kuomintang and the communists. The scale of the atrocities committed by the Japanese shocked the world, not least the rape of the Kuomintang capital Nanking following its capture in December 1937, in which Chinese deaths ran into the tens of thousands. But China, as Germany would find later with the Soviet Union, was not susceptible to quick defeat; however out-gunned and out-generalled, Chinese forces remained in the field, falling back into the interior before the advancing enemy. The 'China Incident', as Japan termed it, was the opening round in a conflict that would eventually merge with that launched by Hitler in Europe.

Italy, under Fascist dictator Benito Mussolini, had also embarked on a course that was bound to unsettle the international system. Dreaming of reconstituting a

Italian dictator Benito Mussolini reviews a military parade in the Libyan town of Benghazi.

25

Roman Empire in Africa, Mussolini had launched an aggressive adventure in Abyssinia in 1935; four years later Italy would also occupy Albania. From 1936 Italian troops — and German — provided covert assistance to rebel forces under Francisco Franco seeking to overthrow the Republic of Spain. All these developments provided the essential backdrop to Hitler's crusade against the hated Versailles settlement that would culminate in the invasion of Poland.

British and French unwillingness to firmly oppose violations of international agreements and law caused growing concern in Wellington. This hesitance derived in part from strategic weakness. Britain faced obvious dangers, for example, in risking the enmity of Italy, which would make implementing the Singapore strategy more difficult. The extent of German rearmament, especially in air forces, had quickly put the British and French at a perceived disadvantage; avoiding hostilities while rearmament programmes closed the gap seemed imperative. But at the heart of the Anglo-French approach lay an overriding desire to avoid another European conflagration. It rested on the belief that the dictators could be bought off, that their aims were limited and could be accommodated by conciliation and negotiation — an appeasement strategy that merely reinforced Hitler's contempt for the Western powers and fed his appetite for expansion.

Labour ministers in Wellington strongly opposed appeasement. Determined to assert a principled approach to international affairs, they soon found themselves at odds with the British government. In strongly opposing appeasement, they echoed criticism in Britain itself, the most prominent by Winston Churchill. At the Imperial Conference in London in 1937 Savage bemoaned Britain's pursuit of 'a policy of improvisation on the policy of peace at any price'.[11] New Zealand had viewed with dismay the non-interventionist stance adopted by London and Paris towards the Spanish Civil War. As German and Italian assistance tipped the balance

in favour of Franco's rebels, Western support for the beleaguered republic remained confined to volunteers, among them some motivated and adventurous New Zealanders who made their way to Spain on their own initiative.

To meet the challenge posed by the dictatorships, New Zealand looked to the League of Nations. Previous governments had paid lip service to the world body. They had taken part in its activities, while always placing more faith in imperial defence arrangements. Savage's government, by comparison, actively promoted it as an alternative basis of security. Implicit in its support for the League was the idea that states might have to back words with force — to 'fight in sorrow for the good of the future', as Nash conceded in 1935.[12] The government praised the League's limited response to the Abyssinian crisis in applying economic sanctions — 'the apparent corpse came to life'[13] — but watched with disappointment as they failed to deflect Italy from its course.

In Labour's eyes, the League's inadequacies stemmed directly from the attitude of members — their lack of will to use the collective security provisions in its covenant. In 1936 New Zealand advanced proposals for reforming the covenant, but to no avail. It was too late for such action. Survival now dominated the approaches of the leading Western powers. Any attempt to apply the principles of the covenant would only impose new commitments far beyond their ability to cover with the forces at their disposal. Although New Zealand continued to proclaim the League, it too eventually muted its calls for action as war loomed. The concept of collective security would remain as a beacon for the future.

Although discredited, the appeasement approach had at least demonstrated the desire of the leading Western powers for peace. When war in Europe came, few in New Zealand doubted that it had been precipitated by Germany or that their country was not morally committed to confronting Hitler. A combination of sentiment, strategy and issues, then, propelled New Zealand into war in September 1939 as the result of a crisis on the other side of the globe. For the second time in a quarter of a century the invasion by Germany of one of its neighbours created a situation in which New Zealanders stood united in their belief in the necessity for forcible action. They had no doubt that the European conflict was New Zealand's war.

War aims

New Zealand entered the war in 1939 with one fundamental aim: to ensure its own security. Given its circumstances in 1939, this depended, it seemed, on the British Commonwealth-Empire emerging at least undefeated from the conflict. If New Zealand had a positive aim, it wanted to see established an international order that provided security to all states; this appeared to demand an effective system of collective security. Since it had gone to war because of the violation of Poland's sovereignty, the restoration of that sovereignty represented another New Zealand goal, one that developments on the battlefield quickly brought to the fore.

In contrast to 1914, Germany did not immediately launch a massive onslaught on France. It concentrated on defeating Poland, leaving only weak forces to cover western Germany. No major Anglo-French push ensued to threaten the German position. Without succour, the hapless Poles crumpled in the face of German attacks from three directions. To compound Poland's agony, on 17 September Russian forces lunged forward to occupy the eastern part of the country. They acted in accordance with a secret protocol of the Russo-German Non-Aggression Pact that had been a major inducement to Stalin to accept a deal with his Nazi counterpart.

The Polish capital, Warsaw, fell to German forces on 27 September. Nine days later all resistance ended.

Having secured his military objectives in the east, Hitler immediately mounted a peace offensive in the west. In a speech to the Reichstag on 6 October, he offered an olive branch to his Anglo-French opponents.

The British government dismissed this overture out of hand. Only a German and Russian withdrawal from Poland would have allowed a settlement based on the restoration of Poland's sovereignty, and this seemed out of the question. Ironically — in light of New Zealand's pre-war approach — and somewhat naïvely, New Zealand leaders found fault with this firm British stance. Above all, they wanted to avoid a repetition of the stalemate that had developed in the First World War. In 1939, the utter destruction of Nazism was not yet a war aim. Anything short of the unconditional surrender of Germany implied the need for compromise. Savage advised the British government of New Zealand's view that 'no door should even at the present juncture be closed that might lead to a peaceful solution whether by international conference or any other feasible means'.[14]

The war continued, though in a curiously non-belligerent way. Unlike the First World War, no Western Front had developed. The French and Germans remained behind their fortifications. As in 1914, a new British Expeditionary Force (BEF) crossed the English Channel. It helped cover the unfortified Franco-Belgium border. Neither side sent their air or naval forces to attack the other's territory seriously, and only occasional clashes occurred. This 'phoney war' would last well into 1940. For the time being the high seas remained the main arena of conflict as marauding German surface raiders and U-boats threatened Allied shipping.

8 Nov – NZ Centennial
Exhibition opens

16 Nov – Major-General Bernard
Freyberg accepts offer to command 2
New Zealand Expeditionary Force

30 Nov – Soviet for
invade Finla

HMS *Achilles* after the Battle of the River Plate, showing the blistered gun barrels.

RNZN Museum, AUG0196

15 Dec 1939

1 Jan 1940

13 Dec – HMS *Achilles* takes
part in Battle of River Plate

17 Dec – Empire Air Training
Scheme established

25 Dec – Freyberg arrives in NZ

A New Zealand War Effort

For 16-year-old Arthur Hunt, a seaman boy on the New Zealand light cruiser *Achilles*, war became a reality soon after dawn on 13 December 1939. A bridge messenger, he was removing empty cocoa mugs from the bridge when, shortly after 6 a.m., the alarms began rattling. 'Shoving the tray anywhere it would fit, I rushed to my action station,' he would later recall; while he did so he saw 'a tremendous spout of water' shoot high out of the ocean on the ship's starboard side. As he ran, so did the rest of the crew, their boots clattering on the deck. To the cheers of members of the gun crews manning the ship's secondary guns, one of them raced aft to the mainmast to hoist a New Zealand ensign.

Shortly after sunrise smoke on the horizon had indicated the presence of an unknown vessel. Quickly identified as a pocket battleship, it was initially thought to be the *Admiral Sheer* but was in fact the *Admiral Graf Spee*. Those on *Achilles* braced for action. It was the first time most of them had found themselves in this position, but few had time to reflect on their predicament as they rapidly took up their stations. For most, like Hunt, this would be in the bowels of the ship, cut off from any sight of the action, though not its sound. They heard the cruiser's engines strain as it worked up to full power, the crash of its first salvo going off at 6.21 a.m., and the muffled whumph of *Graf Spee*'s shells exploding in the sea.

Doreen McGibbon Collection

Arthur Hunt (right) with companion Robert Batt in early 1940.

Seaman Boy Arthur Hunt recalls the action against the Graf Spee:

> *My action station was in the forward magazine and as I changed my boots for the felt slippers that reduced the danger of sparking the cordite, my foot clattered on the deck like a Morse key. Yet real fear, like delayed concussion, did not hit many of us until after the action.*
>
> *As the doors closed behind us we realised that if a hit did necessitate sectional flooding of the ship we would drown behind the doors of the magazine....*
>
> *Down in the magazine it was impossible to know whether each great shudder and muffled crash was an enemy hit or the snarl of our own guns. We went on loading and firing, loading and firing.*[15]

Achilles did not face the German ship alone. She formed part of a three-cruiser group that had been patrolling the congested shipping lanes on the approaches to the River Plate, a tempting target for the German raider. With her were the heavy cruiser HMS *Exeter* and the light cruiser HMS *Ajax*, the latter carrying the commander of the force, Commodore Sir Henry Harwood.

Although *Graf Spee* faced three British ships, she had a major advantage. Her six 11-inch guns outranged those she faced — *Exeter*'s six 8-inch guns and her consorts' 6-inch guns. In attacking her, the British ships risked being destroyed before they closed to within effective range of the enemy. But Harwood did not hesitate. Immediately *Graf Spee* was sighted, *Exeter* altered course to separate herself from *Ajax* and *Achilles*. By attacking from two directions, the British cruisers would make the enemy gunners' task more difficult, forcing them either to divide attacks.

After a few minutes shifting between targets, *Graf Spee* concentrated her main armament on *Exeter* and within 10 minutes had badly damaged her. Shifting one of her 11-inch gun turrets back to the smaller cruisers, which had been scoring hits with their sixteen 6-inch guns, she straddled *Ajax* three times. The *Graf Spee*'s 5.9-inch guns were also firing at them, albeit without serious effect. Although the British cruisers had managed to inflict some damage on their adversary, they were in danger of being annihilated. Further hits on *Exeter* left her struggling to remain in action, with more than 60 of her crew dead or dying.

Achilles meanwhile kept up rapid fire. None of *Graf Spee*'s shells found its mark, but at 6.40 a.m. one exploded nearby. 'As I look,' one officer recalled, 'a huge column of water lifts from right under our ship's side, just to the right of the bridge. With it comes the crash of red hot metal tearing through armour plate, the sound of shattering glass, the cries of men in mortal agony.'[16] Flying splinters mangled part of the director control tower; others tore through the bridge, slightly wounding the captain, Edward Parry. They killed four ratings, and injured another eight men, two seriously.

Achilles' gunnery officer Lieutenant Richard Washbourn, describes the aftermath of the near miss on his ship:

I was only conscious of a hellish noise and a thump on the head which half stunned me. I ordered automatically: 'A.C.P. [After Control Position] take over.' Six heavy splinters had entered the D.C.T [Director Control Tower]. The right-hand side of the upper compartment was a shambles. Both W/T ratings were down with multiple injuries.... AB Sherley had dropped off his platform, bleeding copiously from a gash in his face and wounds in both thighs. Sergeant Trimble, RM, the spotting observer, was also severely wounded.... AB Shaw slumped forward on to his instrument, dead, with multiple wounds in his chest.... The rate officer, Mr Watts, quickly passed me a yard or so of bandage, enabling me to effect running repairs to my slight scalp wounds which were bleeding fairly freely.... When the medical party arrived to

remove the dead, I learned for the first time that both Telegraphist Stennet and Ordinary Telegraphist Milburn had been killed outright. I discovered at the same time that Sergeant Trimble had uncomplainingly and most courageously remained at his post throughout the hour of action that followed the hits on the D.C.T., although seriously wounded.[17]

Even as *Achilles* suffered this blow, the character of the action was changing. Showing a curious lack of offensive spirit, *Graf Spee*'s commander opted not to fight it out. As the German ship turned away and headed towards the River Plate estuary, the action became a chase. After a hectic 82 minutes, the guns fell silent, bringing relief to *Achilles'* sweating gun crews, who had fired more than 200 broadsides. During the rest of the day *Achilles* and *Ajax* shadowed *Graf Spee*, with occasional flurries of action as it turned on its pursuers. By nightfall *Graf Spee* had taken refuge in Montevideo harbour, in neutral Uruguay.

Under international law the *Graf Spee*'s stay in Montevideo could only be brief. As British naval reinforcements rushed towards the scene in readiness for her expected emergence, the heavy cruiser HMS *Cumberland* joined *Ajax* and *Achilles* off the River Plate. The men waited with trepidation: 'We were all as strung as tennis rackets,' one of them recalled, 'wondering at which hour the now refreshed battleship would come snarling into sight, her pulverising guns trained on the three terriers waiting to harry her.'

But the fighting spirit of the enemy commander had been sapped. Judging his chances of escape to be non-existent and unwilling to go down fighting, he took his ship out of the harbour and scuttled it, later taking his own life. The sailors watched with awe and delight as the *Graf Spee* 'erupted in great flashes of orange flame and black smoke, her ruptured steel bursting open in crashing chaos that mingled into a deafening hiss as scalding steam and white hot metal struck the water'.

Achilles' crew observe the scuttled *Admiral Graf Spee*.

The crew of *Achilles* march down Wellington's Lambton Quay on 2 April 1940.

People throughout the Commonwealth greeted with joy the news of this victory, the first substantial success against the Germans in the war. It greatly boosted morale. When *Achilles* returned to New Zealand in early 1940, she received a hero's welcome. Seaman Boy Hunt was one of those who marched up Queen Street in Auckland: 'I think that was the moment most of us realised the magnitude of our victory.'[18]

More than three months after New Zealand had entered the war, the navy had drawn first blood — in spectacular fashion. *Achilles* had performed above expectations in the New Zealand navy's first battle. But she represented only a relatively small part of the war effort that New Zealand had been busy shaping while she had been ploughing the seas off South America in the previous four months. Mobilising the economic and military resources of the Dominion took time.

On a war footing

In September 1939 New Zealand had rapidly passed from a peace to a war footing, thanks to pre-war preparatory work by a small group of officials in the Organisation for National Security. At the highest level, the war brought no change. The government did not follow the First World War precedent of forming a coalition with the opposition party in parliament. The National Party remained out in the cold, despite its strong support for making the fullest possible contribution to the war effort. Party politicking continued.

Those opposed to involvement in the war itself inevitably came into conflict with a government determined to suppress anything likely to undermine the national consensus in favour of its declaration of war. Pacifists felt the brunt of this approach immediately. When Ormond Burton, a decorated First World War veteran, tried to express opposition to the war in a public forum, he was quickly arrested, as were other pacifists who did the same.

Later, communists also found themselves at odds with the government, which banned their paper, *People's Voice*, in 1940.[19] Their association with the Soviet Union seemed to put them on the side of the enemy. Not only had Stalin participated in the assault on Poland but also, in November 1939, he unleashed his forces against neighbouring Finland — an action that led to the Soviet Union's expulsion from the League of Nations. It also led to the possibility of outright conflict with the Anglo-French coalition as the coalition looked for means of helping the Finns in their heroic, and for a time successful, struggle to repel the invading Soviet forces.

Food supplies to Britain

A more pressing problem was to determine how New Zealand might best contribute to the Commonwealth war effort. The experience of the previous war indicated that it would take the united effort of the whole grouping to achieve a positive outcome. In that conflict the Dominion contribution to the imperial effort had been substantial: of the British Expeditionary Force's 60 divisions in 1918, 10 were provided by the Dominions. But the Dominion effort had not been confined to the battlefield. Of major importance to the eventual outcome was the sustenance of the British population and industry by the provision of food and raw materials.

This First World War experience indicated that New Zealand could make an effective contribution in both military and non-military spheres. The latter was the easier, for it demanded no major changes to New Zealand's economic structure or trading patterns. Just by doing what it already did well, New Zealand could help to overcome the potential threat to Britain's capacity to fight deriving from its dependence on imported foodstuffs. During the earlier conflict, Britain had made bulk purchase arrangements with New Zealand that greatly benefited New Zealand. Farmers enjoyed stable prices at a favourable level. A repeat of this arrangement in the new war seemed very much in New Zealand's interest. No time was wasted, therefore, in establishing a new bulk purchase agreement for meat and dairy products.

This not only raised farming to the status of a vital industry but also made the efficient delivery of the produce to Britain a key requirement. Workers in the chain of supply — especially freezing and waterside workers — played an important part in the process; so, too, did the crews of the ships that plied between New Zealand and the United Kingdom. The merchant marine had a vital, if largely unsung, role to play in the war effort. Keeping the produce flowing to Britain placed a substantial demand on New Zealand manpower resources and confronted the government with a problem that would persist for most of the war — determining priorities between military and non-military efforts.

The naval effort

In the military sphere, New Zealand's response also followed similar lines to that of 1914. Of the three services, the best placed to make an immediate contribution was the navy. Constituted as the New Zealand Division of the Royal Navy, it had as its main striking force two modern light cruisers, *Achilles* and *Leander*. These were borrowed from the Royal Navy, as were many of the personnel needed to crew them — nearly half those on board, including the captain, in the case of *Achilles*.[20]

Legal, moral and strategic considerations all impelled New Zealand immediately to place its naval forces at the disposal of the Admiralty. To hold back from such control warships whose crews had heavy British representation would have been awkward. Furthermore, New Zealand recognised the importance of co-ordinating the limited naval resources of the whole Commonwealth, and using available vessels where they could be most effective to the overall plan.

Even before the outbreak of war, plans for one of the cruisers to join the Royal Navy's America and West Indies

Squadron had been implemented. Departing on 29 August, *Achilles* was well out into the Pacific when the war began. Meanwhile, *Leander* headed north-west for Fanning Island, lying just north of the equator; she carried an infantry platoon that would guard the cable station there from any German attempt to cut the link (as had occurred in the First World War). On her return, she settled down to patrol New Zealand waters, on the lookout for any of the 80 German merchant ships believed to be in the Pacific, all potential raiders. Other naval tasks included putting in place examination stations to control access to ports, installing defensive armaments on merchant ships to give them some means of defending themselves, refitting the liner *Monowai* as an armed merchant cruiser and requisitioning three trawlers to increase minesweeping capacity.[21]

The air force contribution

New Zealand in 1939 possessed a small air force, which, like the navy, was organised on British lines and used British equipment. Development had been slow at first, but greater government support in the late 1930s had led to several important developments. Wing Commander Ralph Cochrane, a British officer brought out to New Zealand in 1936 to report on requirements, produced a blueprint that emphasised local defence needs. To provide a strike capacity against raiders in the South Pacific, the government in 1937 ordered twin-engine Vickers Wellington bombers from the United Kingdom and began developing facilities in New Zealand.

New Zealand also helped bolster imperial air capacity by sending selected personnel for short service

An RNZAF Vickers Vildebeeste at Rongotai in 1936. The other biplanes are a Waco, a de Havilland DH89 Rapide and an Avro 626 Tutor.

commissions in the Royal Air Force (RAF) — an arrangement that had the advantage of building up a pool of experienced personnel for the Royal New Zealand Air Force (RNZAF). Several schemes had by 1935 sent about a hundred to Britain for service mainly as pilots, and numbers increased in the next four years. In May 1939 New Zealand agreed to provide 600 pilots and 650 observers/air gunners per annum.[22] Apart from these government arrangements, numerous volunteers made their own way to Britain to join the Royal Air Force.

When war came in September 1939, the RAF had about 550 New Zealanders in its ranks — the most of any Dominion. They were the first New Zealanders in action against the enemy. One, shot down over the North Sea just two days after the declaration of war, had the dubious distinction of being the first RAF officer to fall into German hands and began a very long stint in captivity. By the end of the first week of the war, two others had lost their lives on operations and another in a training exercise — the first New Zealand fatalities of the war.

New Zealand also made a direct contribution. Flight crews had gone to Britain before the declaration of war to pick up and ferry home the first six of its new Wellington bombers. Immediately putting this plan on hold, the government offered the aircraft and crews — 16 personnel in all — to the RAF. New Zealand Flight RAF, the vanguard of many thousands that the Dominion would supply to the RAF during the course of the war, provided the nucleus of a bomber squadron.[23]

New Zealand's Wellington bombers following their provision to the RAF in 1939.

Ministry of Defence

The formation of 2NZEF

The government wasted little time in agreeing to make an army contribution, just as New Zealand had done in the First World War. It had long been assumed that in a new conflict New Zealand would follow the precedent of 1914–18 and raise an expeditionary force of about divisional strength. But the military forces were much less well prepared to implement such a plan than they had been in 1914. Compulsory military training had fallen victim to budgetary shortfalls in 1930, and was not revived even when the international situation later deteriorated. So worried had some senior citizen-soldier officers become by 1938 that they went public with their criticism of the government's apparent failure to take seriously the problems confronting the Territorial Force, the main element of the military forces. The so-called 'four colonel's revolt' had little impact on preparations,[24] but in 1939 some efforts were made to boost recruiting. Even so, the Territorial Force remained short of manpower as the war approached.

Within days of the outbreak of war, the government decided that a 6600-strong 'special military force' would

Volunteers parade at Hopuhopu camp in 1939. On the first day alone 5419 men volunteered. This tempo was not sustained, but by 5 October not quite 15,000 had signed up. Another 45,000 men would come forward in the next nine months.

be raised 'for service within or beyond New Zealand'.[25] Most assumed that it would be despatched as soon as possible to join the British Expeditionary Force in France to take part in a re-run of the First World War's Western Front, this time with the advantage of prepared positions in France's much vaunted Maginot Line. Although the initial announcement envisaged a brigade-sized force, a full division would be required if the force were to operate as a national entity. Because New Zealand did not have the facilities to train a whole division at the same time, the preparation of the force would have to be undertaken in three echelons, each of brigade strength. The first would comprise 4 Brigade.

When recruiting began on 12 September, men flocked to the colours no less eagerly than in 1914. Knowledge that world war could be extremely dangerous — one in six of those sent overseas in 1914–18 had not returned and many others had been maimed — did not deter them.

As in the previous conflict, motivations varied. A break from the monotony of civilian occupations, a desire to see the world, a sense of adventure, a chance to emulate fathers or uncles who had served in the earlier conflict, an opportunity to escape unhappy domestic situations, a sense of duty, a wish to assist kith and kin, a conception of the issues involved — all or any of these reasons could induce a person to join the queues at recruiting offices. The events of the late 1930s had left many imbued with the belief that the time had come for action if the Commonwealth was to survive in the face of Hitler's challenge. Others had more personal reasons: 'I just wanted to be accepted like other men,' one volunteer later recalled. 'It would be difficult for anyone to imagine the fervour and excitement of the time, unless he or she lived in those days. One just *had* to be part of it. Not to be in uniform invited a critical hostility, in fact. People thought you were gutless and scared, and started handing out white feathers … men got them anonymously in the mail.'[26]

Sergeant Pat Kane reflects on his reasons for volunteering for 2NZEF:

> *What motive activated me to volunteer very shortly after the declaration of war in September 1939? I can well recall those fateful words coming over Station 2YA, 'New Zealand is at war with Germany.' Although I hate the thought of war, although the prospect of trying to kill my fellow man was completely abhorrent and violence was alien to my nature, I knew in my heart and knew immediately that I had to join up. I was young, fit and without dependants. I had no excuse not to enlist.*
>
> *Perhaps it was a sense of duty, perhaps a matter of pride, perhaps it was my love of my country, which was then and still is very sincere, perhaps it was my hatred of violence. Maybe I felt I owed the younger generation a duty to do my share to preserve for them our national and British heritage. Perhaps like so many of my silent companions waiting behind the stabilised Alamein Line [in 1942] for the dawn of another day of heat, sweat, flies and boredom, I could give no single, real or truthful reason.[27]*

Those selected for the First Echelon entered camp for three months' training on 3 October. At Ngaruawahia, Trentham and Burnham, they learnt how to march, to obey orders and to endure the inconveniences of army life.

Among the trainees were a number of Maori, for they had not been excluded from volunteering. Many went on to serve with infantry battalions and other units of the division. But the government decided at an early stage that a special Maori unit should also be raised. Unlike that of the Great War, this new unit would be a combat unit, a special infantry battalion additional to those of the division. Recruiting began on 9 October.[28] Those selected for what would become 28 (Maori) Battalion were soon in training, impressing officers involved with their 'boundless and infectious enthusiasm' and 'tremendous pride in their reputation as warriors'.[29]

Despatch of the First Echelon

In announcing the raising of the special force, the government had made clear that it would be despatched only if there were no immediate threat to New Zealand. Although the primary danger to the Commonwealth lay in Europe, New Zealand could not ignore its position in the Pacific. Whereas in 1914 Japan had been an ally of the British Empire, it was now allied to Germany and a potential enemy. Some reassurance could be drawn, however, from Tokyo's response to the events of

A recruitment poster for 2NZEF.

August–September 1939. Far from joining Germany, Japan had been repelled by Hitler's accord with Stalin (achieved even as Japanese and Soviet forces were locked in a desperate battle on the Manchurian-Mongolian border). It announced that it would concentrate on settling the 'China Incident'.

New Zealand faced its first major dilemma of the war. Should it hold back 2 New Zealand Expeditionary Force (2NZEF), as the special force had soon been designated, because of a possible threat from Japan? Or should it send it to Europe to help ensure that the Commonwealth did not lose the war with Germany? The government looked to Commonwealth discussions in November 1939 for answers. Deputy Prime Minister Peter Fraser, who had assumed a key role in New Zealand's war direction as Savage declined, set off for London to take part. A man of considerable strength of will — his opposition to conscription had brought him a spell in prison for sedition in 1917 — he was an able debater with a ready grasp of issues, well read on international affairs and above all a strategist.[30]

Winston Churchill figured largely in these talks. The First Lord of the Admiralty again (as in 1914), he oversaw the service that held the crucial role in imperial defence. He set about allaying Australian and New Zealand concerns, painting a very optimistic picture. He not only discounted the likelihood of war with Japan but also argued that Britain could handle such a situation because of the brighter outlook in the Mediterranean. Italy's decision not to align itself with Germany had come as a relief. So long as the Anglo-French coalition did not suffer a major reverse in France, Italy could be expected to hold its hand, leaving a substantial part of the British fleet free to proceed to the east if necessary, as promised in 1937 (and again as recently as April 1939).

As for the other leg of the Singapore strategy, Churchill described the Singapore base as a fortress that could only be taken after a siege of 'at least four or five months' by an army of 50,000 personnel. The cautious Japanese, he maintained, would never embark on 'such a mad enterprise'. He assured the Dominion leaders that 'the defence of Australia and New Zealand, and of Singapore as a stepping stone to these two Dominions', was the second priority after defeating the principal opposing fleet.[31] In short, their defence would take precedence over British interests in the Mediterranean.

Without authoritative information about the situation in Singapore, Fraser was not well placed to probe these confident assertions about British strategy. But Churchill's persuasive rhetoric left him convinced that the question of despatching 2NZEF was a matter of balancing risks. A strong Commonwealth effort in Europe would help prevent the reverse that might induce Japan — and Italy — to throw in their lot with Hitler. Quite apart from the question of the threat posed by Germany to New Zealand's interests, it would be false strategy to let a potential threat prevent New Zealand from helping to meet an actual danger, the more so because of the importance of the European situation to the implementation of the Singapore strategy, upon which any Pacific defence would depend.

On Fraser's advice, the government decided to despatch the First Echelon as soon as it was ready. Announcement of this decision on 22 November 1939 caused a ripple across the Tasman, for the Australian government found itself under pressure to follow suit. New Zealand's failure to consult its Australian counterpart before acting left a sour taste in Canberra mouths.

New Zealand's support of Britain is often simplistically depicted in quid pro quo terms; that is to say, New Zealand would help the United Kingdom so as to create a moral commitment of British help should New Zealand itself be threatened. But New Zealand's approach rested on recognition of the need to ensure the integrity of the Commonwealth defence system as a whole. As a Dominion, New Zealand already had a moral commitment of British support; it had to help ensure that Britain was in a position to provide that support.

Freyberg's appointment

While in London, Fraser also took up the question of a commander for 2NZEF. Bernard Freyberg, a London-born but New Zealand-raised officer in the British Army, whose exploits in the First World War were renowned, quickly emerged as a strong contender. Initially commissioned in the Royal Naval Division, he had fought with almost suicidal valour at Gallipoli and on the Western Front, had won a VC and three DSOs, and had risen to the rank of brigadier-general at a comparatively young age. Having secured a permanent commission in the British Army, he seemed headed for its highest echelons when the detection of a heart murmur led to his retirement, on medical grounds, in 1937, but he had been recalled to service when war began. After interviewing him, Fraser recommended his appointment and the Cabinet duly agreed. Freyberg would command both 2NZEF and its fighting component, 2 New Zealand Division.[32]

Freyberg arrived in New Zealand late in December 1939 for talks with the government. His visit provided an opportunity to meet with the officers who would be his immediate subordinates in 2NZEF. Not all were enthusiastic about his appointment, resenting the government's recourse to an 'outsider' — a feeling that would provide a negative undercurrent in the hierarchy of 2 Division until well into 1941. For his part, Freyberg had to accept appointments over which he had had no control. Among them was James Hargest, a National Party member of parliament, who, despite being found unfit for service abroad, had used his political connections to secure appointment as a brigade commander.

Major-General Bernard Freyberg inspects troops in New Zealand before the departure of the First Echelon.

In the previous conflict, the NZEF had been made available for service under British command unconditionally. In 1939 such an arrangement no longer seemed appropriate. Freyberg requested a definition of his position vis-à-vis the British officers under whom he would serve. The directive, or 'charter', he obtained defined his role as the commander of a small national contingent. Not only would he have a duty to keep the New Zealand government fully informed of developments, but also he would have the right, if he found himself in a dispute with his superiors, to inform the government of the position — an arrangement that was bound to bring him into conflict with British superiors not fully attuned to the nuances of Commonwealth co-operation.

Freyberg left New Zealand with 2NZEF's First Echelon on 5 January 1940. As they had done twice before, in 1899 and 1914, Wellingtonians turned out to farewell the first troops being sent to an overseas war. Embarked aboard six liners, the 6529-strong force left with the British battleship HMS *Ramillies* as a reassuring consort. As agreed during Fraser's talks in London, the troops headed initially for the Middle East rather than France: 2NZEF therefore would renew New Zealand's 1914–18 association with Egypt.

Sir John White Collection

The First Echelon of 2NZEF at sea.

Empire Air Training Scheme

By the time the First Echelon set out, New Zealand had also agreed to another major effort — the provision of a greatly expanded number of airmen to the RAF. That force would need 50,000 trained aircrew each year, but Britain clearly could provide less than half this number. In October Chief of Air Staff Group Captain Hugh Saunders and Air Secretary Thomas Barrow travelled to Ottawa to take part in Commonwealth discussions aimed at overcoming the shortfall. The resulting Empire Air Training Scheme (EATS), established on 17 December 1939, provided for Canada to become the focus of a training pool through which 28,000 Dominion aircrew would flow into the RAF annually.

This agreement imposed a formidable task on the RNZAF. It had to produce 880 fully trained pilots a year, as well as sending to Canada almost 2000 more partially trained pilots, observers and air gunners. An effort on this scale, more than double that envisaged in the previous May, demanded facilities far beyond those already available in New Zealand. A factory in the Wellington suburb of Rongotai was soon turning out Tiger Moths for use in the programme.

Although EATS aircrew served in the RAF, the formation of Dominion squadrons provided a national focus. These had a majority of members from a particular Dominion. But not all aircrew from a Dominion served in such squadrons because the British insisted on flexibility of posting. As a result New Zealand's airmen were to be found scattered through many of the RAF's squadrons, not merely in the seven 'New Zealand' squadrons that would eventually be formed. The absence of Dominion wings or groups reduced the impact of the national efforts, however, and prevented Dominion officers from commanding significant national units within the RAF. An Australian historian has criticised the arrangement for reducing the contribution of the Royal Australian Air Force (RAAF), and by implication the RNZAF's contribution also, 'to that of cannon fodder'.[33] But New Zealanders found little fault with the scheme, perhaps identifying more strongly with the RAF than Australians or Canadians and being less nationalistic in their approach. Many New Zealanders had made their career in the RAF after the First World War, and now held high rank in it.

By the end of 1939 then, New Zealand had established the pattern of its contribution to the Commonwealth war effort. New Zealand would provide as much as possible of its two main resources — farm produce and personnel — to assist in meeting the threat to its interests. Whereas the provision of farm produce required no fundamental change in existing arrangements, the provision of personnel remained for the time being mainly prospective rather than immediate. Given the need to train the troops and airmen that New Zealand so readily offered, there would be a long delay before they could begin to make their presence felt at the front. Long before this, the enemy had brought the whole Commonwealth war effort into a state of jeopardy, and forced adjustments to New Zealand's plans.

Ground crews refuel de Havilland DH82A Tiger Moths used in the air training scheme. The scheme ensured a steady stream of New Zealand pilots and aircrew to Canada and the United Kingdom. Several adjustments increased the flow until 1942, when the number required began to decline. The flow of pilots to Canada was halted in June 1944, at first temporarily then permanently. In all 7002 New Zealanders passed through the Canadian schools, of the Commonwealth scheme's overall 131,000. Accidents killed 31 men. The Canadian trainees formed the bulk of the 10,000 aircrew provided by New Zealand during the course of the war to bolster the 550 already serving in the RAF in September 1939. The number serving peaked at 6127 in October 1944. Ninety per cent of these airmen served in ordinary British squadrons, the rest in seven 'New Zealand' squadrons — 75 (bomber), 485 (fighter/ fighter-bomber), 486 (fighter), 487 (bomber), 488 (night-fighter), 489 (maritime), 490 (maritime). Despite their title, all these squadrons included men of other than New Zealand nationality.

Evening Post Collection, Alexander Turnbull Library, G-49242½

Jan 1940	Feb 1940	Mar 1940	Apr 1940	May 1940

Rationing begins in UK

5 Jan – Freyberg leaves NZ with 2NZEF's First Echelon

27 Mar – Michael Joseph Savage dies and is succeeded by Peter Fraser

9 Apr – German forces invade Denmark and Norway

2 May – 2NZEF's Second Echelon leaves NZ

10 May – Germany launch blitzkrieg against Belgiur Holland and Fran

Winston Churchill becom UK Prime Minist

New Zealand naval personnel march past during a farewell parade at Parliament Buildings in Wellington on 27 April 1940 before leaving with the Second Echelon, the first of more than 4000 men who would be attached to the Royal Navy during the war.

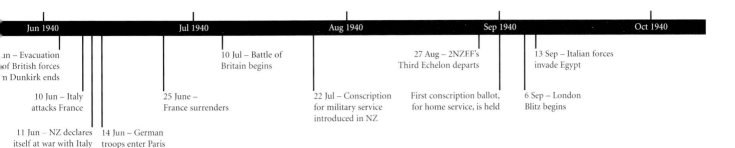

n – Evacuation
of British forces
n Dunkirk ends

10 Jul – Battle of
Britain begins

27 Aug – 2NZEF's
Third Echelon departs

13 Sep – Italian forces
invade Egypt

10 Jun – Italy
attacks France

25 June –
France surrenders

22 Jul – Conscription
for military service
introduced in NZ

First conscription ballot,
for home service, is held

6 Sep – London
Blitz begins

11 Jun – NZ declares
itself at war with Italy

14 Jun – German
troops enter Paris

Backs to the Wall

Shortly after midday on 26 March 1940, a 21-year-old New Zealand flying officer became the toast of the Commonwealth — its first fighter ace of the war. In an unequal dogfight with nine enemy aircraft, Edgar ('Cobber') Kain, flying a Hawker Hurricane, struck twice within a few minutes, sending two German fighters spinning down to earth, his fourth and fifth victims. But his triumph threatened to be short-lived. When another German fighter put shells into his engine, his burning plane also plummeted downwards. Only at the last moment did Kain leap from his cockpit, his parachute carrying him down to a rough landing. Hours later he arrived back at his base bruised, burned and wounded in hand and calf.[34]

One of a small group of New Zealanders serving in the RAF in France, Hastings-born Kain was a section commander in 73 Squadron. Among the pilots in the squadron was distant relation and fellow New Zealander Derek Kain. Crossing to France the previous September, they had operated initially with the British Expeditionary Force's Air Component, supporting the troops on the ground. Within weeks they were flying with the other British air formation in France — the Advanced Air Striking Force. Once battle was joined in earnest, they would have the task of shepherding the force's Fairey Battle light bombers to their targets among the enemy's attacking columns. But while the 'phoney war' persisted there

43

was little to do other than to intercept enemy planes intruding into French air space. A flurry of actions in November allowed Cobber Kain to become the first in his squadron to shoot one down.

Cobber Kain describes the action in which he secured his fifth victory, after his section intercepted nine enemy fighters:

> *I shouted into my 'phone 'Messerschmitts ahead. Let's go!' The Messerschmitts came at us in twos, trying to get on our tails, but it ended up with us on their tails. I got one right in my sights and gave him a full burst. Down he went in flames. A lot more manoeuvring and I found myself dead behind another. He gave me a bit of a chase but I got him. The sky seemed full of planes, darting everywhere. I was too busy to notice my companions but learned later they had done well by themselves, bagging a Nazi each. Suddenly just after I claimed my second Nazi the sky was clear. I breathed deeply then yoicks, the hood over the cockpit was ripped off. A Messerschmitt cannon had let go at me. My engine caught fire. Flames and oil came into the cockpit and I found myself in a steep dive from 24,000 feet. For a moment I thought I was out of it. I jumped....[35]*

While Kain and his colleagues were in action in France, other New Zealand airmen operated out of RAF bases in Britain. Those in Fighter Command, held back from France to ensure Britain's air defence, endured frustrating inactivity. In Coastal Command, aircrew flew patrols over the sea approaches to the British Isles, the monotony only occasionally being relieved by contact with the enemy. For the men of Bomber Command, action was also relatively routine — though more dangerous. Lumbering into enemy territory, the bombers unloaded nothing more lethal than leaflets over German cities.

While a few New Zealand airmen put their lives on the line, back home in New Zealand life went on much as

before. For the time being the war seemed remote. The onset of the perplexing 'phoney war' had allayed earlier anxieties. As the British and French used this welcome breathing spell to marshal their resources, fears of defeat faded. The Germans, many felt, had missed their opportunity. For most the war had brought little more than some inconvenience. They had had to get used to new war-related regulations — petrol rationing, for instance, had been introduced shortly after the war began. In the streets the appearance of men in uniform provided relief from the usual drab suits, and camps and bases at Burnham, Trentham, Hopuhopu and Papakura became hives of activity. Only occasionally would the war intrude in a direct way. They might open their newspapers, for example, to find that a New Zealand airman had been killed or injured, but there were no long casualty lists to bring shock and alarm. There was nothing to shake the mood of growing confidence, even complacency, with which New Zealand in late 1939 began its long-planned celebrations of the centennial of the nation's formation.

Blitzkrieg in the west

The situation changed with shocking suddenness in April 1940 when Germany lunged north to occupy neutral Denmark and Norway. British and French troops landed in Norway, and had some success in the north. A few New Zealanders took part in these ultimately unsuccessful operations, which culminated in the evacuation of Allied forces from Narvik. Mainly airmen, they included the just operational New Zealand Flight RAF, which bombed ports and airfields in Norway and searched unsuccessfully for enemy warships at sea. But momentous events elsewhere soon overshadowed the fighting in Scandinavia.

On 10 May Germany launched a massive onslaught in Western Europe. Neutrality proved no safeguard to Holland and Belgium: airborne troops seized key points as German armoured forces drove across their borders. Another massive concentration burst out of the Ardennes to strike a vulnerable sector of the French defences. Within days the Allies faced a critical situation. Ruthless action, including the terror bombing of Rotterdam, quickly subdued Holland; Belgium, its forts captured, teetered on the brink of surrender; and a German breakthrough at Sedan imperilled all those British and French forces that had pushed rapidly forward into Belgium after 10 May. As the German tank columns thrust across the old First World War battlefields towards Amiens, a disaster of unparalleled proportions loomed.

In the face of a swarming *Luftwaffe*, RAF pilots and aircrew struggled in vain to stem the German flood. The bombers bravely attacked the advancing columns, sometimes with telling effect, but many were soon shot down as their protecting fighters were overwhelmed. A few days before he died in a flying accident on 7 June, Cobber Kain told a correspondent that 'earlier on in the week they'd all been flying half asleep, and had had to keep their eyes open with their hands, so exhausted were they by dawn-to-dusk fighting odds at ten, twenty, and even fifty to one'.[36] Kain himself had managed to shoot down another nine aircraft, bringing his final tally to at least fourteen.

Cobber Kain was one of 44 New Zealanders who lost their lives serving with the RAF in May and June 1940. They included airmen taking part in Bomber Command's operations against Germany itself. As soon as the fighting began in earnest, the leaflets gave way to more lethal cargo. When the RAF mounted its first bombing raid on Germany in May, New Zealanders took part, some flying Wellingtons of the recently designated 75 (New Zealand) Squadron. They experienced the

Cobber Kain (third from the right) chats with other pilots after a mission over enemy lines.

horrors of penetrating deep into the enemy's heartland and the prolonged exposure to numbingly cold temperatures. They felt the helplessness that came with being caught in the beam of an enemy searchlight and buffeted by flak, the fear that an enemy intruder would shoot them down as they landed, and the relief at having survived another mission. These early raids would in time come to be seen as picnics. As the enemy's anti-aircraft defences improved, the carnage they inflicted would render Bomber Command the most dangerous of all the arms to serve in during the war.

New Zealand bomber pilot Cyril Kay describes a raid on the German city of Cologne in 1940:

> *We straightened up for the run-in, intent on crossing the bridge obliquely, so keeping the Cathedral well out under the port wing — and then the flak really began to get our measure. It appeared all about in a pouf of black smoke and a dull red flash, but the worrying bursts were those immediately underneath, unseen but denoting their presence in muffled thuds and a lifting of the aircraft to send it bucking and plunging along.*
>
> *Through it all the crew were tense at action stations. Lofty, huddled inertly over his bomb-sight, sounded quite imperturbable as his steering directions came through the intercom, 'Left … left … left … steady … steady … starboard … steady!' Hurry up, man, were my own impatient thoughts. 'Starboard … steady … steady …' and then at last his satisfied 'Bombs away!'— and so were we, too, in a steep bank and a vigorous change of direction; weaving, climbing and skidding to slide out of one searchlight cone, only to be caught by another, and praying fervently that the fighters had not yet been alerted. Thankfully we escaped at last into the anonymity of the nearest cloud, leaving the flak behind....[37]*

These strikes against the enemy homeland had no effect on the course of operations in France and Belgium.

Allied forces cut off in Belgium by the German advance further south pulled back towards the Channel ports. In a dramatic rescue operation between 26 May and 3 June, the Royal Navy saved 337,000 British and French troops, helped by a flotilla of small boats that had crossed the Channel from Britain. Above the exposed beaches and jetties of Dunkirk and nearby ports, RAF aircraft, flying over from England, sought to shield the defenceless men from the *Luftwaffe*. Although relishing the chance at last to get to grips with the enemy, the pilots soon found themselves having a 'pretty torrid time'. Dunkirk was at the extreme limit of their aircraft's radius of action, so they could operate there only briefly before heading back to base; any delay could mean ditching in the sea. Awareness of their inexperience increased the strain: 'For the vast majority,' Wellingtonian Colin Gray recalled, 'it was the first time we had seen a shot fired in anger and we had to learn fast.'[38]

Although saved from destruction, the British Expeditionary Force had lost all its heavy equipment. Meanwhile the situation on the continent had gone beyond salvation. When the Germans drove south, the French quickly caved in, agreeing on 22 June to a humiliating armistice that came into effect three days later. It had taken the Germans just six weeks to secure the victory that had eluded them in four years of combat in 1914–18.

Britain under threat

For New Zealanders the unthinkable had happened, and with shocking speed. They had observed with mounting anxiety the apparently unstoppable 'blitzkrieg' tactics used by the Germans, the defeatism evident among the French and the narrow escape of the BEF, and the outcome portended an even worse crisis. Its shield having fallen, Britain now stood alone, only the narrow English Channel separating its beaten and disorganised army from a triumphant enemy.

Many worried about the looming danger to kinfolk 'at Home'. The more perceptive recognised that New Zealand, too, was less secure. If Britain fell, all hope of British help in the Pacific against Japan would be gone — and there was no viable alternative. Even if Britain held out, Germany's occupation of the French coastline as far south as the Spanish border posed obvious dangers. German naval and air forces could now more easily place a stranglehold on shipping to and from Britain. New Zealand's economic lifeline had become more tenuous.

Another chilling development increased the dangers. Hitler's success had gained him a new ally. With France teetering, Mussolini threw in his lot with the apparent victor, in the hope of sharing the spoils. Italy's belated attack on France on 10 June made little headway and had no effect on the outcome. But its entry to the war confronted British strategists with a drastic situation, as Peter Fraser, who had become Prime Minister following

Savage's death in March, well knew. What if Japan emulated Mussolini by joining the seemingly victorious Axis? There were tempting prizes now that France and Holland were under German sway, not least the rich oil deposits in the Dutch East Indies (today's Indonesia) and strategically placed air and naval bases on the Indo-China coast (now Vietnam). And barriers to a southward movement were down at a time when the British were in no position to respond. The loss of the French fleet's support had compromised plans to reinforce Singapore. Although that fleet remained out of German hands it was no longer in a position to cover the now belligerent Italian fleet. Britain just did not have enough ships to deal with Italy and Japan at the same time. Promises made to New Zealand and Australia as late as 1939, that Britain would definitely send a fleet to Singapore if Japan attacked, could no longer be fulfilled.

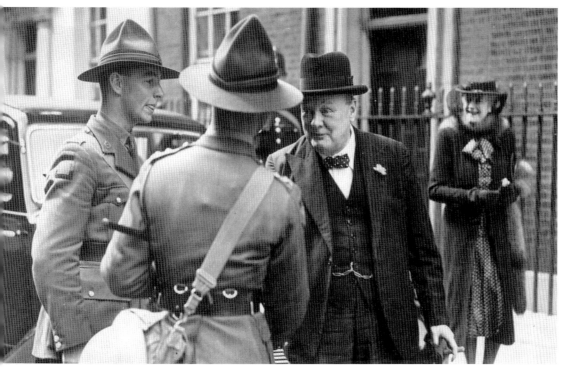

Winston Churchill chats with New Zealand troops in London on 25 June 1940.

Ormond Burton (with a poster) at the front of a Christian Pacifist Society parade in Wellington in April 1940. Pacifists found themselves under increased pressure as the war situation deteriorated, and such parades were banned in June 1940.

Minister of National Service Robert Semple (centre) draws the first marble of the first conscription ballot in September 1940. Others present (from the left) are Colonel OH Mead (Adjutant-General of the Army), Minister of Defence Frederick Jones, JB Black, supervising magistrate FW Stilwell, JS Hunter (Director of National Service) and HL Bockett (Assistant Director of National Service).

It remained to be seen whether the British could sustain their position in the Mediterranean, let alone the Pacific. With huge Italian land forces in Libya and Abyssinia, British strategists feared for the safety of the Suez Canal and vital Middle East oilfields. The entry of Italy into the war, therefore, caused concern to New Zealand quite apart from its effect on Britain's ability to send a fleet to the Pacific. With 2NZEF's First Echelon already in Egypt, New Zealand troops found themselves in a key position, facing the prospect of battle sooner rather than later.

Patriotism rises

The dramatic events in Western Europe provided a blaring wake-up call. New Zealanders reacted like Britons — with a great surge of patriotism. This was spurred by the defiant rhetoric of Winston Churchill, who had replaced Chamberlain as Prime Minister on the day of the German onslaught. In the aftermath of the French defeat, Churchill had to contend with some within his government who favoured seeking terms with Hitler — a debate of great consequence for far-distant New Zealand. Characteristically — and realistically — Fraser indicated that New Zealand would respect whatever decision Britain reached. But, banking on American support in due course, Churchill saw off the challenge. Most accepted that peace on the basis of the existing situation would leave Britain in an impossible position, with subjugation inevitable in the long run. They rallied to Churchill's stirring proclamation of Britain's intention to fight on regardless.

New Zealanders recognised that conducting war in such unfavourable circumstances demanded an even greater effort. Clearly the time had come to get serious about the war, to crank up the war effort. Only by taking extraordinary measures could all the resources of the state be brought to bear against the enemy. Both economic and military fronts demanded action.

British example once again provided a lead, as the New Zealand government assumed emergency powers even before France surrendered. These affected every adult person in the country, placing them at the disposal of the state for use in the war effort and the defence of New Zealand. Their property could also be taken for this purpose.

The new mood also affected direction of the war. Party politicking over the war effort could no longer be tolerated. The only way to remove this was to bring the opposition National Party into the loop. This was achieved, from 16 July, by the formation of a six-person War Cabinet of Labour and National ministers. With the Labour Cabinet still dealing with purely domestic issues, New Zealand's war would now be run by a two-tier system, a clumsy arrangement which nevertheless operated with notable success for over four years.

Conscription

If defeat were to be avoided, all the Dominions needed to do more to help Britain, and quickly. But New Zealand faced difficulties in sustaining even its existing effort. So far involvement in the war had been a matter of choice — and many had opted not to serve. Indeed, after the first surge of volunteering, there had been a fall-off. Not enough men were enlisting to keep the division in the field. Even as this problem emerged, the feeling grew among the public that there should be equality of sacrifice, which demanded some form of compulsion.

At first the government set its face against introducing conscription. Some ministers had been passionate opponents of conscription in the previous war (and even gone to jail for expressing that opposition in public). Bob Semple, for example, had been arrested in 1916 for urging miners 'not to be lassoed by that Prussian octopus, conscription'.[39] But they came round as the recruiting campaign faltered. Even before Germany's triumph, which prompted an upsurge in volunteering, the need for conscription had been accepted. Almost 60,000 had volunteered by the time

conscription came into operation on 22 July 1940.

A new government agency — the National Service Department — had the task of implementing the conscription scheme. Every man between 19 and 45 was liable to have his name drawn in the ballots used for selection. But the process was designed to ensure that those with the least commitments went first, starting with young single men. A 40-year-old father of five obviously had little to worry about at first. Nor did Maori — they were not conscripted. Only volunteers would serve with 28 (Maori) Battalion, and Maori themselves took responsibility for finding the men.

Ironically it was Semple, as Minister of National Service, who drew the first marble when balloting of men got under way in September 1940. The first conscripts found themselves part of Territorial units for home defence, and it was December before the first men were balloted for overseas service with 2NZEF. Not all whose numbers came up found themselves in uniform. Some failed at the first hurdle, deemed medically unfit for service. Automatic exclusion was the lot of all those working in essential industries. Men had the right to seek a reprieve, for example if their enlistment would cause family hardship. Employers could also appeal against the conscription of their workers.

Semple's involvement in the conscription process was the source of considerable mirth among the troops, as for example in the following camp song, sung to the tune of 'Onward Christian Soldiers':

Onward Semple's conscripts, Marching to the war
Death and plague and hunger, Going on before.
Others went before us, Semple went to quad
Brothers we are treading, Where Semple never trod.
Onward Semple's conscripts, Through the mud we plod
To re-divide the Empire, For Semple and his mob.

Armed forces appeal boards dealt with appeals. Most cases were straightforward, and easily resolved. But a small minority — about two per cent — provided big headaches. These involved conscientious objectors, unwilling because of their religious beliefs to take part in war. When conscription had previously been in force, between 1916 and 1918, only members of a few churches had been allowed to stand aside for these reasons. Harsh treatment befell those who refused to accept rejection of their appeals, some even being dragged to the front. In 1940 changed attitudes and the government's inclinations ensured a more liberal approach. Membership of certain churches, the Quakers for example, was still accepted as evidence of consistent attitude. But men outside these churches could gain exemption by convincing the committee that they were sincere in their opinions and not just 'shirkers' or 'lead-swingers'. Of the 3000 men who went before the committees over the next five years, one in five succeeded in gaining full exemption; others were required to serve as non-combatants only.

Most men accepted their fate when drawn in a ballot and passed fit for service. They duly reported to camp for

Evening Post Collection, Alexander Turnbull Library, C-27018-½

The ambulance section of the Manawatu Women's War Service Auxiliary give a demonstration of first-aid procedures at Milverton Park, Palmerston North.

training that would end with their embarkation for Egypt. Apart from essential work and the appeal system, the only way men could avoid this process was by joining the navy or the air force. Only volunteers could enter these services — and there were long waiting lists. The crisis led to nearly a thousand more men being called up for air training, and courses were shortened in duration to increase the flow of pilots to Canada or Britain. The navy, too, were looking for more men — to follow those that had left before the crisis began. These included 10 yachtsmen sent to Malaya at British request and more than 400 personnel who left with 2NZEF's Second Echelon in May 1940. These latter included reservists available for immediate service in the fleet, and men destined for training in the Royal Navy's air component, the Fleet Air Arm. None would serve in separate New Zealand units. Although many New Zealanders became naval airmen during the course of the war, the navy did not emulate the RAF by forming 'New Zealand' squadrons. As with the other New Zealand naval personnel made available, they joined British units as individuals.

The new mood affected more than just the service personnel. Those involved in the other leg of New Zealand's war effort — the food producers — also faced a new challenge. Their efforts to supply the British population had been made more difficult by the German victory in western Europe. With the Germans operating further south, more of the ships plying between New Zealand and British ports would inevitably be sunk. But the German successes had made that supply line even more important, by cutting Britain off from continental food sources, especially in Belgium and Holland. Dairy farmers in New Zealand could help meet the shortfall. The need to meet increased production targets left them working much harder to produce thousands of tons more bacon and cheese for export to Britain. Other farmers met British requests for certain products. A notable example was linen flax, needed for the production of aircraft fabrics, parachute harnesses and other war equipment.

Preparations on the home front

Most New Zealanders applauded these efforts to increase their country's support of Britain. Driven by the huge upwelling of patriotism, they clamoured for a more direct role in the war effort. Some took matters into their own hands. Even as the panzers drove across France, men began forming unofficial militias in many parts of the country, emulating their counterparts in Britain. Patriotic funds benefited from the new mood as people gave more generously than ever.

Ever since the war's outbreak, women had been impatient with their expected role as mere bystanders in a men's war. They yearned for direct involvement. Many wanted to demonstrate their commitment to the cause by wearing a uniform, like their male counterparts. Some could achieve their aspirations by offering their services for 2NZEF as nurses or later as voluntary aids (VADs as they were termed). For most others voluntary organisations remained the only forum for action. Many women had thrown themselves into such work with great gusto.

Women seized the opportunity provided by the new mood to enhance their role. A new organisation emerged — the Women's War Service Auxiliary (WWSA). A countrywide effort, this provided an umbrella framework for 250 district committees, which organised activities at a local level. Women in uniform now became a familiar sight as they underwent courses in first aid, truck driving, and other useful skills.

Men also organised themselves for emergencies. Almost as if they were in the front line, expecting to hear the drone of approaching *Luftwaffe* bombers, local bodies set about making civil defence arrangements under the broad direction of the National Service Department. Volunteers joined sections charged with a range of duties covering law and order, fire fighting and public utilities. Boy Scouts, members of the Red Cross, volunteer firemen — all were pressed into service in the sections. Although prompted by a crisis in Europe, this Emergency Precautions Scheme, as it was termed, would stand New Zealand in good stead should the position in the Pacific turn nasty.

From August, those over 15 years of age wanting a more military oriented role could join New Zealand's 'Dad's Army' — the Home Guard. Organised by local bodies, this had originated in the unofficial militias appearing after May. Many Home Guard units were tiny, especially in rural areas, but in larger towns some were of battalion size. Home Guardsmen wore makeshift uniforms at first, with an armband, and they had little in the way of equipment. But enthusiasm more than made up for these deficiencies, especially in the early stages.

An appeal by the National Patriotic Fund offered people the opportunity to contribute to meeting the needs of those in uniform.

Community pariahs

In the new mood prevailing, anyone who seemed to threaten the unity of the country or its war effort bore the brunt of public disapproval. This applied especially to citizens or former residents of the enemy states. Events in Europe had highlighted the danger of internal subversion. Axis sympathisers — the so-called Fifth Column — had undermined resistance to the German onslaught in both Scandinavia and Western Europe. The several thousand Germans or Italians living in New Zealand were seen in a new light. Some Germans adjudged pro-Nazi had been taken into custody as soon as the war began; now some pro-Fascist Italians suffered the same fate. For these men — 45 in all — internment on Somes Island in Wellington harbour followed. Those aliens who remained in the community, some of them Jewish refugees from Hitler's Europe, endured public hostility. In retrospect it is clear that the public greatly exaggerated the danger. Ugly incidents occurred, but the government wisely resisted the call to increase the number of internees.

'Conshies' (conscientious objectors) who refused to serve after their appeals had been rejected also faced public hostility. Over the course of the war their numbers would reach 1200, though a third of them eventually joined the forces. In the bleak outlook of 1940, the public had little patience with such men. Any sign of leniency towards them would have produced an outcry. But the government had no intention of taking such an approach, despite earlier attitudes of some ministers. It had no sympathy for men it considered to be shirking their responsibilities as citizens.

At first defaulters were detained in military camps, but late in 1941 special work camps were established for them at Whenuaroa, near Reporoa, and Hautu, near Turangi, the latter serving at first as a 'punishment' camp. Smaller camps would later be formed in the Manawatu, Canterbury and Southland. Put to work on a range of manual tasks, including clearing scrub, developing farms and track building, the defaulters lived like prisoners of war; they even had secret radios to keep up with news of the outside world. For some it would be a very long

Conscientious objectors at Hautu detention camp in November 1943.

war: the last defaulter did not regain his liberty until May 1946.[40]

Jack Rogers, a Methodist and 'dedicated and sincere Christian pacifist', was one of the 1200 men — about 40 per cent of those who sought exemption on grounds of conscience — who refused to accept the decision of the appeal board. He was detained at Trentham and Strathmore. Early in 1942 at Strathmore, when he refused to work he found himself under considerable pressure to desist, as he recorded in his diary:

> *Over 1½ hours Greenberg [Controller-General of Defaulters Detention Camps] accused me of being a self-imposed martyr, an insane anarchist, and claimed to be sick to death of this 'comedy and humbug'. He used every means of persuasion, reason, ridicule, threat (you will go to Hautu [a punishment camp] where you will be kept in a single cell with a ti-tree fence all around and left to rot) and emotional pressure (effect on mother and father).*
>
> *He discussed the war and ridiculed my pacifist position (I would let the Japs come and rape my loved ones) and accused me of gross muddlement and confusion of thought and said all we pacifists were guileless victims of men who sat in their homes in front of the fires in comfortable chairs at no risk of sacrifice....*[41]

Raiders in New Zealand waters

Despite the shocking events of May–June 1940, New Zealanders still believed themselves far from immediate danger. As the mail steamer *Niagara* pulled away from the wharf in Auckland on 18 June, few of those who lined her rails expected any trouble until they neared their destination, Britain. Passengers were still settling themselves down as the *Niagara* headed out into the Hauraki Gulf, anticipating the long journey ahead,

when a thunderous explosion rocked the ship. As she began to settle, all on board took to lifeboats. It soon became apparent that the *Niagara* had fallen victim to enemy action.

Just five days earlier the German raider *Orion*, a disguised merchant ship, had brought the war to New Zealand. Creeping into the Hauraki Gulf in darkness, she spent seven hours laying mines between Couvier Island and the mainland. Although the toiling German crew tensed as four steamers passed, none spotted the blacked-out intruder; neither did *Achilles*, nor an armed merchant cruiser that proceeded through the area during the night. By the time *Orion* slipped away out to sea, 228 of her lethal weapons lay in wait for vessels entering or leaving Auckland.

Evidence that a raider had been in New Zealand waters galvanised the authorities into action. Aircraft and warships searched for the intruder — all to no avail. Meanwhile the navy set about clearing the menace lurking in Auckland's approaches. All did not go smoothly. When a minesweeper struck one of the mines and sank, five men lost their lives — the only New Zealand servicemen killed in action by German forces within New Zealand territorial waters during the war. *Orion*'s intrusion had brutally reminded New Zealanders that distance alone did not render them immune from attack.

Two months after the *Niagara* went down, *Orion* claimed another victim near New Zealand — the refrigerated cargo ship *Turakina*. Intercepted about 260 miles off Cape Egmont, the merchantman bravely opened fire with the ship's deck gun and began broadcasting a warning signal. A 12-minute pounding by *Orion*'s guns left her on fire and dead in the water. Her gunners' continuing resistance forced *Orion* to finish her off with shell and torpedoes. This unequal struggle, the Tasman Sea's first gunnery duel, cost the lives of 35 of the *Turakina*'s crew. At some risk — for the warning signal had sent warships, including *Achilles*, rushing towards the area — *Orion* lingered to pick up all the survivors before slipping away.

Depending on secrecy and unpredictability, *Orion* headed south of Australia in search of further victims. Not till November did she return to New Zealand waters, this time accompanied by another raider, *Komet*, and the supply ship *Kulmerland*. After several weeks of fruitless searching for prey, they came upon and sank the 500-ton inter-island vessel *Holmwood* between the Chatham Islands and Lyttelton on 25 November.

The presence of the enemy remained unknown to the New Zealand authorities, for *Holmwood* had sent no warning signal. Oblivious to the danger, the 16,000-ton liner *Rangitane* put to sea from Auckland that same morning, laden with meat, butter and cheese. More than a hundred passengers included a number of servicemen en route to the United Kingdom for air force or naval service. No-one sensed danger. 'Everyone was laughing,' Aircraftsman Alan Jones recalled of a boat drill held

during the day, 'It couldn't happen to us.' But in the pre-dawn darkness next morning the sound of clanging sirens and heavy crashes had them leaping from bed. Less than 480 kilometres off East Cape, *Rangitane* was under fire. Hastening up on deck, Jones could see a raider on either side of the ship and the supply ship in front. 'You could see some of the shells ricocheting off.'[42] But others hit, and people were being killed. Although faster than her adversaries, *Rangitane* had no hope of getting away. By the time she hove to, the enemy salvoes had killed or mortally wounded 10 people, including four women. German boarding parties were astounded by the wealth of cargo they found, but there was no time to tarry. *Rangitane* was soon consigned to the deep — the largest vessel ever to fall victim to a raider.

Taken aboard the raiders, most of *Rangitane*'s survivors would later be landed on Emirau Island in the Bismarck Archipelago. For Jones and some of the other captured servicemen, however, the final destination was more distant. Taken back to Europe on the raiders, they ended up in POW camps in Germany with the dubious distinction of being captured nearest to home of all the New Zealand POWs held there.

So far no warships had been able to get to the scene of action quickly enough to catch the raiders, despite warning signals. Able to move much faster, aircraft had a better chance of interception. But the air force had only two lumbering flying-boats for the purpose, its pre-war plans to have modern Wellington bombers available for such operations having been upset by the government's decision to offer them to the RAF. Nobody questioned the wisdom of leaving the Wellingtons in Britain; they were being used at the vital point. But something needed to be done to improve air force striking power in New Zealand. 'The public are becoming restive at the repeated evidence that raiders can visit our shores with impunity,' Fraser warned Churchill.[43] The British authorities were unhappy about diverting resources to meet what was an intermittent threat at best. But they let New Zealand have some twin-engined Lockheed Hudson medium bombers. New Zealand also

Niagara survivors. When the *Niagara* went down, she took with her half of New Zealand's small arms ammunition, intended to help Britain make up losses suffered at Dunkirk. The other cargo included £2.5 million worth of gold bullion (later salvaged). *Orion* had struck a telling blow indeed.

wanted *Leander* brought back to the South Pacific, but the Admiralty sent an Australian cruiser instead.

Neither of these steps stopped New Zealand from suffering another incursion. Just as the Hudsons arrived in mid-1941, the raider *Komet* entered New Zealand waters. She used a captured whale-chaser, *Adjutant*, to lay small minefields in the approaches to both Lyttelton and Wellington harbours before making off into the vastness of the Pacific, undetected and unmolested. Neither minefield caused any damage — in fact their existence remained unknown until after the war, when captured documents provided the first clue.

Battle of Britain

Even as Germany brought the war to the South Pacific, most New Zealanders remained preoccupied by the mortal danger facing the 'mother country', seriously threatened by invasion for the first time in one and a half centuries. They feared that the outcome of the coming struggle would determine their own fate.

Despite the weakness of its army, Britain was not defenceless. To get to grips, the Germans would have to cross the English Channel. This would be a dangerous operation with the Royal Navy, much more powerful than the German navy (the *Kriegsmarine*), lurking to the north and covered by the RAF. Hitler knew the operation would be no cakewalk. Even though, on 16 July, he directed that preparations begin for a landing in England (designated Operation Sealion), he hoped that the British would remove the need for it by making peace. While the *Luftwaffe* set about neutralising the RAF, small ships to carry the invasion force were gathered in French and Low Country ports from all over Western Europe.

Britain's defenders included many New Zealanders — at sea, on land and in the air. Seamen felt the brunt of German attacks first. They included many of the naval reservists who had left New Zealand in May. On arrival in Britain, these men, among them Peter Phipps (a later

admiral), had been assigned to small minesweeping ships that operated in two groups in the English Channel. *Luftwaffe* attacks on shipping in the Channel in late July put these minesweepers in the front line. Evading bombs became a daily task as they shepherded merchant ships in or out of British ports and swept mines in the entrances.

Meanwhile, on shore, New Zealand soldiers prepared to repel the invader. Part of 2NZEF's Second Echelon, they had come to Britain after a last-minute diversion of their convoy away from the Red Sea. This was because of the threat posed by Italy, which had forces in north-east Africa that could have attacked the troopships. As a result of this change of plan, the troops had disembarked in Scotland on 16 June, just as the French reached the point of collapse. A sign of Commonwealth unity, the arrival of New Zealand and Australian troops at this dark hour helped boost British morale.

New Zealanders who volunteered for 2NZEF in England in training before setting out for the Middle East.

New Zealand soldiers with a fallen enemy aircraft in southern England.

The New Zealanders went by train to Aldershot, where they began an intensive training programme. Although they expected to go to Egypt when safe transit could be arranged, the government in Wellington soon agreed that, as long as they were fully equipped and trained, they could be used against the invader. In such an event Freyberg, who had arrived from Egypt on 24 June to take command of 2NZEF (UK), could deploy two infantry brigades: a composite brigade had been formed from a variety of units to serve alongside James Hargest's 5 Brigade. The units included 28 (Maori) Battalion, which had formed part of the Second Echelon.

Because of shortages afflicting the whole British Army at this time, Freyberg struggled to secure enough equipment for his men. Nonetheless, on the day after Hitler issued his directive for a landing, 2NZEF(UK) was made available for use in the defence system if needed. Six weeks later, action became a real possibility. With invasion seemingly imminent, the New Zealanders moved forward to the Maidstone area in Kent in early September. There they formed part of a reserve ready to deal with airborne landings in the vicinity. Their job would be to attack any German forces that managed to get ashore in the Dover–Folkstone area.

As the troops took up their positions, the question of whether they would fight the enemy on British soil was being determined in the sky above them. In this contest, upon which the fate of the Commonwealth depended, other New Zealanders played key roles. Members of Fighter Command — the famous 'few' — they included aces like Alan Deere, Brian Carbury and Colin Gray, who excelled at the difficult task of shooting down enemy aircraft.[44]

If the exploits of these pilots thrilled New Zealanders, so too did the fact that one of their own — Air Vice-Marshal Keith Park — had a key role in directing the RAF's efforts. His command, 11 Group, covered south-east England and the vital approaches to London.[45] Born in Thames, he had served in the First World War, initially with the NZEF at Gallipoli and later with the Royal Artillery on the Western Front. He ended the war as a fighter pilot after joining the Royal Flying Corps in 1916. Like a number of his compatriots, he pursued a post-war career in the RAF — though only after the New Zealand permanent forces had rebuffed an attempt to join them. By 1940 Park was a dynamic and experienced commander. He had demonstrated his abilities during the Dunkirk operations, even flying over to the scene of action himself. Now he faced an even greater challenge — the most severe yet to have confronted an RAF officer.

At first things went badly for Park's command. For 10 days in August a battle raged in the skies as the *Luftwaffe* sought to overwhelm the defenders. When later in the month the Germans began to bomb the airfields from which the fighter squadrons operated, the prospect of defeat loomed. The RAF was losing aircraft quicker than it could replace them. But on 6 September German tactics changed, and the *Luftwaffe* started bombing London. The RAF used the respite to recover its strength, and soon began inflicting heavy losses on the bomber formations heading for the capital.

Fighter pilot Colin Gray recalls a close call on 31 August 1940, the worst day experienced by Fighter Command during the battle:

> We had not been sent off in the morning, but just after lunch … we were sitting quietly in the dispersal hut when the silence was rudely shattered by the ominous jangle of the 'operations' telephone, which immediately produced the customary sinking feeling in the pits of our stomachs as we strained to hear the message. Sure enough, '54 Squadron, scramble.' Out we ran to our respective aircraft, strapped ourselves in, with the assistance of the ground crews, and started up. However, before we could taxi out, an airman came running out of the dispersal hut waving his arms. We got the message and switched off, but no sooner returned to the hut than it happened all over again. '54 Squadron, scramble!' Unbelievably we were stopped once again, just as we started our engines.

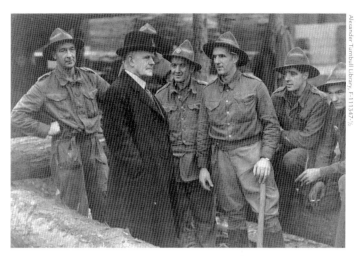

New Zealand High Commissioner William Jordan meets members of a New Zealand forestry company in the west country of England in 1940. The sappers were among the New Zealand troops who arrived in the United Kingdom with the Second Echelon. Their first task was to fell trees to form roadblocks to hinder the invader. Two further companies arrived later in 1940, bringing their numbers to more than 500. Once the immediate danger passed, they operated sawmills in the vicinity of Cirencester until September 1943. One company then proceeded to Algeria, and later to Italy, while the other two were disbanded and the men returned to New Zealand.

Air Vice-Marshal Keith Park.

The third time we had not even reached the door of the hut before an airman burst out yelling to us to scramble. It was a warm day, the engines were already hot, and Merlin engines could be easily 'flooded' under these circumstances. Some of the less experienced pilots had trouble starting. I was first out onto the airfield with my section, waiting for the others to get into position, and had just turned on the radio in time to hear a panic stricken shout over the R/T, '54 Squadron take off, take off, for Christ's sake take off'. I had never heard the controller use this sort of language before, and it was obvious that something was very wrong, so I opened my throttle and for Christ's sake took off…. As we crossed the boundary, I looked back to see the airfield disappear in a cloud of smoke and rubble.[46]

New Zealand fighter ace Colin Gray, during later service in the Mediterranean. The number of New Zealanders serving in Fighter Command rose from 65 to 95 during the battle. In all, 105 took part. These were all men who had already joined the RAF when the war began, for the first New Zealand trainees under the Empire Air Training Scheme were only reaching Canada as the battle drew to a close. Although only four per cent of the total number of RAF fighter pilots in the battle, the New Zealanders were the second most numerous non-UK nationality after the Poles.

As the battle reached a climax in mid-September, the fighting became a test of endurance for these men. As a German formation was detected over France or crossing the Channel, they would be scrambled. Rapidly climbing to get above their prey, they would dive among the enemy formation when it arrived, evading if possible the fighters that were trying to protect the bombers. For a few frantic minutes they would endure the horrors, and the exhilaration, of air combat. In a sky filled with aircraft, turning, twisting, diving, firing, they would struggle to get an enemy plane into their gun sights, the closer the better. For some there would be the exultation of victory, as the enemy plane fell away on fire or exploded.

But there were also casualties. Pilots might find themselves struggling to get out of their burning plane. Many suffered horrific burns before freeing themselves to parachute to earth, perhaps eventually to end up in the care of renowned expatriate New Zealand surgeon Archibald McIndoe, who specialised in treating such injuries. Others failed to make it out of their stricken aircraft. One in five of the New Zealand fighter pilots involved died.

Another 29 New Zealanders lost their lives flying with Coastal and Bomber Commands, both of which played important subsidiary roles in the battle. Coastal Command airmen flew anti-invasion patrols, while Bomber Command mounted raids on ports on the continent where shipping was being gathered. It also bombed airfields from which the *Luftwaffe* was operating against Britain. The squadrons taking part in these operations included 75 (New Zealand) Squadron.

All these efforts ensured that when their navy reported naval preparations for Sealion complete, the Germans were still not in control of the air above the Channel. Hitler did not formally call off the invasion. But British intelligence soon picked up the fact that invasion craft were being dispersed. Never strongly committed to the operation, Hitler now turned his attention eastwards. Ignoring the non-aggression pact, he resolved to invade

RNZAF Museum

the Soviet Union. Destroying the communist giant and securing living space (*lebensraum*) for the German people in the east had long been one of his primary goals. By defeating the Soviet Union, he rationalised, he would force the British into submission by removing what he believed to be the reason for their stubborn refusal to come to terms — the possibility of Soviet intervention.

On 2 October 1940 Hitler ordered the dismantling of much of the preparations for Sealion. German planes continued to make daylight raids on London and other British population centres during October, but night attacks became more prevalent. The strategic purpose had changed: no longer designed to facilitate a landing, the raids were intended to weaken British will to resist. The blitz would continue well into the following year. Oblivious to the German intention to attack Russia, Britons (and New Zealanders) assumed that the invasion threat would re-emerge in the summer of 1941.

In fact the danger of invasion had passed for good. The Battle of Britain had been won. In the most significant wartime role ever undertaken by a New Zealander, Keith Park had emerged with colours flying. His careful husbanding of resources, his tactical insight and his leadership had played a big part in the successful performance of 11 Group. Committing his squadrons separately and immediately to break up the enemy formations, he had ensured the failure of the German invasion plan merely by avoiding defeat. During the battle he resisted the more aggressive approach based on committing massed formations of fighters — big wings — championed by other officers, recognising that the time taken for them to form up was a major disadvantage. But he proved more successful in the war in the air than in the battle over tactics. Later in 1940 he was shunted off to a training command.

The German defeat had immense strategic consequences. The *Luftwaffe* had been badly mauled, losing 1700 aircraft. Many of its most experienced pilots had fallen victim to the RAF, and were now either dead or in British POW camps. The Luftwaffe would never

fully recover from this reverse. From New Zealand's viewpoint, Britain's escape from invasion came as a great, if for the moment temporary, relief. The Commonwealth's vital bastion, and New Zealand's main market, had been preserved as a base for operations against German-occupied Europe. The outcome of the battle also encouraged Hitler to follow his inclination to have a showdown with his ideological enemy to the east, starting a conflict that would ultimately settle Nazi Germany's fate. But these consequences were not readily apparent in October 1940. The outlook remained uncertain. Even as it had lost its most powerful ally, France, Britain had acquired a new enemy well placed to threaten its position in a vital theatre, one in which New Zealand troops were located.

Bombing-up one of 75 Squadron's Wellingtons prior to a mission over the continent.

Oct 1940	Nov 1940	Dec 1940	Jan 1941	Feb 1941

28 Oct – Italy attacks Greece

8 Brigade Group begins
deploying to Fiji

31 Oct – British victory
in Battle of Britain

26 Nov – *Rangitane* sunk by
raiders off East Cape

9 Dec – British forces
launch offensive against
Italians in Egypt

Special work camps established for
'defaulters' near Reporoa and Turangi

NZ Women's Land Service established

12 Jan – 2NZEF's
Second Echelon sets
off from UK for Egypt

22 Jan – Allies take
Tobruk in North Africa

14 Feb – First Gerr
troops land in Li
under Rom

New Zealand troops take a break during the retreat in Greece.

Mar 1941   Apr 1941   May 1941   Jun 1941   Jul 1941

5 Mar – 2 NZ Division begins deployment to Greece

21 Mar – Rommel launches offensive

24–30 Apr – Evacuation of Allied forces from Greece

16 May – Italian forces in Abyssinia surrender

20 May – Germany launches airborne attack on Crete

1 Jun – Evacuation of Allied forces from Crete ends

8 Jun – Allied forces invade Lebanon-Syria

22 Jun – Germany invades Soviet Union (Operation Barbarossa)

Mediterranean Disasters

While New Zealanders anxiously followed events in Western Europe, the Middle East also held their attention — if only because of the large number of New Zealand troops there. The first had arrived in February 1940, moving into camps at Maadi and Helwan on the southern outskirts of Cairo. Like their predecessors in 1914, they had begun an intensive training programme in the surrounding desert. The soldiers revelled in the chance to explore the city and its surrounds in their time off, becoming acquainted with a very different culture to their own. They also became aware that not all Egyptians welcomed their presence. Many resented the limitation of their country's independence that the British military occupation represented. Nationalist-inspired attacks on isolated individuals were not uncommon, and some soldiers died. The fact that Egypt was neutral in the conflict — and would remain so until 1945 — provided a curious backdrop to the New Zealanders' preparation for possible conflict on its soil.

The diversion of the Second Echelon to Britain disrupted plans for the build-up of New Zealand's force in Egypt. Several companies of railway sappers, recruited at British request, arrived to bolster support services, but it was not until September 1940 that another sizeable body of New Zealand troops joined the First Echelon at Maadi. The Third Echelon, formed around 6 Brigade, had been allowed to leave New Zealand only after careful consideration of the country's security outlook in the Pacific following the defeat of France. In taking this step, the government in Wellington adhered to its strategical approach: it accepted that New Zealand, 'in the last resort, must stand or fall according to the decision in the main theatres of war and that as a corollary it would be wise to have all possible forces at decisive points rather than to disperse them in reserves all over the world'.[47]

The Third Echelon arrived in Egypt just as the British position there came under threat. Ever since Italy had entered the war, the huge concentration of Italian forces in North Africa had been a source of worry. To the south-east, in Abyssinia, lay more than 350,000 troops, though their relative isolation reduced their menace. With superior British sea power preventing any supply or reinforcement from Italy, Italian troops in Abyssinia had little capacity for wide-ranging or sustained operations, though they did have the distinction of capturing, in August 1940, the first British colonial territory to be lost during the war — the undefended British Somaliland.

If only because of their location, the 250,000 Italian troops in Libya represented a much more dangerous threat. Yet although they dwarfed the 36,000-strong British force in Egypt, the threat posed by these Italian forces was more apparent than real. Operations would quickly reveal their poor equipment, weak morale and command deficiencies. For the time being, however, their sheer numerical preponderance aroused concern in Cairo, and many recalled the determination with which Italian troops had fought on the Allied side in the First World War.

Italians invade Egypt

On 13 September 1940, just as the Battle of Britain reached its climax, British fears were realised when a large Italian force under Marshal Graziani invaded Egypt. But this proved to be no blitzkrieg. Within three days, Graziani had halted at Sidi Barrani, just 100 kilometres inside the border, to wait for supplies.

With invaders on Egyptian soil and few troops to cover the approaches to the Nile valley, the British High Command in Cairo looked to use New Zealand units. In Freyberg's absence (he was in Britain), some units were provided to meet particular purposes, though none came into contact with the Italians. Upon his return to Egypt

Sir John White Collection

Maadi Camp.

New Zealand troops detrain after arriving in Cairo.

in late September Freyberg was irritated to find his force dispersed in this way, and his efforts to re-concentrate it brought him into conflict with his superiors. For the first time he confronted the problems of serving as the commander of a small national contingent within a British command structure. Only by threatening to invoke his charter was he able to get his way.

Even as Freyberg grappled with his superiors, startling British victories reduced the chances of an early clash between New Zealanders and Italians. First, the Mediterranean Fleet struck a telling blow against the Italian navy at Taranto, sinking several battleships in a surprise attack by torpedo bombers flown off a British aircraft carrier. Then the Italian forces in Egypt suffered a crushing defeat at the hands of Lieutenant-General Richard O'Connor's small Western Desert Force. A raid launched against the sedentary Italians at Sidi Barrani on 9 December proved so successful — nearly 40,000 prisoners were taken — that O'Connor drove into Cyrenaica, the eastern province of Libya, capturing the stronghold at Bardia on 5 January. Three weeks later the port of Tobruk was in British hands and O'Connor's troops were pressing rapidly westwards.

Although not directly involved in this offensive, 2 New Zealand Division provided a number of New Zealand units to support the advance, mainly signallers, drivers and engineers. The sappers extended water pipelines and operated water points. They also salvaged enemy vehicles from the battlefield, disposed of mines and bombs, repaired demolished bridges, operated water barges and ferried troops and supplies along the coast. Some fell victim to enemy mines. A few New Zealanders took a more active role in the fighting. As members of the Long Range Patrols, they ranged deep behind enemy lines, gathering intelligence and launching surprise attacks on airfields and supply convoys deep in Cyrenaica.

By February 1941 the British position in the Middle East seemed secure. Although the Italian forces in Abyssinia had repelled a British attack in November 1940, a new offensive launched in mid-January 1941

New Zealand gunners have smoko in the desert during training manoeuvres.

A Long Range Desert Group patrol at Siwa oasis in western Egypt. At first known as the Long Range Patrols, the Long Range Desert Group was an irregular British unit formed in June 1940. Initially most of its members were New Zealand volunteers, but from December it included Britons and Southern Rhodesians as well. These latter were grouped in one squadron, the New Zealanders in another. By 1942 the LRDG was 350-strong. In all 325 New Zealanders, mainly drawn from 2 NZ Division's Divisional Cavalry, would serve with this highly effective unit during the course of the war. So popular was service in the LRDG that at one stage more than 800 put their names forward for 40 places available.

proved more successful — beginning an advance that would culminate with the final surrender of Italian forces four months later. While no New Zealand units took part in these land operations, the cruiser *Leander* provided a New Zealand naval contribution. Part of the naval forces covering the theatre in the Indian Ocean, she sank the Italian auxiliary cruiser *Ramb I* in the Indian Ocean on 27 February 1941.

On 7 February at Beda Fomm O'Connor had crushed the remnants of the Italian army that had attacked Egypt. As another 25,000 men trudged into captivity, the Italian position in North Africa seemed on the point of extinction. Little stood in the way of a drive by O'Connor into Tripolitania, Libya's other province, and the capture of Tripoli. But there would have been risks. With

Benghazi port out of action, O'Connor's force would have been fighting at the end of a supply route stretching back many hundreds of kilometres to Tobruk — a dangerous proposition should it encounter substantial resistance. And this became more likely with Hitler's response to the Italian débâcle. Although not overly worried by the military impact of the Allies taking the whole of North Africa, he feared that Mussolini might in that event throw in the towel. Some German forces would therefore be provided to help Mussolini hold Tripoli. A week after O'Connor's triumph at Beda Fomm a German light division began landing in North Africa, to be followed shortly after by an armoured division. With them came Major-General Erwin Rommel to command this *Deutsches Afrika Korps* (DAK).

POWs, both in boats and swimming, come over to HMS *Leander* as their raider, *Ramb I*, burns in the background.

Greek interlude

The advent of the DAK would prolong the war in North Africa for more than two years. But it was not Rommel's force that proved to be the New Zealanders' first German opponents; but rather the troops of Field Marshal Wilhelm List's Twelfth Army. And the action took place not in the sandy wastes of North Africa but in the rocky terrain of a Balkan peninsula on the other side of the Mediterranean.

The New Zealand division went into action for the first time in Greece. It did so because of yet another aggression by Mussolini. Even as his forces took on the British in Egypt, he launched an invasion of Greece on 28 October 1940 — with equal lack of success. With the help of some RAF squadrons, the Greeks held the invaders and threw them back into Albania. In support of this effort, New Zealand had its first involvement in Greece — a detachment of 19 New Zealand railway survey sappers, sent to the Athens area to survey railway connections for airfields used by the RAF. This deployment embarrassed Freyberg, when he learned of it, for he had not been consulted about it by the High Command.

Defeating dispirited Italian troops was well within Greek capacity; the same could not be said of German forces. As the Italians fell back into Albania, the possibility of German intervention increased. What were the British to do about this danger? To support Greece against aggression, as Britain had promised in 1939, would be difficult. Yet Churchill also saw tempting possibilities. Might not intervention there encourage Turkey and Yugoslavia to join a Balkan front against the common threat to them all? But when the Greeks were sounded about possible help, they revealed reluctance to agree to a course that might, they feared, merely ensure a German attack without protecting their country, given the limited forces Britain could make available. And Yugoslavia and Turkey showed no interest in joining any front against Germany.

This discouraging response did not stop Britain from sending an expeditionary force to Greece. Its task would be to hold a line on the Aliakmon River, south of the port of Salonika (Thessaloniki), where an important Allied bridgehead had been held for more than two years in the First World War. Misunderstandings between British and Greek representatives and between Cairo and London, misplaced assumptions about the political impact of British intervention in the Balkans, and over-confidence that a successful defence would be possible in the rugged terrain in northern Greece — all played their part in inducing the British government to accept a commitment in which political objectives and military capacity were badly out of kilter.

The Greek intervention has since been dismissed, somewhat unfairly, as just another Churchill-inspired fiasco — similar to that at Gallipoli 26 years earlier. But whereas Gallipoli had been a feasible plan poorly executed, the Greek intervention offered no hope of a successful outcome, given the correlation of forces and the location. Not only could the Germans bring overwhelming force to bear — they had a huge preponderance in both ground and air forces available — but also they would face defenders weakened by division over strategy. Naturally wanting to protect Salonika, the Greeks insisted on also attempting to hold a forward line on the Bulgarian-Greek border, thereby dissipating Allied strength.

The British decision had serious implications for New Zealand. Among the units earmarked for the proposed expeditionary force (codenamed Lustreforce) was the New Zealand division, now concentrated at last in Egypt after the arrival of the Second Echelon from Britain. Informed of the British plan by British Commander-in-Chief General Archibald Wavell on 17 February, Freyberg was appalled. The plan, he confided to his diary, 'violates every principle of war'.[48] Probably assuming, incorrectly, that the New Zealand government had already agreed to the use of the division in spite of the dangers, he kept his doubts to himself and began preparing for the operation. He would later complain that his opinion on the military merits of the plan had not been sought by Wellington. But Fraser had received a cable from him on 23 February reporting that his division was now ready for combat. Freyberg's failure to mention any misgivings about the Greek plan misled Fraser into believing that he had no professional doubts about it. This misunderstanding would lead to recriminations later.

By the time Churchill approached the New Zealand government about what he described as 'perhaps, the most severe proposal ever put before Dominion Governments',[49] New Zealand troops were already crossing the Mediterranean. Obscure though the diplomacy behind the commitment may have been, Fraser had no illusions about the prospects of a Balkan front being formed. But, like Churchill, he recognised that assisting the Greeks was 'an inescapable matter of honour'.[50] Behind the War Cabinet's acceptance of New Zealand participation lay several other considerations: the mistaken belief that Freyberg did not regard the operation as militarily unwise, the fact that Australians would also be involved, an acceptance that risks had to be taken in war, an expectation (unjustified as it transpired) that substantial air support would be provided, and a belief that if the worst happened the force could be evacuated. After the campaign, Fraser insisted that his government 'would take the same course again in the same circumstances'.[51] His chief adviser, Carl Berendsen, maintained later 'there was in honour and decency no option at all'.[52]

As New Zealand and Australian troops took up positions on the Aliakmon Line, the situation became more menacing. Yugoslavia's adherence to the Tripartite Pact on 25 March 1941 exposed the Balkan front as a chimera — even if a coup in Belgrade two days later briefly raised hopes again. Hitler responded to this sudden development by unleashing German forces against both Yugoslavia and Greece on 6 April. The collapse of Yugoslav resistance followed within days, opening the way for German forces to drive into Greece through the Monastir Gap in Yugoslavia. On the morning of 10 April, New Zealand and German troops fired on each other for the first time in the war, when a Divisional Cavalry troop pushing up to the Yugoslav border clashed with a motorcycle patrol.

German units pushing south from Monastir outflanked both the Greek defences on the Rupel and the Commonwealth/Greek positions on the Aliakmon.

New Zealand troops dig in on the Aliakmon Line.

The retreat in Greece.

Withdrawal became the only sensible course. Repeated attacks by an unchallenged *Luftwaffe* could not prevent the movement of the troops southwards. The sappers came into their own, blowing up bridges and roads to delay the enemy or hastily opening obstructions on the route. Infantrymen and gunners fought a series of rearguard actions to hold open vital road junctions. These actions tested the troops, and in some cases they failed. At Pinios Gorge, 21 Battalion had a savage encounter with the enemy that left it scattered and in disarray.

By 20 April the Australians and New Zealanders, now fighting as an Anzac Corps, were back on a line at Thermopylae. But the capitulation of the Greek Army soon ruled out the possibility of the Anzacs emulating those ancient Greeks who had made a famous stand at this position in 480 BC. Threatened with being outflanked once again by German forces to their west, the Anzacs fell back to the south behind a rearguard.

Army nurse Jo Adamson recalls the final stages of her unit's evacuation:

We left Kephissa on buses. Prior to leaving we had to dump most of our personal luggage. We were then taken to a station three miles out of Athens and lay in the cornfields. German planes came over frequently and we had to seek shelter under the trees. At 9.30 p.m. we were packed into trucks with our luggage — there were 20 people in ours. We had a long, tiring journey. The road had huge craters, and even dead horses blocked the road. The Germans had been machine-gunning them. The roads were [through] steep, high hills, with the sea on one side. We went through the Gulf of Corinth and arrived at a small village where we had our breakfast. Planes flew over frequently and we experienced machine-gunning. We had to jump from the trucks and shelter in the fields.

One of the trucks ahead of us with our sisters tipped over on this road, and we [spent] two hours giving them first aid and tending them. We had ambulances and they were tended

Nurses from the New Zealand General Hospital shelter from enemy planes in a cemetery during the retreat in Greece.

New Zealand troops watch a column of Italian POWs passing through Athens.

War History Collection, Alexander Turnbull Library, PA1-q-296-008-1244

Sergeant Jack Hinton won a VC for his bravery in fighting German forces at Kalamata before being wounded and captured. He was one of 1826 New Zealanders taken POW in Greece. The brief campaign had cost the lives of 291 New Zealanders, and nearly 400 had been wounded.

to in those. We had to seek refuge in a cemetery because, with the Germans being overhead, they could see any movement, so we spent most of our time there. We had to walk the last few miles carrying our luggage.... This was in the night-time so we couldn't be seen.

We were taken over to an Australian destroyer [HMAS Voyager] and felt at last we had a place of refuge. We had 500 [aboard] for the trip so we were really squashed together. We had some attempted dive-bombing there, but we brought two planes down....[53]

The ensuing evacuation mirrored that at Dunkirk in its effectiveness. The Royal Navy took off 50,000 Commonwealth troops, including most of the New Zealand division. But 2000 New Zealanders were among the 14,000 men left behind. The more adventurous took to the hills, and some eventually managed to get away from Greece in small boats. The rest surrendered to the Germans, though not without spirited resistance in places.

Defending Crete

The vagaries of the evacuation left the New Zealanders split between Egypt and Crete. Most of 6 Brigade went direct from Greece to Alexandria. The remainder of the division landed in Crete with the expectation that it too would soon proceed to Egypt. But evidence of impending German invasion changed this plan. The troops found themselves preparing to defend the island, joining a motley collection of British, Australian and Greek units.

The New Zealanders arrived on the island exhausted after their ordeal on the mainland. A few days' rest in Crete's balmy spring weather worked wonders in reviving their morale. But their fighting capacity proved more difficult to restore. Most had only their personal weapons. All heavy equipment had had to be abandoned, and even

Greece 1941

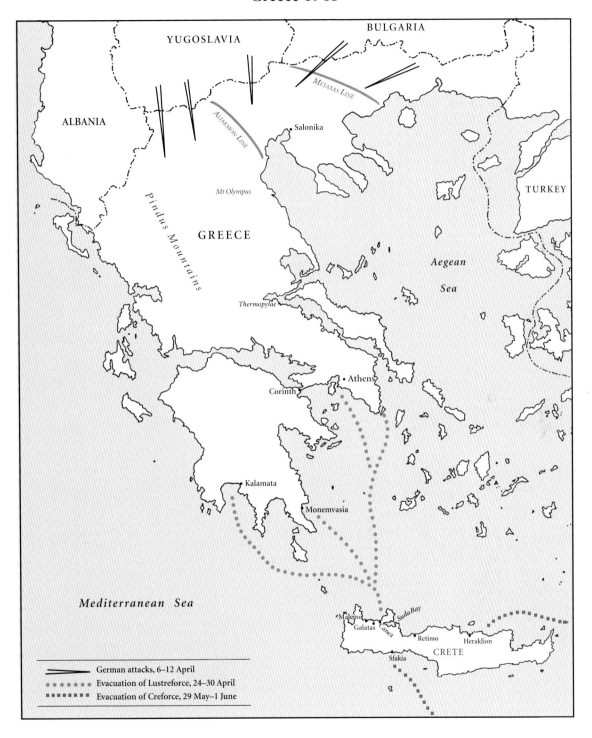

YUGOSLAVIA

BULGARIA

ALBANIA

Metaxas Line

Salonika

Aliakmon Line

Pindus Mountains

Mt Olympus

GREECE

TURKEY

Aegean Sea

Thermopylae

• Athens

Corinth

Kalamata

Monemvasia

Mediterranean Sea

Maleme   *Suda Bay*
Galatas *Canea*
         Retimo   Heraklion
Sfakia   CRETE

― German attacks, 6–12 April
····· Evacuation of Lustreforce, 24–30 April
▪▪▪▪▪ Evacuation of Creforce, 29 May–1 June

rudimentary tools such as spades and shovels were in short supply. The other nationalities were in the same boat.

The task of putting the garrison into a state of defence fell to Freyberg, who assumed command of all the forces on Crete (designated Creforce) on 30 April. Finding equipment for his troops proved a major task in the next three weeks. Much was done, but many deficiencies would remain when the test came. Freyberg also grappled with the problem of most effectively disposing his force — a task made more difficult by the island's geography. The island's three main airfields — at Maleme, Retimo, and Heraklion — and main port at Suda Bay, Creforces' vital supply conduit, all lay on its northern coast, relatively close to the now enemy-occupied Greek mainland and exposed to air attack.

Despite the problems he faced, Freyberg enjoyed one huge advantage: he had detailed foreknowledge of his opponent's plans well in advance of their implementation. ULTRA intelligence, derived from the decoding of enemy wireless signals, warned that the Germans would mount an airborne attack on the island — designed to seize one of the airfields or the port to allow rapid reinforcements to be flown or shipped in. So clearly was the German plan exposed that Churchill, in London, hoped that Crete might provide the opportunity to inflict an embarrassing defeat on German forces that had so far, on the ground at least, carried all before them.

The ULTRA intelligence had its roots in pre-war work by Polish code-breakers on overcoming the obstacle presented by the supposedly unbreakable automatic coding machine (Enigma) used by Germany's armed forces and other agencies. Building on this Polish effort, British code-breakers at Bletchley Park, north of London, succeeded in breaking some German codes, helped by over-confidence on the part of the Germans as to the security of their signals traffic. Although never complete, and subject to breaks, the ability to read parts of the German operational signal traffic had immense importance in the Allied prosecution of the war, especially in the crucial Battle of the Atlantic. To prevent the Germans from learning that their Enigma machines were compromised, knowledge of the 'ULTRA secret' was confined to a limited group and great care was exercised in the use of the material in the field. At the time of the Greek campaign, procedures were still being developed, but ULTRA intelligence proved of considerable assistance during the retreat on the mainland.

German JU52s dropping paratroops near a New Zealand position in the Galatas area.

A German plane crashes on 20 May 1941. Paratroops can be seen landing at left.

It is still an open question whether Freyberg knew that the ULTRA intelligence derived from wireless interceptions. The cover story attributed it to a well-placed spy in Athens, and no commander could safely assume that information from such a source was absolutely reliable. Whether or not he knew the 'secret' — and he seemed to indicate much later that he did — he knew when the invasion would come, and he did not need ULTRA to discern likely German objectives, the airfields and the port. Although the main attack would clearly be airborne, he over-estimated the potential threat posed by a planned seaborne reinforcement. Perhaps believing that the paratroopers' loss of their main advantage — surprise — had lessened the airborne danger, he prepared to meet both seaborne and airborne attack, a decision that weakened the all-important defence of the airfields. He assigned Maleme airfield to James Hargest's 5 New Zealand Brigade, Retimo to a mainly Australian force, and Heraklion to a mainly British force. A large force stationed near Canea, available to move east or west as required, included two New Zealand brigades, Lindsay Inglis's 4 Brigade and the newly promoted Howard Kippenberger's composite 10 Brigade.

For more than a week the New Zealanders endured a savage assault by the *Luftwaffe* that made all daytime movement dangerous in the extreme. They knew that invasion was imminent, even that it would come on 20 May. But the day began much as the preceding ones had, with heavy air attacks. A lull then developed, during which many prepared to have breakfast. As they did so, the sinister whirr of gliders passing close overhead provided the first hint of trouble. The troops hardly had time to take in this sudden development when they heard the drone of an approaching air armada. Within minutes German transport planes passed overhead, disgorging strings of paratroopers. The sky filled with a mass of coloured parachutes.

For a brief moment the defenders gazed at this spectacle in awe. Then grabbing their weapons they began firing at the bobbing figures descending on them. Many of the Germans died before they hit the ground, others as they struggled to release themselves from their parachute harnesses. The toll among the thin-skinned gliders was equally severe. 'It was a great sight but very scaring,' a watching gunner recalled. 'It reminded me of the duck-shooting season to see all these fellows coming down.'[54]

New Zealand soldier Peter Wildey recalls the German invasion on 20 May 1941:

Well, we were having breakfast. We'd just finished it, I think, when all of a sudden two gliders came in.... everyone was looking at them; they didn't have a clue what they were. So I opened up my Tommy gun. They were at a very low altitude. They were lucky to get through without hitting the Cemetery Hill area. I had a hundred-round magazine on [the Tommy gun], and I managed to pour the whole lot into those two [gliders]. I couldn't help hitting some, just raking it from stem to stern....

After I got going, the others started joining in. Shortly after that, just right on their heels, these big transports came in, great big tri-motor things. The chaps just started pouring out of them. We fired at them as they were coming down, as hard as we could....

That first bit of action would have been about an hour, I suppose. We were shooting, and ducking and diving. One big German was coming down right on top of me. I was getting bursts of the Tommy gun into him and he took out a hand grenade, and I could see it coming right for me. I flattened out but it landed just the other side of a line of vines — it was in a little vineyard — and I didn't get a scratch. But I didn't get another squeak out of him. I think I must have killed him. Others were coming down and they were swinging in the air, from side to side like a pendulum. I think that was a ruse to make it hard to shoot them. I cottoned on, and I waited until the end of the swing and kept my Tommy gun pointing there till they came back the next time and I managed to shoot at two or three. Whether I killed them or wounded them, I don't know.[55]

71

At first the fighting was confined to the western part of the island. The Germans, landing in the vicinity of Maleme and in the Suda-Canea area, were horrified to find many more defenders on the ground than they had expected. Despite their bloody reception enough troops reached the ground safely to secure a tenuous foothold in two areas — west of Maleme airfield in an area Freyberg, in a major tactical error, had left unoccupied and in the Prison Valley, south-west of Canea. But by the end of the day neither of these concentrations had been able to make any progress towards securing their objectives. Nor had the second wave, which had attacked Retimo and Heraklion in the afternoon. The German commanders in Athens feared that the operation had failed; without an airfield or the port, the paratroops could not be reinforced. The prospect of a humiliating defeat loomed.

A crucial mistake during the night let the Germans off the hook — and sealed the fate of Creforce. At Maleme, 22 Battalion, commanded by First World War VC winner Lieutenant-Colonel Leslie Andrew, held the key positions, covering not only the western edges of the airfield but also the substantial hill overlooking it. All day the *Luftwaffe* had ceaselessly attacked its companies, and those near the airfield came under increasing pressure from Germans advancing from the west. Unable to communicate with these companies and assuming, incorrectly, that they had been overrun, Andrew feared that the rest of his battalion would be cut off. He decided to pull back to positions closer to neighbouring battalions, which had shown no sign of supporting him. Pre-attack orders had been to counter-attack should the airfield be threatened; the failure of battalion commanders to adhere to these orders, and the lethargic performance of Andrew's superior, Hargest, contributed to the collapse of the defence of Maleme airfield.

The Germans wasted no time in turning this development to their advantage when they discovered the absence of defenders on the hill next morning. Although the airfield was still under artillery fire, they began flying in elements of a mountain division later in the day, tipping the balance their way. A chain of New Zealand errors of judgement and a lack of dynamic leadership had allowed the Germans to escape from a frightening predicament.

Despite the reverse at Maleme, Freyberg remained confident of victory as he oversaw plans for a counter-attack to regain the airfield. While the troops of the two battalions assigned to this task, 20 and 28 (Maori), prepared to move forward, they heard encouraging sounds of battle out to sea. The Royal Navy had intercepted seaborne reinforcements on the way to Crete and was in the process of destroying or dispersing them. The evidence of this action in the seas to the north not only removed one of Freyberg's biggest anxieties but also encouraged him in the belief that he had won the battle. He was mistaken: the counter-attack on Maleme failed, partly because of his own actions. Reluctant to leave a gap in the defences near Canea/Suda, he had insisted on an Australian battalion replacing 20 Battalion before it moved off, ensuring a fatal delay. Misunderstood ULTRA reports of a possible sea landing in this area had influenced him.

Maori company commander Captain Parekura Tureia recalls the closing stages of the counter-attack at Maleme just after dawn on 22 May 1941:

> *As it was daylight now with the sun well overhead we had to keep well under the trees and then word came through that the Hun were attacking — then without waiting for his attack we charged. The chaps in a twinkling of an eye went into it with a perfect line — the din of the yelling was terrific. There was Major Dyer on my right urging the boys along and Arnold on my left all yelling together with machine gun bullets flying over our heads; for 400 yards we charged with never a sight of the enemy. By jove they must have bolted like frightened rabbits. We did not see them and as we approached the edge of the trees into the clearing we stopped as it was suicide to proceed any further into the open.*[56]

The counter-attacking troops made a valiant attempt to reach the airfield. They advanced with great purpose and courage, overcoming numerous German pockets as they neared the airfield. No-one fought with more determination than platoon commander Captain Charles Upham. This Christchurch-born farm manager had proved a natural leader of men, and his ruthless dedication to his infantry skills and almost pathological hatred of Germans rendered him increasingly conspicuous. His actions this night would go a long way towards securing him the first of the two VCs he won during the war — a feat without parallel in the twentieth century.

By daylight the Maori had been held up short of the objective, but some men of 20 Battalion had reached the airfield's edge. They could go no further. With the *Luftwaffe* back in the skies, any attempt to cross it would have been suicidal. The delay in starting the attack had left the troops too little time to complete their task. But the force itself was almost certainly too small to dislodge the Germans, who now included fresh troops airlifted in; Freyberg himself later suggested that the only slight hope would have been to have hit the airfield with everything available.

The failure of the counter-attack decided the fate of Creforce. As German strength grew, the exhausted New Zealanders fell back to the east. On several occasions — at Galatas and 42nd Street — they drove the Germans back in ferocious counter-attacks, fighting in which Sergeant Clive Hulme earned 2NZEF's third VC of the war. At 42nd Street Maori soldiers were in the van. One of their number recalled later their prowess with the bayonet: 'so much so that the efficient and let me say brave Hun turned tail and ran throwing away everything he had. What a chase for a mile....'[57] Such local successes provided some temporary relief, but they had no hope of changing the overall situation.

Junior officer Allan Yeoman describes his platoon's part in the charge at 42nd Street:

> *We were still allotting posts to our section commanders when we heard a scurry in front and soldiers came running back towards us.... Like a shot we lined the road and awaited the attack with men almost shoulder to shoulder. The German scouts were apparently almost as surprised as we were ourselves and it was quite a few minutes before the encounter battle began. Then their machine guns opened up from about 200 yards away. They were screened from view by the standing oats and barley, but the streams of bullets whipped through this and cracked above our heads viciously. We soon found, however, that it was unaimed fire and that the Germans were just as shy of us as we were of them. Then word came down the line like wild-fire.*
>
> *'The Maoris are charging on the left.'*
> *I turned to Captain Trousdale. 'What about it, Sir?'*
> *'OK, Mr Yeoman — off you go.'*
> *With a wild whoop we shinned up the bank and went over the top. Our weariness was forgotten. We had only one bayonet to five men — but that didn't matter. In a matter of seconds we had the Germans on the run. The boys didn't want to stop. Had we let them they would have chased the enemy indefinitely. But we knew that no charge on such a wide front could remain intact — and had to call it off after we had chased them for about a mile.*[58]

By 27 May, when Freyberg was authorised to evacuate his force, weary troops were already trudging over the mountains towards the tiny port of Sfakia on the island's southern coast. Helped by the failure of the Germans to detect this movement (the main German forces pushed rapidly east to Retimo and Heraklion), most of the western part of Creforce succeeded in reaching the Sfakia area. Over four nights, the Royal Navy took off 10,500 men from Sfakia — a number slightly increased by the personal intervention of Prime Minister Peter Fraser in Egypt; he persuaded the British naval commander to send one extra ship on the final night, ensuring that a few hundred extra troops could be taken off.[59]

Another evacuation at Heraklion rescued the mainly British garrison there.

Although most of the combat troops were taken off, 6000 men remained at Sfakia, many New Zealanders among them. Forced to capitulate on 1 June, they soon began a depressing march back over the mountains. As in Greece, many took to the hills before capture, or managed to escape there. Some would remain at large for years assisted by Cretan civilians, who paid a high price for their resistance to the occupiers. But nearly 2200 New Zealanders went into the bag on Crete — the largest group of New Zealand POWs taken in any single battle of the war.[60]

For the POWs, depression at being captured was compounded by the difficult conditions in which they were held near Galatas before being transported to the mainland, where they joined those captured in Greece in unpleasant transit camps at Corinth or Salonika. In due course all would be taken north by train. Officers and NCOs went to camps in Germany itself, and most of the rest to camps in the expanded Reich — in Austria or just south of the Austro-Yugoslav border. As allowed under the Geneva Convention (the agreement covering POWs and other aspects of warfare), the Germans put the latter to work, many on farms. Most settled down to make the best of their lot, but a small minority, not content to sit out the war in captivity, took often fleeting opportunities to escape from the transit camps or trains. A trickle of men made it safely to neutral Turkey or directly to Egypt, some after epic adventures. One such was young subaltern, Sandy Thomas, who was wounded and captured in Crete, escaped from a hospital in Athens and reached Turkey after taking refuge for a time in the ancient monastic community on Mount Athos. Another POW, Sergeant John Denvir, who escaped from a camp in Slovenia, part of occupied Yugoslavia, took a less conventional route; joining partisans fighting under Tito, he rose to command a battalion and was wounded several times before eventually being evacuated.[61]

Meanwhile, back in Egypt the rest of the New Zealanders reflected on their first experience of combat. Even if their tactical direction left much to be desired, the troops themselves had fought with great élan and skill. They knew that they had done as well as might have been expected, given the odds stacked against them from the start, especially because of the lack of air support. Although opportunities to grapple with the enemy had been limited on the Greek mainland, they had had more than their fill of combat on Crete. They had responded with great fortitude and courage to a new form of warfare, and had inflicted heavy casualties on the paratroopers, killing more than 3000 of them — a toll so high that Hitler forbade the use of the paratroops in any further divisional-scale air assault operations. But the Greek campaign had been a searing introduction to modern warfare for 2 New Zealand Division as well: nearly 1000 men (670 of them on Crete) had died and 4000 were now in enemy hands.

As the troops recovered in Egypt from their ordeal, Freyberg's capacity as a commander came under scrutiny. Fraser, who was visiting Egypt, found to his

Exhausted sappers rest at Sfakia while they await evacuation.

War History Collection, Alexander Turnbull Library, F-10739-½-DA dismay that the general had never considered the Greek expedition a viable enterprise. His doubts increased when it became evident that some of Freyberg's senior subordinates believed he had botched his task in Crete. Unfazed by his own errors during the battle, Hargest went behind his commander's back to express adverse comments to the Prime Minister; in London, Inglis voiced similar criticisms in briefing Churchill. Others kept their opinions to themselves until after the war. After consulting senior British officers, Fraser wisely decided not to make any change in the division's command. Freyberg was enjoined to convey to Wellington any doubts he might have about future operations. With the air cleared, Fraser and Freyberg went on to establish a very effective relationship over the next four years.

Fraser also reminded British leaders that Dominion support could not be taken for granted. Submitting a list of searching questions to the British authorities, Fraser probed the basis on which the operations in Greece had been mounted, though the answers he received were not all entirely accurate.

The Greek campaign had not merely led to a series of defeats. It adversely affected the Allies' overall strategic position in the main Mediterranean. At sea the naval position had been jeopardised by the grievous losses sustained by the Royal Navy while supporting Creforce. Four cruisers and six destroyers, as well as many smaller craft, had been sunk and others damaged. More than 2000 men had lost their lives, including New Zealanders serving on British ships; British fatalities at sea during the battle for Crete in fact exceeded those on land. The damage to the Mediterranean Fleet would have been all the more worrying had the Italian navy been more aggressive; its will to fight had been further undermined, however, by the sharp reverse it suffered off Cape Matapan in March 1941.

On land, the resources diverted to Greece were sorely missed when the German-Italian forces in Tripoli went over to the offensive even before the German attack on Greece. Rommel had wasted no time in launching a raid that recaptured El Agheila on 21 March 1941. This sudden onslaught surprised Berlin for Rommel had been instructed to adopt a defensive stance; because ULTRA sources had indicated this German approach, Cairo was also surprised. Rommel's initial operations proved so successful that he pressed deeper into Cyrenaica. Confusion quickly developed among the British forces, and they pulled back in disorder as far as Egypt, leaving only the port of Tobruk as an important enclave behind the Axis lines.

Rommel's success jeopardised the whole Allied position in the Middle East by threatening Egypt. The recapture of Cyrenaica had, moreover, provided airfields from which to attack the British outpost of Malta. So strategically important was this island, lying astride the Axis supply route between Italy and Libya, that Hitler's advisers had urged him, unsuccessfully, to use the airborne forces against it rather than Crete.

The capture of Crete provided a springboard for further assaults on the British position in the eastern

War History Collection, Alexander Turnbull Library, C-8055-½

An injured Maori soldier is assisted ashore at Alexandria, Egypt.

Sir John White Collection

Freyberg with Prime Minister Peter Fraser.

Mediterranean. German successes in Greece put a sinister light on other developments in the region. Following a pro-German uprising in Iraq, the Vichy authorities in Lebanon-Syria had allowed German aircraft to land en route to provide assistance. The possibility of the Germans establishing a base in this area, in the British rear, set alarm bells ringing in Cairo.

To remove the danger, an Allied force invaded Lebanon-Syria on 8 June 1941. The Vichy troops resisted strongly, with some support from *Luftwaffe* units based in Greece and the Dodecanese Islands. Although no New Zealand ground units took part in the fighting, the cruiser *Leander*, which had joined the battered Mediterranean Fleet just after the evacuation from Crete, operated with the supporting naval force for a fortnight. She skirmished with Vichy naval forces, endured air attacks and carried out shore bombardments in support of the advancing Allied troops. Her stint with the Mediterranean Fleet came to an end shortly after the successful completion of the operation on 14 July, and she began the long journey back to New Zealand. Meanwhile a mainly Indian force had occupied Iraq to remove the danger from this direction.

By this time fears about the situation in the Mediterranean had been further allayed by evidence that Hitler had set himself against pursuing a Mediterranean focused strategy. From the Allied viewpoint, Germany seemed to stand to gain much from such an approach. Overstretched, at the end of a long supply line and disorganised by recent defeats, British forces in the theatre of war were vulnerable. By placing itself in a position to exploit the oil resources of the Middle East, moreover, Germany could have removed a significant threat to its war-making potential. But for Hitler the German operations in the Balkans and North Africa had always been merely sideshows to his real purpose, which was revealed less than a month after the Allied surrender in Crete.

On 21 June 1941, Hitler launched Operation Barbarossa — the invasion of the Soviet Union. More than 3.5 million men, thrusting forward in three great concentrations, seemed within a few weeks to have decisively defeated the Red Army — or so the endless columns of Soviet POWs suggested. By November 1941 German forces stood at the gates of Leningrad (St Petersberg), had occupied most of the Ukraine, and were mounting an offensive towards Moscow. Behind them other Germans were busy annihilating Jews, communists and other perceived enemies in the occupied territories — a barbaric process which differentiated this conflict from those fought in Western Europe or North Africa.

Operation Barbarossa completely changed the strategic picture. The Commonwealth acquired a new and formidable ally, albeit one that initially seemed in danger of early defeat. Setting aside previous political differences, even hostility, Britain set about helping the Russians. In New Zealand the new conflict had one immediate minor political impact: the Communist Party switched its stance to supporting the war.

The Russo-German conflict lessened the significance of the German victories in the Balkans for the Commonwealth position in the Mediterranean theatre. With Egypt under threat from Rommel, it was a blessing in disguise that Crete had not been held by Commonwealth forces; its continued defence would have proved a distraction from the task of meeting the approaching Italian-German forces. Even as the expansion of the conflict rendered the Commonwealth position in the Middle East less precarious, it had the opposite effect in the Pacific. With the Soviet Union embroiled in the west, an important constraint on the Japanese had been removed. Moreover the need to provide assistance to the Soviet war effort siphoned off resources that the United Kingdom might have sent to bolster the position at Singapore. This assumed growing significance as the possibility of war loomed in the Pacific. In such a conflict New Zealanders knew they would stand much closer to the front line than they had been so far in the war.

German troops advancing in Russia. This campaign on the Eastern Front would dominate the German war effort from June 1941.

Australian War Memorial, PO2018.061

NZ Army takes control of the Home Guard

Japanese troops move into southern Indo-China

12 Aug – Churchill and Roosevelt sign Atlantic Charter

27 Sep – Japan joins Germany and Italy in Tripartite Pact

400 RNZAF personnel arrive in Singapore

The destroyer USS *Shaw* explodes during the Japanese attack on Pearl Harbor.

– NZ troops in
action in Libya
ation Crusader)

NZ assumes
esponsibility for
ce of all British
ossessions in the
uth-west Pacific

7 Dec – NZ declares
war on Finland,
Hungary and Romania

8 Dec – Japan attacks
Pearl Harbor, Philippines
and Malaya, and the US
enters the war

NZ declares war on Japan

10 Dec – Hitler declares
war on the US

13 Dec – NZ declares war
on Bulgaria

24 Dec – Roosevelt and
Churchill meet in Washington
to discuss strategy

10 Jan – All NZ home forces
mobilised and direction of
labour authorized

Nazi murder of Jews
intensifies as first death
camp set up

15 Feb – Singapore
falls to Japan

War Comes to the Pacific

While New Zealanders at home were waking up on 8 December 1941, dramatic events far to their north-east were transforming the war. In the pre-dawn darkness 275 miles from Hawaii, where it was still 7 December, nearly 200 Japanese dive and torpedo bombers and fighter planes had lifted off their carriers. To resounding '*Banza*i' hurrahs from ground crews and sailors, they set off on their 'divine mission', heading for the island of Oahu.

Swooping down on the American naval base at Pearl Harbor at 7.50 a.m., these planes wreaked havoc among the warships tethered on 'battleship row'. By 8.25, when the last of them headed back out to sea, seven of the US Pacific Fleet's nine battleships had been sunk or heavily damaged. Fifteen minutes later a second wave arrived to attack airbases and other installations, inflicting further damage but suffering some themselves as the surprised Americans began to respond. By 10 a.m. the Japanese planes were gone, leaving more than 2400 Americans and Hawaiians dead or dying. Deciding against a third strike, the commander of the Japanese fleet, Admiral Nagumo Chiuchi, ordered his force to withdraw to the north-east.

This was no isolated attack, for the Japanese objective of neutralising American naval and air power in the region and the Singapore base demanded wide-ranging action.

79

Shortly after midnight Japanese forces had struck the international settlement in Shanghai. Less than two hours later — and 70 minutes before the planes appeared over Pearl Harbor — Japanese troops began landing on beaches at Kota Bahru in northern Malaya. In a few hours more went ashore at Singora and Patani in southern Thailand, and Japanese air forces struck the Singapore and US bases in the northern Philippines, destroying many aircraft on the ground at the latter. Japanese planes also bombed Hong Kong and US facilities on Guam and Wake Islands.

These dramatic events propelled New Zealand into a new conflict: from 11 a.m. on the 8th the country was at war with Japan. Inextricably linked to the struggle in Europe, this was nonetheless a new and separate war. Japan did not come to German aid. There was no strategic co-ordination of German and Japanese action, as might have occurred if Japan had launched an attack on the Soviet Union while Germany was at its throat, and little co-operation except in some intelligence and limited supply matters.

Japan took the opportunity of the distraction of the European powers to seek to create its own self-sufficient economic sphere — the Greater Asian Co-Prosperity Sphere. This would go beyond China, hitherto the main focus of Japanese action, to encompass South-East Asia. (Neither Australia nor New Zealand figured in Japanese plans in other than vague terms.) In effect Japan sought to supplant the South-East Asian empires of the European powers and the United States (which had held the strategically important Philippines since taking them from Spain in 1898) with one of its own. Although it sought to use Asian nationalism and proclaimed itself as a liberator of subjugated Asians, its brutal treatment of populations brought within its orbit soon demonstrated the essentially exploitive nature of its imperial grab. In the circumstances, American power presented the main obstacle to achievement of Japan's goal, and the American-Japanese contest thus became the key to the outcome of the new conflict.

The Pacific War, as it became known in the West, had its roots in East Asia. It emerged out of the undeclared war Japan had been fighting in China for more than four years and greatly expanded the scope of the Second World War. It also raised the stakes for the British Commonwealth. The fate of the British Empire was at issue at a time when Britain was in no position to respond decisively. For New Zealand, as a Pacific state, the clash of empires inevitably posed a potential threat to its physical integrity. New Zealand's fate depended on the United States, an alien though friendly power, prevailing in the deadly struggle initiated by Japan. In this conflict, racial hatred would, as on the Eastern Front, lead to many breaches of the then prevailing rules of war by both sides.

The path to war

If the explosion in December 1941 came as a shock to New Zealand, it was not entirely unexpected. Throughout 1941 war had become steadily more likely as the United States increasingly resisted Japan's efforts to expand its Co-Prosperity Sphere in East Asia by force. During 1940 it had urged Britain not to agree to Tokyo's demands for the closure of the Burma Road, a limited supply route to the beleaguered Chinese. When Japanese troops moved into southern Indo-China in July 1941, the United States tightened economic sanctions, froze Japanese assets and, crucially, banned the export of oil to Japan. It demanded Japan's withdrawal from both China and Indo-China.

Japanese strategists believed their country had stark alternatives — submission or war. Forced by the oil embargo to deplete its vital oil reserves, Japan could not delay a decision for long. Only by seizing the oil-rich Dutch East Indies could it avoid strategic strangulation. Yet war offered no certain salvation, so great was the disparity in resources between the United States and Japan. Conscious of the huge industrial potential of the

The Pacific Theatre

SOVIET UNION

MONGOLIA

MANCHURIA

Sakhalin

Aleutian Is

Peking •

KOREA

JAPAN

CHINA

Hiroshima

Tokyo

Chungking •

Nagasaki

Okinawa

Midway (US)

Kohima •

Iwo Jima

Imphal •

Formosa

Hawaiian Is

BURMA

Hong Kong

Mariana Is

Wake (US)

Pearl Harbor

Rangoon

FRENCH INDO-CHINA

Saipan

THAILAND

PHILIPPINES

Guam (US)

Pacific Ocean

Leyte

Truk

Palau

Marshall Is

MALAYA

Caroline Is

Singapore

BORNEO

Manus

Nauru

Tarawa

Gilbert Is

SUMATRA

Ocean I

JAVA

Rabaul

Pheonix Is

DUTCH EAST INDIES

NEW GUINEA

Solomon Is

Ellice Is

Port Moresby

Guadalcanal

Samoa

Indian

Coral Sea

Fiji Is

Ocean

New Caledonia

Tonga

Cook Is

AUSTRALIA

Sydney

Auckland

Tasman Sea

NEW ZEALAND

Wellington

- - - - - Japanese Empire, 1932
— — — Limit of Japan's expansion, July 1942

United States, Vice Minister of the Navy Yamamoto Isoroku warned against such a course: 'We can run wild for six months or a year,' he predicted, 'but after that I have utterly no confidence.'[62]

When the Japanese government, with a certain resignation, opted for war, Yamamoto (now commanding the Combined Fleet) had to confront the problem of embarking on this apparently unwinnable contest. While diplomatic negotiations to ease the sanctions continued, he conceived and pressed the only course that seemed to give Japan any hope — a devastating pre-emptive strike against the American fleet at Pearl Harbor to neutralise the superior American naval power. This would be inflicted by a carrier-borne air attack, just as the British a year earlier had mauled the Italian fleet at Taranto. Behind this cover Japanese forces would, at the same time, invade the Philippines, Hong Kong and Malaya. Once the go-ahead for these plans had been given on 1 December, Japanese forces began to move towards their assigned positions.

In the lead-up to 8 December, New Zealand had shown increasing sensitivity to the United States' approach to Japan. When Britain in 1940 closed the Burma Road for three months, New Zealand had protested, fearing that the United States would be antagonised and that Tokyo would be encouraged to make more demands. This divergence faded in 1941, however, as the British took a firmer stand with the Japanese. Both Britain and New Zealand denounced their commercial treaties with Japan and supported the American tightening of sanctions. Meanwhile staff talks between British and American officers had indicated encouraging Anglo-American co-operation, even if these talks involved no commitment. American observers began attending British-Dutch planning meetings in the Pacific. Even so, Wellington — and London — remained fearful that the United States might still stand aside if Japan attacked the Common-wealth alone. Not till very late in the piece were such doubts finally allayed, before being swept away entirely with the bombing of Pearl Harbor on 8 December.

Bolstering Singapore

Behind New Zealand's growing attention to the American position lay concern over British capacity to confront Japan. This concern had been greatly increased shortly after Italy had entered the war in June 1940, when Churchill spelt out the implications to Fraser in a brutally frank cable. Up till then Britain had been relying on the French Fleet to cover Italy while Britain sent a fleet to Singapore — even at the expense of the British position in the Mediterranean. But, with France on the verge of defeat, such a course could no longer be contemplated. If Japan attacked, Churchill warned, New Zealand and Australia would have to look to the United States to ensure the British position in the region.

This repudiation of the Singapore strategy remained hidden from ordinary New Zealanders, who continued to see in Singapore a reassuring bastion of British power. The government, however, grimly accepted that the very foundation of New Zealand's defence preparations in the previous two decades had been suddenly knocked away. Previous assumptions that the Dominion would experience only limited raids no longer held good. Fraser resisted any inclination to indulge in recriminations about Britain reneging on previous promises. Instead, he conceded that his government had always recognised that previous assurances about Singapore might prove untenable. Accepting that it was all a matter of priorities and that safeguarding the position in 'the central and critical theatre of war' must take precedence over reinforcing Singapore, Fraser assured Churchill that New Zealand was 'quite prepared to accept the risks which they recognise are inevitable if the most effective use is to be made of Commonwealth naval forces'.[63] This was the response of a strategist, capable of seeing the big picture. Fraser was sure of his country's long-term objective — to ensure the ultimate victory of British arms — and conscious that that objective could not be achieved on the periphery of British power, however vulnerable that left New Zealand to short-term attack, even invasion. In this situation Fraser looked to establish closer ties with the United States.

In the event, Singapore remained at the heart of New Zealand defence planning. In August 1940, Churchill revived Britain's commitment to the strategy. As New Zealand and Australia prepared to send further forces to the Middle East, he sought to allay their concerns about the situation in the Pacific. Reiterating earlier priorities, he assured them that their countries' defence ranked second in priority to the defence of Britain: 'If … contrary to prudence and self-interest, Japan set about invading Australia or New Zealand on a large scale, I have the explicit authority of Cabinet to assure you that we should then cut our losses in the Mediterranean and proceed to your aid, sacrificing every interest except only the defence of the safety of this Island on which all depends.'[64]

A British historian later concluded that this assurance by Churchill was 'not wholly rational', that it involved 'simpler, and more primitive considerations than those of grand strategy'.[65] After all, it made no strategic sense to do anything that might lose the war merely in order to save two peripheral parts of the Commonwealth, not crucial to British survival. In restoring the promise, Churchill must have assumed that it would never have to be fulfilled. Strategic logic seemed to rule out a Japanese thrust southwards while the superior US fleet lay astride its flank in the Hawaiian Islands. Only by going to war with the United States could Japan nullify this threat, but to take on both superior naval powers would lead to almost certain disaster. Churchill expected that Japanese policymakers would back down because war offered them no prospect other than eventual defeat. This assumption lay at the heart of the British — and American — attitude as the crisis deepened.

Men of the New Zealand aerodrome construction squadron hard at work on an airfield in southern Malaya.

RNZAF Museum, HIST1456

83

Hopes in London that the US government might agree to send part of the US fleet to Singapore came to nothing. The Americans wisely refused to take the risk of dividing their force in this way. But they did agree to increase US naval strength in the Atlantic so as to allow Britain more leeway in sending reinforcements to Singapore. The Admiralty aimed to establish a substantial fleet in the east by March 1942, including seven battleships and an aircraft carrier.

Events overtook these plans. As tension mounted in late 1941, Churchill favoured sending a small, powerful detachment of the British fleet to Singapore, not to fight the Japanese but rather to deter them from going to war in the first place. Evidence of British resolve, coupled with the likelihood of having to fight the world's two leading naval powers, would, he reasoned, have a powerful impact on Tokyo's strategists. Despite Admiralty misgivings, the politicians prevailed. On 2 December, Force Z — the powerful new battleship HMS *Prince of Wales* and the older battlecruiser HMS *Repulse* — arrived at Singapore amid a blare of publicity.

Airman Sid Wells on ground defence duties at Kallang in Singapore in late 1941. A Brewster Buffalo stands behind him.

For the residents of Singapore and those preparing to defend the base, the appearance of these naval leviathans provided a huge boost to morale.

New Zealand also made limited efforts to improve the defences of the base. Unlike Australia, which provided an infantry brigade in February 1941 and another four months later, it did not send ground troops to Singapore. The only New Zealanders involved in army units were a few resident in Malaya or Singapore, who joined local defence battalions (as they also did in Hong Kong). Colonial mines administrator John Mackie, for example, was a subaltern in the Perak Volunteers, a part-time unit that carried out rudimentary training. New Zealand confined its assistance to naval and air activities.

Following the arrival of Force Z at Singapore, *Achilles* set off, as planned, to join it. A number of New Zealand officers and seamen attached to the Royal Navy were already in the area. They included a specially recruited contingent of yachtsmen, 32-strong by December 1941, manning patrol craft, and a sprinkling of men in larger units.

New Zealand had also made a direct, if somewhat belated, contribution to the air defences of the base, despatching about 400 RNZAF personnel to the area, mostly members of an aerodrome construction squadron. Formed by inducting recruits from the Public Works Department and private construction companies, it arrived in October 1941. The men toiled in the tropical heat to build aerodromes at Tebrau and Bekok in southern Malaya.

Meanwhile in New Zealand a fighter squadron was being formed for service in Singapore — its first such unit. Pilots newly out of training schools formed most of the complement of 488 Squadron, which began its deployment with considerable anticipation in October 1941. Bound for the Empire's greatest base in the east, they expected shortly to form part of a highly effective defence organisation, and to be equipped with modern aircraft.

What they found was very different from expectations. Big guns guarded the base, but the rest of the defence infrastructure left a lot to be desired.

The state of the air forces available in Singapore indicated how far down the pecking order the island lay. The best British air resources were reserved for the active theatres in Western Europe and the Mediterranean, while the need to support the Soviet effort after June 1941 took priority over Singapore's needs. To South-East Asia Britain sent Brewster Buffalos; it relied upon Australia and New Zealand to provide most of the pilots to man the five squadrons of these American-built fighter planes deployed in Singapore, Malaya and Burma. These men, most just out of training schools, did not appreciate just how out-classed their Buffaloes would be when they came up against the main Japanese fighter plane — the Navy Zero or its army equivalent.

The commanding officer of 488 Squadron, Wilfred Clouston, an Auckland-born veteran of the Battle of Britain, who had joined his unit in Singapore, set about the task of bringing his inexperienced pilots up to operational standard. This proved difficult, not least because of the tropical weather conditions and shortages of essential equipment and spares. Stationed at Kallang

on Singapore Island, the squadron was still working up when the Japanese struck.

New Zealand air force participation was not confined to the 155 men of 488 Squadron. New Zealanders were well represented in the RAF fighter squadrons, including 26 men in 243 Squadron. Others flew with squadrons operating obsolete Vickers Vildebeeste torpedo-bombers, Hudson bombers or Catalina reconnaissance planes.[66]

The Fijian bastion

During 1941, New Zealand looked more seriously at the danger of a Japanese incursion into its own waters. Seizure of a base in the islands to the north seemed an essential prerequisite for such an attack. Although a glance at the map indicated the importance for New Zealand security of both Tonga and Fiji, little had been done to improve their defences before the fall of France. Work had then started on airfields at Nadi and Namaka, in Fiji. In November 1940 the first New Zealand troops,

Soldiers of 30 Battalion at lunch while on manoeuvres in Western Fiji.

Brigadier WH Cunningham, the officer commanding the forces in Fiji, takes the salute from New Zealand troops marching past during an Anzac Day parade in Suva in 1941.

8 Brigade Group, had deployed to Fiji and had begun expanding defence installations on Viti Levu. Under the watchful guidance of sappers, they built gun-pits, reservoirs and tunnels, cursing the heat and their inadequate equipment.

As the outlook in the Pacific darkened in late 1941, preparations became more urgent. In November, New Zealand, which was responsible for the defence of Fiji, agreed to an American request to construct three further airfields. An aerodrome construction squadron, later reinforced by a 1000-man Civil Construction Unit, arrived in the colony to carry out this project. So effectively did they apply themselves to the task that the airfields were up and running well ahead of schedule. A seaplane base was later constructed at Lauthala Bay, and two reconnaissance squadrons deployed there, making it less likely that an approaching raiding force could slip through undetected.

Coastwatchers extended the reach of New Zealand's surveillance effort in the islands to the north of Fiji. Some were servicemen, but the navy, which ran the scheme, also used civilian government officials already in the islands and familiar with local conditions. The coastwatchers carried out their lonely task as far north as the Gilbert and Ellice Islands, reporting by radio any passing ship or air movements.[67]

Preparing to defend New Zealand

Behind the island screen, New Zealand looked to its own defences. At the main ports, heavy guns stood ready to repel intruders. The system installed before the First World War had been upgraded at Wellington and

The crew of a 6-inch howitzer ready for action during an exercise by the Northern Field Force in the Franklin area in 1941.

War History Collection, Alexander Turnbull Library, PA1-q-291-029-078

Auckland during the 1930s. To meet the possibility of the Japanese landing elsewhere and moving on any of these points overland, a mobile force was provided by each of the three military districts. Divisions were created for this particular purpose in each district to provide some cohesion to the forces that would provide the main resistance to such intruders.

But this was a system with many defects. The troops would have little in the way of air support. The Hudson bombers might provide some striking power, but only training aircraft were available to support them. European operations had already demonstrated the disadvantages that lack of air support imposed on troops. A lack of field guns and tanks compounded this problem. All that New Zealand did have in relative abundance was manpower, but even here there were barriers to efficiency.

Part-time soldiers of the Territorial Force manned the port guns and the field divisions. They went into camp for just two weeks a year, a period far too short to allow them to develop real expertise and cohesion. Although fully manned, thanks to conscription, units suffered constant disruption as men were withdrawn for overseas service with 2NZEF. During 1941 men called up for full-time service provided a cadre upon which to build in an emergency, increasing readiness.

Older, less fit men with previous military service also had a part-time role to play in the defence system. Members of the National Military Reserve, formed in May 1939 — 'retreads', as they became known — provided a useful presence in areas away from the main concentrations of forces. Organised in nine mounted squadrons and 20 infantry companies, they patrolled less accessible areas of the country, albeit on a part-time basis. By December 1941 more than a thousand were serving full-time as coastwatchers or guards at vital points.

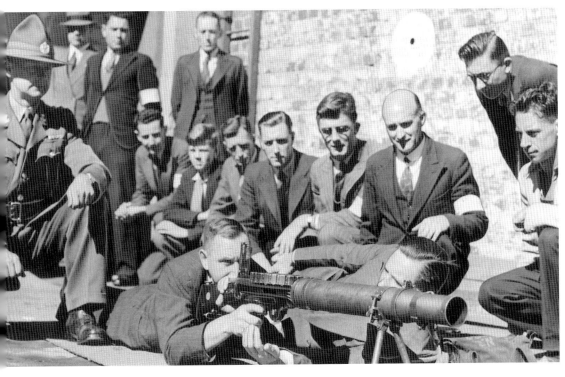

Home Guardsmen receive instruction in the use of a Lewis gun during their lunch hour in April 1941.

Behind them all lay the Home Guard, comprised of older men, teenagers, and others who spent their spare time preparing themselves for battle with varying degrees of enthusiasm. 'On Saturdays we paraded — with our armbands on — some in shorts, some in gardening clothes,' a Home Guard officer later recalled.[68] An assortment of rifles armed about half the 100,000 men spread throughout the country by mid-1941. Others made do with broomsticks for drilling purposes. As uniforms and equipment appeared, the Home Guard assumed a more organised form, especially after the army took control of it in July 1941. The Home Guard performed useful services, especially by relieving more effective soldiers of some routine tasks, but their fighting capacity in the event of a full-scale Japanese invasion remained doubtful.

A Home Guard officer, Captain TEY Seddon, recalls the changing mood in the force in 1941:

Quite early in our own Company's training we essayed 'manoeuvres'. We en-motored [set off in vehicles] and found ourselves at Mount Marshall and there over hills covered with gorse and good cover we had our first experience in field craft. The results were not carried out to the complete satisfaction of the military authorities, but manoeuvres certainly had in them much of the element of surprise — both for the umpires and ourselves! However, they were early days. The parades were happy meeting days and the outings joyous experiences — almost picnics. But the news of the successes of the Axis Forces in Europe and the serious position in the East and the menace of the Japanese advance towards Australia and

A cartoonist's comment on one of the hazards of service in the Home Guard.

The Book of the Gua

New Zealand caused a different, a new spirit to be associated with the Home Guard movement. Seriously, intently, the Guardsmen applied themselves to their training and every parade was marked by an earnestness and a determination to make ourselves into an efficient unit of Home Defence. Rumours were rife. The Home Guard was to be the first line of Defence! The Home Guard would collaborate with the National Reserve. Yet nothing official was given out. Presently the scheme for the defence of Wellington was detailed, and our Marshall Battalion was given a defined area. Men from our unit then found themselves given a frontage and told that that was theirs to hold. The Company's area was inspected and the platoon sections allotted. Every officer, non-commissioned officer and guardsman sought to make himself acquainted with every aspect of the territory given to us to defend.[69]

Defeat in Malaya

On the eve of the attacks on Pearl Harbor, the Philippines and Malaya, New Zealanders had undoubtedly become more concerned about the position in the Pacific. Nonetheless, like many of the British residents and service personnel in Malaya and Singapore, they tended to underestimate Japan's fighting capacity. A sense of racial and cultural superiority underpinned such attitudes. Japan's victory over the revolution-weakened Russians earlier in the century had not proved a real test, in the opinion of many; nor had the conflict in China. Many had convinced themselves that Japan would easily succumb to Western power once directly applied.

This complacency partly explains the lack of urgency evident in Singapore in late 1941. An officer on one of the ships of Force Z, arriving just days before the

The battleship *Prince of Wales* arrives at Singapore.

Japanese invaded Malaya, recalled finding that 'the whole atmosphere in Singapore was pretty slap-happy', which contrasted sharply with that in Alexandria, which he had just left. In Singapore, he concluded, 'nothing seemed to be worrying anybody'.[70] Poor leadership in the top echelons of the British command compounded the problems.

Within days of the outbreak of the new conflict doubts about Japanese fighting ability had been completely dispelled. During 8 December the commander of Force Z, Admiral Sir Tom Phillips, took his fleet to sea. Far from disappearing among the islands of the Pacific to present a lurking menace to Japanese sea movements, as Churchill had envisaged, if it failed in its primary purpose of deterring the Japanese from going to war, the British Fleet would take the fight to the enemy. Unwisely, Phillips set off up Malaya's east coast to attack

reported landing forces without having ensured air cover. Finding no sign of the Japanese and uneasily aware that a Japanese aircraft had spotted his force, he set course for Singapore, and might have made it safely but for a report that Japanese were landing at Kuantan. His diversion to this area proved fatal, for it allowed more than 80 Japanese land-based bombers from Indo-China to intercept his force. Their bombs and torpedoes quickly sent both *Prince of Wales* and *Repulse* to the bottom. Two of the six New Zealanders serving in the ships were among the 800 men lost — almost certainly New Zealand's first casualties of the Pacific War.

Less than a week after Force Z's arrival at Singapore had provided reassuring evidence of British sea power, it had been annihilated in a blow that cast gloom over every British and Commonwealth resident in Malaya and Singapore — and elsewhere. Long schooled in the superiority of the British fleet, New Zealanders were horrified by the rapid demise of the British capital ships. The disaster put an end to plans for *Achilles* to join the force; she was at Port Moresby when recalled to Auckland.

On land the picture was soon equally depressing. Rapidly defeating the mainly Indian forces in northern Malaya, the invading Japanese moved rapidly south. Once again Allied troops suffered the consequences of weakness in air support. The full effects of the poor leadership and the failure to provide modern equipment, particularly aircraft (partly because of the need to supply the Soviet Union with *matériel* to keep it in the fight), became apparent. Adept at outflanking movements through the jungle, the Japanese overcame successive blocking positions as they advanced down both sides of the peninsula. Amphibious operations kept the British forces off-balance; in attempting to disrupt one of these, at Endau on 26 January, a number of New Zealand Vildebeeste aircrew lost their lives, as the Japanese smashed the raid with ease.

As the enemy approached Johore in southern Malaya, the New Zealand aerodrome constructors hastily

Australian War Memorial, 127898

Japanese troops cross a jungle stream as they push southward on the Malayan peninsula.

destroyed the airfields they had built and pulled back to Singapore. They would be evacuated to the Dutch East Indies (now Indonesia) in early February. On 31 January 1942, when the last of the British forces in Malaya had crossed the causeway to the island of Singapore, the causeway was blown up. The siege of Singapore began.

Meanwhile New Zealand airmen had been fighting a losing battle in the skies over the island. Soon after the Japanese onslaught began, Clouston's squadron had begun flying interception patrols, but it did not become fully operational until 3 January. With 243 Squadron, it provided Singapore's main air defence. A heavy air raid on Kallang on 9 January caught many of the planes on the ground, causing severe losses. Even when the planes got into the air they had little prospect of driving off the Japanese, as became apparent when 488 Squadron had its first clash with the enemy on 12 January. The Japanese airmen ran rings around the lumbering Buffaloes, shooting down two and damaging five for no loss.

With great bravery, the mainly Australian and New Zealand pilots sought to overcome the odds against them. They had some successes. Maori pilot Flight Sergeant Bert Wipiti, flying with 243 Squadron, helped to down the first Japanese bomber destroyed over Singapore. His compatriot and fellow squadron member Flight Sergeant Geoffrey Fisken, a Wairarapa farm labourer in civilian life, proved especially skilful at air combat. 'We were outnumbered 16 to one and every time we went out, it was nothing to see 200 or 300 Japanese aircraft in the sky,' he later recounted. 'Anybody who tried to dogfight was just a bloody fool … you were dead in five minutes. The Japanese could out-manoeuvre you easily with their Zeros.'[71] Diving from high above enemy aircraft in hit-and-run attacks, he claimed six victims before being wounded on 1 February and later evacuated.

Frustrated by their inability to meet the Japanese on equal terms, the beleaguered pilots of 488 Squadron welcomed the prospect of using nine Hurricanes that arrived by sea on 13 January. But their hopes proved

New Zealand airmen at an airbase in Singapore after a mission in their Brewster Buffalo fighters.

Flying Officer Geoffrey Fisken, the leading Commonwealth fighter ace of the Pacific War.

short-lived. An enemy bombing raid on Kallang airfield on the 27th destroyed or damaged eight of the Hurricanes, as well as most of 243 Squadron's surviving aircraft. Almost incapable of putting any aircraft in the air, 488 Squadron was withdrawn to the Dutch East Indies on 2 February, and its ground staff followed soon afterwards. The remnants of the other squadrons also flew south.

The fall of Singapore

The Japanese began their assault on Singapore on 8 February 1942. Despite enjoying a numerical superiority over their adversary, the demoralised defenders quickly faltered. The vaunted citadel of British power in the Pacific fell in a week. More than 130,000 men laid down their arms — the worst military disaster suffered by the United Kingdom since the loss of the American colonies in the eighteenth century. Many civilians were killed attempting to make their escape from the island by ship in the final days; some fell victim to atrocities as the triumphant Japanese caught up with them.

In the fighting in Malaya and Singapore, 35 New Zealand airmen lost their lives. About 40 New Zealanders serving in the Royal Navy also died in operations in Malayan waters — or in Hong Kong, which had fallen to the Japanese on Christmas Day. The naval dead included 14 of the specially recruited RNVR yachtsmen. On land, the campaign also took the lives of a few New Zealanders serving with local colonial forces. Just before the fall of Singapore, one New Zealand-born officer, serving with the Indian Army, apparently suffered the ignominious fate of being summarily executed for spying for the enemy.[72]

The Japanese onslaught left a number of New Zealanders in Japanese hands. The first to be taken were

A pall of smoke from the naval base hangs over beleaguered Singapore city in February 1941.

Imperial War Museum, HU337

92

9

coastwatchers in the western parts of the Gilbert Islands, who had no choice but to surrender or were quickly rounded up when Japanese forces arrived soon after the Pearl Harbor attack. Seven captured on Butaritari were taken to Tokyo to begin nearly four years of captivity. They were fortunate; when the Japanese seized the rest of the island group nine months later, 17 of their colleagues were murdered by their captors — the worst atrocity inflicted on New Zealanders during the war.

In all, about a hundred New Zealand servicemen and women and several hundred civilians became POWs of the Japanese, mainly in the first few months of the Pacific War. They languished in camps spread throughout South-East Asia, with most in Singapore. Some were also held in China or Korea, and in Japan itself. Although Japan had never ratified the Geneva Convention on the treatment of POWs, it seemed to indicate that it intended to observe the spirit of the agreement. In practice it failed to do so. New Zealand POWs endured years of harsh treatment, made worse by the contempt that many of the Japanese guards, in keeping with their own military code, felt towards men who had surrendered. Conditions varied from camp to camp, but imprisonment by the Japanese was invariably a more trying experience than that endured by New Zealand POWs in Europe. Largely devoid of the Red Cross parcels that helped succour those held in Germany and Italy, without adequate medical facilities and subject to regular humiliation by their guards, the prisoners of Japan struggled to survive as malnutrition and disease took their toll.[73]

New Zealand RAF pilot Flight Lieutenant RD Millar recalls his capture in Java in April 1942:

> *The interrogation commenced, the gist of which was that they were trying to convict us of being guerrillas. Keblewhite was the spokesman for our party, putting across a good story,*

as near the truth as possible.... About half way through the interrogation two other Japanese Officers arrived.... One of these Officers, a very sadistic looking individual, after listening for a few moments said something to the Captain, who nodded his head. The 'Sadistic Type' then drew his sword and indicated to Keblewhite that he get down on his knees. He refused. The Captain then ordered him, through the Japanese and Chinese interpreters, to get down on his knees, which he did. The sadistic type proceeded to indicate to him by grunts and gestures that he was to pull his shirt collar down and tuck it in, and to stretch his neck out further, the officer in the meantime holding his sword up in the air and drawing his thumb along the edge of same, all the time looking highly delighted. The Captain asked why we had not committed 'Hari-kiri', to which Keblewhite replied that it was not part of our religion. After about an hour or more of this Keblewhite was allowed to stand up again, and the Captain said that we all had to die at dawn the next day. How did we wish to die, bayonet, cut-throat, sword-cut-head-off, or shoot. We said that we preferred shooting, thank you.

We were taken to cells in the Dutch P.O.W. Camp.... Here we were given a meal of rice and vegetables ... and left to wait for dawn and execution. The cells were built to hold four or five persons, but there were ten of us in each of these cells.

Dawn broke, but apart from the usual activity among the Japanese guards nothing else of importance was apparent. In due course breakfast ... was served.... The morning and afternoon, the night and the next morning passed without anything happening....[74]

As the POWs adjusted with difficulty to their new situation, New Zealanders at home worried about what lay in store for them. The shield provided by the Singapore strategy had proved illusory. For the first time they faced the possibility of a hostile power moving into the South Pacific in strength. New Zealand's strategic isolation threatened to become a source of danger, rather than of security.

15 Feb – Singapore falls

19 Feb – Darwin bombed
by Japanese aircraft

8 Mar – Japanese submarine *I-25*
enters Cook Strait

9 Apr – Japanese attack
Trincomalee, Ceylon

Death camp set
up at Auschwitz

2 Mar – Capital of Dutch East Indies
(Batavia) captured by Japanese

Alexander Turnbull Library, F-66963-½

Members of the Territorial Force, equipped with gas masks, prepare for possible invasion.

27 Apr – Rationing
begins in NZ with
sugar and hosiery

12 May – US assumes
responsibility for
defence of South-west
Pacific islands

4 Jun – US victory in
Battle of Midway

13 Jun – First US troops
land in Auckland

7 May – US victory in
Battle of the Coral Sea

28 May – Clothes
rationing begins

1 Jun – Tea rationed

30 May – First RAF 1000-
bomber raid on Germany

The Invasion Threat

The fall of Singapore left most New Zealanders fearful that their own country could now become a target. Their worries grew as the Japanese juggernaut lurched on, seemingly unstoppable. In the east, British and Indian forces fell back in Burma, abandoning Rangoon to the enemy in March. To the south the Japanese flooded into the Dutch East Indies, taking the capital, Batavia, on 2 March. Most worrying, from a New Zealand viewpoint, was the appearance of Japanese forces in the South Pacific, as they took Rabaul and entered the northern Solomon Islands. Australia had already been violated; on 19 February aircraft launched from aircraft carriers in the Timor Sea had bombed Darwin, killing several hundred people — the first, and most destructive, of more than 60 raids on the town.

After Singapore fell, only a few New Zealanders remained in action against the Japanese. Expatriate Frank Quayle was one of several who operated behind the lines in Malaya. Members of stay-behind parties, they secreted themselves in the jungle and later supported a guerrilla effort that relied heavily on indigenous Chinese communists.

In far-off Burma more than a dozen New Zealand pilots helped man the only RAF unit in the country at the outset, 67 Squadron, and there were a handful in 113 Squadron, which arrived with its Bristol Blenheim medium bombers from the Middle East in January 1942.

New Zealand pilot Vic Bargh describes his method of attack in the Buffalo:

> *We were using what they call a rolling attack. You had to be above them. And when you saw them coming, you pulled up steeply and rolled over on your back as you were coming up. You could see everything below you, you see. Well, we were quite used to flying the aeroplane; it didn't matter a damn whether we were upside down or right way up. You just curled over at the top — when you lost a lot of speed, you'd turn into a dive, and you twisted around so you came in from behind. Straight in behind.... I did it twice, and I lived.*

Like their counterparts in Singapore, these airmen fought a losing battle against superior forces. The fighter pilots soon became aware of the shortcomings of their Buffaloes. 'I learned very quickly,' pilot Flight-Sergeant Vic Bargh later recalled. 'I never really got caught. He who fights and runs away, lives to fight another day.'[75] As in Singapore, the Buffalo pilots brought down a few Japanese bombers, but they suffered many casualties. Some of the New Zealanders were killed in action; a few were captured. Eventually Bargh and the other surviving pilots pulled back into India to avoid annihilation.

In the Dutch East Indies, other airman tried to hold up the enemy, although they were operating under very

Peter Fraser arrives in Hawaii with Admiral Chester Nimitz (left) and South Pacific commander Vice-Admiral Robert Ghormley.

difficult conditions. Evacuated by ship from a hospital in Singapore, flying-boat pilot Sid Scales rejoined his squadron at Tjilatjap in southern Java, and flew at least one reconnaissance mission. But the Japanese moved fast, and he was eventually left with no way out: 'We finished up in a big convoy of trucks at an aerodrome called Tasik Malaja, and the next thing we knew was that a Japanese motorcycle patrol was going round and round the perimeter and we were all POWs.'[76]

At sea other New Zealanders continued to resist the Japanese. Some were aboard British warships destroyed in a series of vicious naval battles in Dutch East Indies waters. New Zealand's own cruisers, *Achilles* and *Leander*, joined a small force of cruisers and destroyers operating out of Suva as the Anzac Squadron, under the command of an American officer. The New Zealand seamen endured the tedium of escorting troop and cargo ships — without even an encounter with the enemy to relieve the monotony. Only New Zealand's armed merchant cruiser *Monowai*, also active in the area, had such an experience. While proceeding south of Fiji on 16 January, she came under fire from a Japanese submarine that surfaced near her. But the Japanese commander quickly broke off the action when he became aware of *Monowai*'s hitting power.

Three weeks after the fall of Singapore the Pacific War at last arrived in New Zealand waters — though no one realised it at the time. Nosing into Cook Strait on 8 March 1942, the Japanese submarine *I-25* launched an aircraft to make a pre-dawn reconnaissance flight round the harbour looking for American shipping. A few days later, it did the same over Auckland and the Hauraki Gulf before making off towards the Fiji area. A couple of months later the submarine *I-21* made a similar reconnaissance of Auckland after coming south from Fiji. No ships fell victim to Japanese submarines in New Zealand waters at this time, nor indeed later; better pickings for such predators existed across the Tasman on the east coast of Australia, especially off Sydney.

America at war

Japan's entry to the war had immense strategic consequences. Above all, it precipitated the United States into active hostilities with Germany. Even if American warships in the Atlantic had for months been used in ways that compromised US neutrality, full-scale American participation in the war still remained unlikely, however much President Roosevelt might favour such a course. Adolf Hitler solved Roosevelt's problem at a stroke. Determined to support his ally, the German leader declared war on the United States on 10 December 1942.

Hitler's gratuitous action added a new and formidable enemy to the anti-German coalition just as the first cracks appeared in Germany's war effort. Even as Japanese planes struck at Pearl Harbor, Germany was suffering its first serious reverses. In North Africa a British offensive launched three weeks earlier had relieved Tobruk (see Chapter 8). More significantly, the Soviet Union had risen from the dead. Aided by 'General Winter', its armies had gone over to the offensive against German forces that had reached the outskirts of Moscow. As the Germans fell back from Moscow, they were haunted by the spectre of the catastrophe that had befallen Napoleon's Grand Army in Russia some 150 years earlier.

Most New Zealanders were greatly relieved when America became involved in the war in Europe. Like Churchill, they saw victory as inevitable once the huge, virtually invulnerable reservoir of American strength was mobilised for war. They applauded efforts to co-ordinate the Anglo-American war effort. Immediately after Pearl Harbor Churchill had hurried across the Atlantic for talks with Roosevelt. The two leaders had little difficulty in agreeing that the Allies should give priority to defeating the more dangerous enemy, Germany. This strategic decision, which had great bearing on the nature of New Zealand's ongoing war effort, provided the solid foundation for harnessing the Western Allies' resources. The Joint Chiefs of Staff in Washington now became the key to how those resources were used.

With the United States taking responsibility for the war in the Pacific, New Zealand's security depended on American power. Strengthening its ties with the United States assumed new urgency. In late January 1942 Walter Nash arrived in Washington to head the newly established New Zealand Legation — the first post established by New Zealand in a foreign capital. His tasks included sitting on the Pacific War Council, a body that Roosevelt grudgingly established in Washington to meet Allied powers' desire for some access to strategic formulation at the highest level. But the council in no sense acted as a coalition policymaking instrument. With Pacific war strategy firmly in American hands, it served more as a source of information than of consultation.

For New Zealand, American control of the Pacific theatre meant adjusting to American war planning that did not necessarily accord with its perceptions or wishes, as when the American authorities defined operational areas in April 1942. Australia found itself in the massive South-West Pacific area, New Zealand in the South Pacific area. This pleased neither Canberra nor Wellington. But the Americans disagreed with their contention that the two Dominions formed a single strategic entity; they regarded New Zealand's defence as a purely naval problem. Thus New Zealand's war effort would henceforth be carried out within a framework controlled by the US Navy, under Admiral Chester Nimitz, the Commander-in-Chief Pacific. Posing a land and sea defence problem, Australia stood in a different position to New Zealand, in Washington's view. It would be the responsibility of the ambitious General Douglas MacArthur, who had escaped south from the Philippines when the Japanese invaded. This neat solution to the problem of what to do with MacArthur, which owed as much to army-navy rivalry as it did to strategic reasoning, ensured that Australia and New Zealand would not be closely associated in most of the Pacific fighting after the wind-up of the Anzac Squadron in April 1942.

Maori soldiers of 2 Maori
Battalion train in New Zealand.

World War II Official Album, Alexander Turnbull Library, PA1-q-292-09-4

Fears of invasion

The disasters at Pearl Harbor and off the Malaya coast shocked New Zealanders, but did not panic them. With the Singapore base still standing as an apparent bulwark to any southward Japanese advance, the scene of action remained distant. Above all, the United States, though staggered by the Japanese attack, was far from being knocked out. But Singapore's fall and the seemingly unstoppable Japanese advance soon changed perceptions. A great fear gripped the public.

At no stage did the government's military advisers regard invasion as imminent. Quite apart from the distances involved, they reasoned that New Zealand had neither the resources nor the strategic location to make it a target worth taking risks to attack in strength. Only when Japan had secured complete freedom of action in the Pacific would such an operation be worth the trouble, perhaps to remove a possible springboard for an attempted American resurgence in the western Pacific. Such freedom could only be gained by neutralising American naval power. But, although reeling from the losses at Pearl Harbor, the US Navy was still in business. It made its presence felt with a series of raids on Japanese-held islands, culminating in a carrier-borne attack on the Japanese homeland itself, the famous Doolittle raid.

If Japan did defeat the American forces, it would have the capacity to isolate New Zealand completely. New Zealand had no industry to provide the shells and bombs necessary to modern warfare, let alone the tanks and aircraft to use them. Without re-supply capacity, protracted defence would be impossible. An invasion implied a situation in which Japan, moreover, could bring overwhelming air power to bear to support its troops — and the disasters of 1941 left no-one with any illusions about what that would entail for the defenders.

On this reasoning, then, New Zealand would face a hopeless situation if invasion became a real prospect. But this assessment provided no excuse for inaction. The public, less concerned by strategic reasoning than by evidence of action, would clearly not be satisfied with half measures. In any case, defences were needed against contingencies less extreme than invasion. Japan could be expected to mount raids on outlying Allied territories with a view to disrupting the Allied war effort in more vital areas. Such raids could be made more difficult, and perhaps deterred, by the preparation of defences.

Intelligence trump card

For a small minority, including Fraser but perhaps not other members of the War Cabinet, assessment of Japanese plans was not merely guesswork. Intelligence about movements of Japanese warships provided an indication of Japanese intentions. This integrated Allied effort, in which New Zealand played a small but valuable part, centred on enemy radio traffic. The distinctive techniques of Morse code senders were a giveaway as to a particular ship once the link had been made. Photographing a ship's signals as sound waves as they appeared in a cathode ray tube (radio fingerprinting) provided a means of tracking it. Ships' positions could also be determined by intersecting the bearings of radio signals as picked up in two or more places. New Zealand service personnel took part in these radio direction-finding operations.

Just as in Europe with the breaking of the Enigma ciphers, the jewel in the crown of Allied intelligence was the ability of Allies to read some enemy messages. Japanese signals picked up in New Zealand were forwarded to intelligence organisations in Australia and Hawaii; there code-breakers succeeded in deciphering and decoding some of them, with telling effect on the course of the naval war. This material was returned to Wellington in the form of top-secret intelligence summaries provided by the US naval authorities. These authorities were concerned about possible leakages that might alert the Japanese to the fact that their signals were being read, which would lead at best to a change of codes and at worst to a change of system that might shut out the code-breakers indefinitely. Protecting the source placed severe constraints upon what Fraser or his Australian counterpart John Curtin could tell the public about Japanese intentions, as gleaned from this intelligence.[77]

There were other dangers. New Zealand's intelligence organisation, which produced its own weekly summaries using material received from the Americans and elsewhere, made a serious blunder in May 1942. Four of the summaries, bound for the intelligence centre at Colombo, were aboard the steamer *Nankin*, and these fell into German hands when the German raider *Thor* intercepted the steamer. Placed in the ordinary mail, they had not been destroyed with other secret papers as the enemy approached. The summaries, which may have allowed the Japanese to deduce that their naval signals were being read, were made available to the Japanese authorities belatedly in August 1942 but they do not appear to have been of great value to them.[78]

Defence preparations escalate

As the situation worsened, the authorities continued to regard the Fijian bastion as the key to limiting the scale of attack on New Zealand. Another 600 men had been sent there immediately war began, along with additional anti-aircraft guns. More substantial reinforcements followed in January 1942. Men being trained as reinforcements for the Middle East were hastily formed into three infantry battalions and sent, as 14 Brigade, to Fiji to bolster what was designated 2NZEF in the Pacific. Sufficient battalions now existed to form a light division that from May 1942 would be informally referred to as 3 Division. By the middle of the year more than 10,000 New Zealand servicemen and women garrisoned the islands, practising battle tactics, building installations, cursing the tropical heat and wondering what would happen if a Japanese task

Anti-aircraft gunners fixing shell fuses during a training exercise.

Alexander Turnbull Library, C-27016

100

force appeared over the horizon. They may have been fortunate that their efforts were never put to the test: a senior American officer criticised the preparations in mid-1942 as sounding 'too much like the old textbook stuff to be very impressive' and providing evidence that the New Zealanders were still unaware how radically different the war was to the First World War.[79]

Regular officer Frank Rennie recalls the early stages of 14 Brigade's service in the islands:

> The first week or so was unquestionably the most uncomfortable of my service, and it says a lot for the morale and spirit of this new battalion that it emerged in such good shape under conditions which would have tested any well-established unit. Most of us were off colour when we arrived because of the vaccinations, and it was mid summer and very hot. It took time for reasonable food to be produced and in the meantime the troops got into the pineapples and other tropical fruit which surrounded the camp. With the inevitable touch of dysentery which emerges before hygiene standards are enforced, it was an 'eye of the needle' situation if ever there was one.
>
> That was difficult, but not as trying as the absence of mosquito nets (and New Zealand blood, even with vaccine, seemed to be appetising) and beds....
>
> The primary task of 14th Brigade was the defence of the airfield at Namaka (now Nadi); 30th Battalion, which had been in Fiji for some time, was based in the Momi area to prevent landings and infiltration from the sea and 35th Battalion was in defended localities along the foreshore, covering the airfield and its seaward side. Our Battalion was in reserve, with the primary role of counter-attacking the airfield area, as well as preparing defended localities for occupation to prevent penetration. Our priorities were to familiarise ourselves with the area by 'walking the course' and to prepare fire positions.[80]

Members of the Elmwood Home Guard, Christchurch North Battalion, dig shelters.

Lower Hutt Home Guardsmen parade for inspection by Brigadier Norman Weir.

Eleven hundred miles to their south, New Zealand was undergoing an unprecedented mobilisation. Fully manning the coastal defences had been the first priority after Japan's entry to the war. Within days of Pearl Harbor nearly 6000 Territorials of specific units had been called into camp. The rest were scheduled to follow within weeks for their now extended annual training. But before this could happen the government mobilised the whole force. Men left their employment and headed for camp. By mid-January 43,000 men had joined their units, and were preparing for possible combat.

A Territorial soldier called up in December 1941 recalls a peptalk soon after entering camp:

> *…we were all called on parade in front of dozens of trucks and told that the Japs were expected 'somewhere' on the coast and we were issued with one round each for our rifles! When the guy next to me asked the Sergeant what would happen after the round was fired — he said, 'Throw bloody stones!'* [81]

The call-up was not confined to Territorials. More than 21,000 'retreads', and others now allowed to join the National Military Reserve, stood to arms. Many of these reservists were obviously not in good shape for active military operations, and the army wasted no time in winding up the Reserve. Fitter men went into Territorial units, the rest into the Home Guard, which also became more active. In order that Territorials could concentrate on training, home guardsmen performed useful service in preparing fixed defences. They installed barbed wire on beaches and elsewhere and provided guards for key points.

As units prepared to confront the enemy on the battlefield, others toiled away on a huge range of defence works. Tons of concrete were poured to stud beaches and access routes with pillboxes, gun emplacements and tank blocks. Underground headquarters were built, including

a headquarters under Parliament Buildings. Preparations began to install much heavier guns at Wellington and Auckland. The construction of air-raid shelters reminded civilians that they, too, would be in the firing line if the worst happened.[82]

Enemy at the gates

Lacking the intelligence information available to the authorities, many in New Zealand believed that at any moment a Japanese fleet could appear off some part of New Zealand (probably in the far north) and throw a sizeable force ashore. They saw the feverish defence preparations; they heard news of continuing disasters as the Japanese drew nearer and they responded to rumours. The sense of crisis heightened when the government announced, on 10 January, drastic measures to ensure that New Zealand's farms and factories remained in business. All men of military age and some women became liable to direction into essential industries.

Although the nearest Japanese forces were still thousands of kilometres to the north, New Zealand went onto a war footing. The nightly task of blacking out homes to ensure no light was exposed now became more relevant. Any chink of light showing would soon bring an irate warden knocking on the door. People began preparing for an emergency by collecting essential items. Some buried valuables.

The prospect of invasion evoked varied reactions among the public. Resignation and fear mingled with a certain sense of bravado: 'We would be prepared, act quickly and with courage, die rather than surrender,' one youthful Hawke's Bay woman recalled. 'We talked of little else, while those with realistic attitudes towards our prospects of making more than a token gesture against Japanese invasion kept their mouths shut and let it all go on around them.'[83] Many women feared violation by rampaging Japanese soldiers.

Australian War Memorial, PO2018.098

USS *Lexington* belches smoke after attack by Japanese torpedo bombers during the Battle of the Coral Sea in May 1942.

Some looked for ways of doing their bit for their endangered country. In Hamilton, men and women came together to raise funds to help equip local Home Guard units. This spontaneous Awake New Zealand movement caught on. Soon other communities had followed Hamilton's lead.

The War Administration

The unifying effect of the crisis also left its mark on politics. While both main parties had agreed to postpone the general election scheduled for 1941 because of the looming danger in the Pacific, strong political in-fighting had continued during several by-elections held even after Pearl Harbor. National criticised in particular the government's failure to crack down hard on strikers.

The deteriorating situation in early 1942 bolstered calls from various quarters, including the influential RSA, to bring the parties together in the administration of the war effort. Labour remained implacably opposed to forming a coalition ministry; but private talks eventually bore fruit, and in June a War Administration — a kind of super-War Cabinet of 13 ministers — was established. With both the War Cabinet and the ordinary Cabinet also still in existence, the arrangement appeared to be 'unbearably clumsy'.[84] But despite its drawbacks it worked reasonably effectively at first. It brought a truce in political strife, for the parties agreed to put off the delayed general election until after the end of the war.

Pacific versus Mediterranean deployment

Japan's entry to the war brought into question the future role of New Zealand's most effective military formation — 2NZEF in the Middle East. Since the war, a myth has developed in New Zealand, and even Australia, that

following Japan's onslaught the Australian government immediately demanded the return of its troops from the Middle East to protect the homeland, while New Zealand in contrast deferred to British requests that its division remain where it was. On the basis of this myth, some commentators have denounced New Zealand's approach as evidence of a lack of independence, of a willingness to put New Zealand itself at risk rather than upset the British government. In reality a British request, not an Australian demand, lay behind the removal of two of Australia's three divisions from the Mediterranean theatre. They formed part of a four-division reinforcement of the Commonwealth forces in South-East Asia.[85]

With shipping already committed to moving these troops to the east, the means did not exist immediately to redeploy 2 Division to the Pacific, even if New Zealand had asked for its return. The movement of Australian and British divisions in accordance with overall Allied strategy had priority; action not in accordance with this strategy must await its completion. By the time the Australian divisions had been re-deployed, Japanese warships were marauding the Indian Ocean. They attacked targets in Ceylon on 4 April. The movement of troopships in the Indian Ocean would be far too risky. But that was the only route a returning New Zealand division could take. Axis air forces in Sicily and Tripolitania rendered passage through the western Mediterranean — and thence around either of the Capes — out of the question.

Allied strategy provided another reason for leaving 2 Division to continue its fight with Rommel's forces, a fight in which it had recently proved its mettle and for which it was trained. Fraser accepted the basic precept underpinning the Allied coalition effort — that the defeat of Germany must take priority. New Zealand, he believed, should continue to make its small contribution where it could best achieve the Allied objective. The fact that Roosevelt urged New Zealand to retain 2 Division in the Middle East underlined the point.

Fraser may also have recognised that in the event of full-scale invasion 2 Division would not suffice to ensure the country's defence, and the forces already in New Zealand could deal with anything less than invasion. But the people's fears had to be allayed, and a solution to his political problem soon appeared in the form of an offer by the US government on 10 March to send American troops to New Zealand. This proposal, which was conditional on New Zealand leaving 2 Division in the Mediterranean theatre, offered a safer and easier reinforcement to bringing home 2NZEF. As a first step American troops began relieving New Zealand troops in the islands to the north — at Fanning Island on 26 April and Tonga on 9 May. On 13 May the Americans agreed to take over responsibility for the defence of Fiji, though it would be 18 July before this process was completed. After that date, the only New Zealanders who remained were 260 men attached to the Fiji Defence Force (including its commander) and some gunners manning coastal guns until they could be relieved by American units. American garrisons in the islands to the north provided a reassuring shield to New Zealand.

Tokyo plans its next moves

Notwithstanding the fact that Japanese maps of New Zealand and even occupation currency were prepared (and later found by Allied troops), Japanese strategists at no time gave serious consideration to an invasion of New Zealand — for the very reasons earlier identified by the military authorities in Wellington. New Zealand just did not figure as a Japanese priority at this stage of the war; it was a long-term objective that would depend on the development of the situation. That the possibility did exercise the minds of some agencies in Japan explains the evidence of certain preparatory actions, including the gathering of intelligence about the country, continuing pre-war efforts.[86]

Surprised by the ease with which they had secured their main objectives in early 1942, Japanese strategists struggled with the tricky question of what to do next. Within the top naval echelons opinion was divided. Staff officers in Tokyo wanted to invade Australia, but the army dismissed such a scheme as impossible while most Japanese troops were still embroiled in China. The Combined Fleet, the navy's primary striking arm, focused on bringing the main American fleet to battle and decisively defeating it. To do this, it looked to lure the American fleet into a trap by mounting an operation against American-held Midway Island, an outlier of the Hawaiian Islands and near enough to Pearl Harbor to ensure an American response. Annihilation of this fleet would leave Japan with a free hand in the Pacific for an indefinite period.

That the Combined Fleet's approach eventually prevailed was of vital moment to New Zealand. If Japan won the showdown, the conditions needed for an invasion would be created. For the time being, however, Japanese objectives in the South Pacific ruled out any major attack on New Zealand. Australia and New Zealand were merely to be cut off from the United States by the occupation first of Port Moresby and then of the islands to the east and south-east of New Guinea — New Caledonia, Fiji and Samoa.

With the benefit of decoded Japanese signals, the Americans soon perceived Japan's intentions. Taking a calculated risk, they sent part of their fleet, including

The aircraft carrier USS *Yorktown* on fire after an attack by Japanese bombers during the Battle of Midway.

several aircraft carriers, southwards to counter the operation in the South-West Pacific. The Japanese force bound for Port Moresby was intercepted in the Coral Sea on 7 May. The ensuing battle was notable for the fact that the opposing fleets never came in sight of each other (for the first time the aircraft not the big gun proved decisive). Although a draw tactically — both sides suffering similar losses and damage — the Americans won strategically. The Japanese turned back, abandoning their attempt to seize Port Moresby by sea.

Japan's plan to cut off Australia and New Zealand foundered in the battle. Australian troops later foiled its attempt to attack Port Moresby overland in a difficult campaign on the Kokoda Trail, inflicting the first significant defeat of the war on the Japanese army. Orders for the second stage of the planned operation, the capture of New Caledonia, Samoa and Fiji, were cancelled in July. Unaware of the limitations on Japanese plans, many in New Zealand and Australia believed that the Battle of the Coral Sea had saved them from imminent invasion by halting a seemingly inexorable southward thrust by Japanese forces.

Showdown at Midway

Although the Coral Sea success boosted Allied morale, it paled in significance before the showdown looming in the Central Pacific. In a typically complicated Japanese plan, which included landings in the Aleutian Islands in an unsuccessful bid to lure away elements of the US Fleet, the Combined Fleet bore down on Midway Island in early June. With a formidable armada of battleships, it dwarfed the American naval forces available to counter it, though, crucially, there were three US aircraft-carriers to Japan's four. Midway's land-based bombers, and the American ability to read parts of the Japanese naval signal traffic, offset this numerical disadvantage. The Americans prepared to ambush the oncoming Japanese armada.

The ensuing battle was a near-run thing, the outcome being determined by the fortuitous appearance of American dive-bombers over the unprotected Japanese aircraft carriers on 4 June. The mortal damage inflicted on three of its carriers in the space of five minutes shattered Japan's hopes in the war. The fourth soon succumbed as well, though not before Japanese airmen had heavily damaged an American carrier (which was later finished off by a Japanese submarine). It was not just the loss of the carriers that was disastrous to Japanese hopes; with them went the cream of Japanese naval air crews, rendering any recovery even more difficult.

Midway proved to be the decisive battle of the Pacific War. In New Zealand the outcome brought relief — coming on top of the Coral Sea success, it confirmed the revival of the American fleet. The danger of invasion now receded further into the future, being contingent on Japan turning the tables in another encounter and regaining the strategic initiative. But the skill of American fleet commanders, the important intelligence advantages enjoyed by the American naval authorities, and not least the immense scale of American warship building all seemed to render unlikely any such revival. New Zealanders could breathe easier — and another development soon reinforced their growing belief that the worst was over.

The Yankee 'invasion'

Less than a fortnight after the Battle of Midway effectively removed the danger from Japan, an invasion of a very different kind began. The Yanks arrived in New Zealand. The first, a regiment of the US Army's 37 Division, landed at Auckland on 13 June and moved into camps hastily built by the Public Works Department in the vicinity. Next day, units of 1 Marine Division began landing at Wellington. They were soon settling into a camp near Paekakariki, 45 kilometres north of Wellington.

Neither division remained long. The army regiment had come south only because of a lack of accommodation in Fiji until the New Zealand troops there had been withdrawn. Twelve days after landing in Wellington, the marines received orders to prepare for a landing at Guadalcanal. By the end of July the camps in both Auckland and Wellington were empty.

No official announcement had been made of the American 'invasion', and the sudden appearance of unfamiliar troops was greeted with surprise — and sometimes consternation. The naval successes and the evidence of an American presence in the South Pacific greatly eased earlier anxieties; a Japanese descent on New Zealand would clearly not be uncontested. Indeed it soon became apparent that, far from being attacked, New Zealand would become a support base for the counter-offensive being planned by the Americans. Anxious to maintain production, the government wasted little time in beginning the process of standing down elements of the mobilised Territorial Force. The first returned to civilian employment in July. As they did so, New Zealand eyes were focused on the Middle East, where the success of the Allied campaign in North Africa hung in the balance.

US Marines march off Paekakariki Station following their arrival in 1942. Apart from the initial arrivals, New Zealand played host to two other Marine divisions (2 and 3) and two Army divisions (25 and 43) between 1942 and 1944.

War History Collection, Alexander Turnbull Library F-36341-½

| Jun 1942 | Jul 1942 | Aug 1942 | Sep 1942 |

21 Jun – Tobruk captured by Rommel

1 Jul – First Battle of El Alamein begins

Camp for Japanese POWs established near Featherston

US government initiates the Manhattan Project to build an atomic bomb

24 Jun – War Administration formed

Mahatma Gandhi interned for demanding India's independence from England

28 Jun – 2 NZ Division narrowly escapes destruction at Minqar Qaim

A German tank crew member is taken POW by New Zealand troops.

War Administration collapses

23 Oct – Second Battle of El Alamein begins

7 Nov – Allied forces land in Morocco and Algeria (Operation Torch)

15 Dec – Wage-price freeze introduced in NZ

4 Nov – Allied victory at El Alamein

Defeating Rommel

During the late afternoon of 30 November 1941, hundreds of New Zealand soldiers found themselves in an unenviable predicament on a sandy ridge in western Libya. Dug in on the Sidi Rezegh escarpment, they watched with trepidation German tanks and troops in the distance forming up for an attack.

As soon as the approaching enemy infantry came within range, the New Zealanders brought them under a withering fire. They could see the attackers faltering. But their relief proved short-lived. Mortar bombs began to drop in their positions, systematically seeking out the anti-tank guns that provided their protection from the lurking enemy armour. Shortly after 5 p.m., with all these guns knocked out, the tanks drove into the New Zealand positions.

As the light faded amid dust and smoke, tanks moved from section to section. Menaced by their guns, the men in the foxholes had no choice but to raise their hands. 'When I rose from my trench what a sight met my eyes in the growing darkness,' a company commander later recounted. 'We were ringed in by Hun tanks and their infantry were collecting the prisoners.'[87]

Operation Crusader

This disaster befell the men of 24 and 26 Battalions less than a fortnight into their first engagement with the enemy in North Africa. On 18 November, as part of 6 Brigade, they had crossed the wire separating Libya from Egypt to take part in Operation Crusader — another in the British Middle East Command's series of efforts to relieve beleaguered Tobruk. With the rest of 2 Division, they entered the battle with confidence that this would be no repeat of the Greek fiasco; this time they had ample armour and air power in support.

Unbeknown to the troops, the question of air support had been the subject of exchanges between Churchill and Fraser. The latter, anxious to avoid previous mistakes, had queried the RAF's capacity to counter possible *Luftwaffe* interference with the operation. Churchill reassured him, though only by juggling the figures: a senior officer sent to the Middle East from London had performed 'an entirely political conjuring trick' in order to provide 'the Prime Minister with figures which he must have known bore little relation to the reality of the forthcoming battle'.[88] The episode was a further demonstration of the limitations on New Zealand's distant control of its force.

During the battle the *Luftwaffe* certainly made its presence felt. Yet even if the troops had to endure dive-bombing and strafing on numerous occasions, this was no re-run of the hammering they had suffered in Greece. The RAF was present in strength and vigorously contesting control of the skies. Fears that after the offensive opened the enemy might gain superiority by flying planes into the theatre from elsewhere, perhaps even Russia, came to nothing.

In Operation Crusader it was not the air force but the armour that let the troops down. As they moved

Fires from distant action on Belhamed hang over the desert battlefield. The New Zealand division suffered the highest casualties of any division engaged in Operation Crusader on the Allied side. The 879 dead included 80 wounded killed by an air attack on the ship conveying them from Tobruk to Alexandria. Seventeen hundred men had been wounded, and another 2042 had gone into the bag as POWs. The losses were all the more disturbing because on 27 December 1941 Freyberg learned that the 8th Reinforcements training in New Zealand would be held back for home defence purposes. They would not leave New Zealand until December 1942.

Sir John White Collectic

westwards, they had no inkling that a faulty tactical approach put them in jeopardy of being left unsupported. British tank commanders conceived their role as meeting and defeating Rommel's armoured units, something like a naval force seeking out the enemy fleet and decisively defeating it. With this mindset, they tended to fight their own battles, leaving the infantry to their own devices — a very different approach to that adopted by Rommel's forces, in which tanks, anti-tank artillery and infantry were used in a tactically integrated fashion.

Nor, at this stage, did the New Zealanders fully appreciate the threat posed to effective operations by another British tactical mindset — that the brigade group provided the most appropriate sized unit for desert operations. To be sure, a brigade was more mobile than a division; but it packed less punch than a division, which could bring to bear the concentrated firepower of all its field guns in attack or defence. Brigade groups — the so-called Jock columns — operating independently offered the enemy the opportunity to defeat them separately. An *Afrika Korps* officer later likened these independent brigade groups to mosquitoes: a nuisance 'but in the end no more violent in their sting' and 'never really strong enough to do irreparable damage'.[89]

Freyberg strongly disagreed with the brigade-based tactical approach, partly because he believed in concentration, partly because he was determined to resist dispersal of his force. But such tactics soon affected his division in Libya. After taking Fort Capuzzo, the New Zealanders had pressed on towards the Libyan coastal towns of Sollum and Bardia. Hargest's 5 Brigade was ordered to cover the enemy stronghold at Sollum, while Inglis's 4 Brigade cut the Bardia–Tobruk road and isolated Bardia. On 22 November 6 Brigade was directed westwards to Sidi Rezegh, on an escarpment that was the key to the relief of Tobruk. It soon found itself up against determined opposition. An attempt to seize the tactically important Point 175 failed bloodily, with 25 Battalion losing 100 men — the worst disaster to befall a New Zealand battalion on a single day in the whole war.

The division took the position the next day. Meanwhile 4 Brigade had also been ordered to drive westwards towards Tobruk. At Bir el Chleta, on 23 November, it scattered the *Afrika Korps* HQ, but then found its way blocked by a well-defended escarpment — Belhamed.

Even as the New Zealanders attacked westwards, developments elsewhere on the battlefield were rendering their position precarious. The British tank brigades had driven towards Tobruk with the intention of bringing Rommel's tanks to battle. But a failure to concentrate the British force had diminished its striking power. Rommel fell on the separated brigades and dispersed them. Uncontained, he then thrust to the east. Although a blunder on his part, for it amounted to a punch into thin air, this 'dash for the wire' threatened to cut off the New Zealanders.

Oblivious to the danger, the men of 4 and 6 Brigades continued to attack westwards towards Tobruk. On successive nights they completed the occupation of Belhamed and Sidi Rezegh. On 27 November 4 Brigade linked up with the Tobruk garrison at Ed Duda on the last escarpment before the port.

By this time Rommel, running short of tanks and supplies, had abandoned the frontier area. Heading back towards Tobruk, he overran a surprised 5 Brigade HQ and other units. Brigadier Hargest was among more than 700 men who surrendered. Driving on to the north-west, Rommel saw an opportunity to destroy the New Zealand division, by falling on the other New Zealand brigades, which were still consolidating their newly captured positions.

When 6 Brigade came under attack on 30 November, the New Zealanders were not well placed to resist. To their consternation and anger, nearby British armoured units failed to respond as German tanks overran both 24 and 26 Battalions. On the following day, 4 Brigade suffered a similar fate on Belhamed escarpment. The Germans destroyed another infantry battalion and a field regiment. Commander of the divisional artillery Brigadier Reginald Miles was among the POWs; he had strolled forward to be with the gunners, looking, in one observer's opinion, 'for all the world as though he were going duck-shooting'.[90] Some of 4 Brigade managed to pull back into the Tobruk area; other elements of the brigades eventually withdrew during the night of 1–2 December to Bir el Chleta, where they linked up with a South African brigade.

Sergeant Charles McDonald describes the overrunning of his 20 Battalion unit at Belhamed on 1 December:

Shortly after dawn the order was passed along 'Stand by for A.F.V. attack.' Visibility was bad, a haze making it difficult to pick up objects beyond five hundred yards. About fifteen minutes after the warning order three tanks passed across my front about four hundred yards away. They had brushwood tied at the back to raise a dust. At first I was not sure whether they were enemy as our artillery did not fire at them, but when they stopped I saw their gun flashes firing towards Brigade area. Then more tanks came into view with anti-tank guns towed by motor vehicles. I immediately opened fire....

For the first part of the attack the nine tanks I could see did not engage us. With the arrival of their supporting weapons they turned on us, edging slowly up. We had been firing continuously for some time and I was beginning to consider the advisability of conserving ammunition. During a pause I looked to my left and was surprised to see some of our men with their hands up, three hundred yards away. I could not understand what had happened. There was still plenty of enemy movement in our front and we carried on shooting and getting heavy fire in return. The tanks closed in to shorter range and fired heavily on us with guns and machine-guns. About fifteen minutes later Mr. Guthrey shouted to me to put my hands up and I did, not understanding the reason until I saw three tanks a short distance away to the left. Surrendering was something I had never considered possible and yet here it was.[91]

Rommel had virtually swept all before him — even if Tobruk remained beyond his grasp. But his force was now largely spent, as became apparent when he tried to relieve besieged Bardia and Sollum on 3 December and 5 Brigade resolutely blocked his way. He decided to pull back to Gazala, west of Tobruk, and eventually to El Agheila. By doing so he lived to fight another day. But by leaving the battlefield and retreating, he left the British with a victory of sorts. Despite the severe mauling he had inflicted on the British forces, Tobruk had been relieved. When Bardia and Sollum eventually fell, more than 30,000 Axis troops surrendered.

Meanwhile the New Zealanders nursed their wounds. They had performed well, they knew, but the cost had been very high. Casualties amounted to 4600. The dead included two members of parliament serving with 2NZEF — two of the total of four MPs who lost their lives on active service during the war. Operation Crusader's 'butcher's bill' exceeded that of all 2 Division's other battles in the whole war.

As in Greece a large number of New Zealanders had gone into the bag as prisoners. Some had the good fortune to be liberated when advancing Allied forces

Wounded New Zealanders are prepared for evacuation at Bir el Chleta during Operation Crusader.

overran the transit camps in which they were being held; and a few managed to escape and return to Allied lines. But most made the dangerous journey across the Mediterranean to Italy, eventually to find themselves languishing in large POW camps in the north of the country.

The North African campaign

Strategic and geographical influences shaped the nature of the campaign in which the New Zealanders became involved in November 1941. It was fought by two coalition forces whose strength was determined by requirements elsewhere. On the Axis side, the German divisions provided the backbone and Rommel, though nominally under Italian command, dominated the tactical approach of the Italian-German forces. But he was fighting in a campaign regarded by Hitler as a sideshow to events on the Eastern Front, where the great bulk of German forces were deployed. This determined the level of reinforcement provided to the *Afrika Korps*, and ultimately limited its effectiveness.

New Zealand railway sappers constructing the Western Desert railway in October 1941.

On the Allied side, the North African campaign was also ultimately a sideshow to the defence of the United Kingdom. But for the time being it was the only show — the only place where British ground forces could engage the enemy. And it was fought for major strategical stakes — control of the Suez Canal, protection of Middle Eastern oilfields, and the opportunity to strike at the soft underbelly of Axis Europe if successful. As with Rommel's forces, requirements elsewhere determined the level of reinforcements. Many of the divisions engaged in North Africa were Commonwealth — South African, Australian, New Zealand — or from the Indian Empire. 8th Army, as the Western Desert Force had been re-designated in September 1941, also included contingents from five occupied European countries. The British High Command in consequence had 'a lot of children to humour'; a senior New Zealand officer wrote later that they 'must have been difficult children'.[92] The problems of using Dominion forces had been indicated by their reaction to the Greek fiasco and by Australian insistence upon replacing Australian troops besieged in Tobruk in the face of British reluctance to do so.

Geography dictated that the campaign be fought along a narrow coastal strip of the continent. The terrain and soft sand placed severe limits upon the operation of vehicles any distance to the south. Along the coastal strip, however, there were few natural obstacles to provide strong defence lines. Opportunities for outflanking always existed, except at El Agheila or El Alamein where the ability to operate inland was particularly constrained. In consequence, these two points became in effect gateways to the main bases of the two opposing sides — El Agheila to Rommel's base in Tripoli and El Alamein to the Allied base in the Cairo/Suez area. Once outflanked, a force might be forced into prolonged retreat before a new stand could be made — as in Rommel's pull-back to El Agheila after the Crusader offensive. The troops dubbed the see-sawing of the contending armies across this desert battlefield the Benghazi Stakes.

The second main influence on the campaign was the

difficulty of bringing in supplies in an area in which distances were great and roads limited generally to a single main route along the coast. Sustaining an army in the desert demanded large supplies of petrol, ammunition, water and food, all of which had to be brought in from outside. The further an army operated from its supply point the more difficult became its operations, since everything had to be trucked up to the front. This placed a premium on the few sizeable ports along the coast, and especially Tobruk. Without Tobruk, Rommel's forces operating in eastern Libya had to rely on far-off Benghazi and Tripoli for their supplies.

While the Commonwealth effort depended, ultimately, on defeating the Italian-German units on the desert battlefield, action elsewhere provided the essential prerequisite to success, both in enhancing 8th Army's capacity to fight and diminishing that of its opponent. In this logistical struggle, New Zealand made a big contribution, though one less visible than that of its fighting division.

As early as 1940 railway sappers had arrived in Egypt from New Zealand. They immediately set to work extending the Western Desert line beyond Mersa Matruh, but the defeat of Graziani's army soon reduced the urgency. Not till mid-1941 did they return to the task in earnest. Working seven days a week, and using Egyptian labourers, they pushed the railway rapidly westward, reaching Capuzzo early in 1942 and eventually extending it to Belhamed — a distance of 440 kilometres from Mersa Matruh. (German sappers completed the link with Tobruk in 1942.) Other New Zealanders undertook the often dangerous task of operating the trains that used the line to bring up supplies.

Although the Western Desert railway line was perhaps their most important contribution to the Allied effort, railway sappers operated as far afield as Persia (Iran) and the Sudan. The surveyors and constructors were also active in building and maintaining lines in Syria in 1942–43.

The troops fighting in the arid forward areas had reason to be grateful to New Zealand sappers, who ensured their water supply. Elsewhere others helped with the facilities needed to maintain a steady flow of supplies by improving port facilities, clearing debris from captured harbours and even building a reserve port in the hellish heat at Safaga on the Red Sea coast.[93]

The British position in the Middle East depended on its naval predominance, which ensured the flow of supplies from Britain and beyond to Egyptian ports. Many New Zealanders took part in these operations while serving with the Royal Navy. But the navy also had the capacity to harass the enemy's lines of commun-ication — for Axis supplies also had to pass across the sea, albeit the shorter route from Greece or Italy to Tripoli or Benghazi. British submarines inflicted a heavy toll on this sea traffic — sometimes with fatal consequences for Allied POWs being conveyed across the Mediterranean to Italian POW camps. Forty-four New Zealanders were among more than 600 killed when a torpedo sank the *Jantzen* on 9 December 1941. A similar incident in August 1942 involving the *Nino Bixio* took another 118 New Zealand lives.

The Mediterranean Fleet provided cover for the ships used to carry supplies to Tobruk and Benghazi ports while those ports were in Allied hands; it also sought to intercept enemy convoys carrying supplies to their own troops. During these operations, New Zealand suffered its worst naval disaster. While attempting to intercept an Italian convoy on 19 December 1941, the cruiser HMS *Neptune* struck mines and sank. She carried an unusually large number of New Zealanders because she had been earmarked eventually to join the newly constituted Royal New Zealand Navy. All but one of the crew died, including 150 New Zealanders.

The main focus of Allied operations against the enemy supply chain lay in the island of Malta, lying astride the route between Italy and Tripoli. Recognising its significance, German military planners had urged Hitler to take it rather than Crete, but without success. Operation Crusader drove home to Rommel the threat posed by this dagger aimed at his lines of communication, and German and Italian air forces began to attack Malta with much greater intensity from bases in Sicily.

Almost 200 New Zealand airmen took part in the Malta operations against both this bombing campaign and enemy shipping. Two of the three air commanders on the island during the course of the North African campaign were also New Zealanders. When Italy first entered the war Air Vice-Marshal FHM Maynard had occupied the hot seat. In July 1942 Battle of Britain veteran Keith Park took up the task, having previously spent half a year commanding the air forces in Egypt.

New Zealand transport south of Mersa Matruh prior to the Minqar Qaim escape.

Efforts to disrupt the flow of Axis supplies to North Africa were not confined to the regular forces. In September 1942 Special Operations Executive parachuted a sabotage group into Greece to destroy a viaduct on the main railway line running south to Athens — a supply route to Rommel's force. Two New Zealand sapper officers, Captains CE Barnes and Arthur Edmonds, played a key role in this operation. They laid the charges that brought down the Gorgopotamos viaduct on 25 November. Plans to evacuate them immediately could not be implemented, and they remained in Greece with the Allied military mission for some time supporting resistance forces. In June 1943 in an even more spectacular operation, other saboteurs, including New Zealander Donald Stott, destroyed the Asopos viaduct. At least ten New Zealanders served for periods with the military mission in Greece between 1942 and the end of the German occupation in late 1944.[94]

Syrian interlude

Early in 1942 it seemed likely that the New Zealand division would soon return to the desert. But the government stepped in to ensure that it received a less onerous assignment — as part of the British forces occupying the recently occupied Vichy territory of Lebanon-Syria. Leaving 5 Brigade to follow a month later, the division began moving to Syria in February 1942, a development much appreciated by troops delighted to pass through biblical lands. In Syria, they came under the command of General Sir Henry Wilson's 9th Army.

When the division departed to Syria, the non-divisional sappers provided New Zealand's continuing army contribution to the Western Desert campaign, as they toiled on railways, ports, water points and other lines-of-communication tasks. One small group of New Zealanders, those serving with the Long Range Desert Group, remained in action with the enemy. Sometimes they swooped in to attack isolated enemy installations,

but their main task remained to gather information about terrain, enemy movements and defence positions. On one occasion, later in the campaign, they set up a temporary airfield into which aircraft flew to refuel, thereby allowing air strikes on targets in Cyrenaica that the enemy thought were out of range of such attack.[95]

Meanwhile in Syria, the division spent much time improving defences. Although the area lay in a backwater for the present, Allied strategists foresaw the possibility of a German thrust down from the north through Turkey that would endanger the British position in Egypt. But the troops gave little thought to such contingencies. For them the three-month sojourn in Syria amounted to 'a pleasant holiday and many interesting things to do and see'.[96] The men's tourist streak reasserted itself as they explored the neighbourhood.

Freyberg saw the interlude as an opportunity for refresher training in light of experience of the 1941 battles. He considered Operation Crusader to have merely confirmed the dangers inherent in the British tactical approach of using brigade-sized 'battle groups' rather than full divisions. The advantages of the latter were particularly apparent when it came to artillery support. The gunners spent much time in Syria reassessing their tactics, developing techniques for improving the speed and weight of fire. The 'stonk' — a concentration of all divisional fire on one point — became a New Zealand byword.

Halting Rommel

Rommel, now commanding the Italian-German *Panzerarmee*, eventually cut short the New Zealanders' pleasant and undemanding stay in Syria. After pulling back to El Agheila, he did not wait long before lashing back at the forces that had followed him up, starting the next race in the Benghazi Stakes on 21 January 1942. In no time he had forced 8th Army back to the Gazala Line, about 65 kilometres west of Tobruk. A lull developed, but on

27 May he attacked again. Out-manoeuvred, the Allied army fell back to the east, exposing Tobruk. This time no resolute defenders stood in his way. The port's capture, on 21 June, not merely earned Rommel a field marshal's baton; it also left him able to concentrate on invading Egypt without a flanking threat to his line of supply and with his supply problems eased by use of the port.

As these events unfolded, the New Zealanders made 'a lightning move' back to the Western Desert. Pressing westward from Alexandria, they passed demoralised and disorganised troops 'coming pell-mell back down the road'.[97] Shocked by the stench of defeat that hung in the air, they took up positions in the fortified area at Mersa Matruh the day before Tobruk fell.

When Rommel's army arrived on the scene, things did not go well at first. Freyberg had insisted on a more mobile role for his division than being tied up in a defensive box. The New Zealanders moved south to Minqar Qaim, only to quickly find themselves in a precarious position. Amidst the confusion of battle, it became apparent that the pull-back of other Allied units had placed them in jeopardy, for 21 Panzer Division had moved between them and the rest of the Allied forces to the east.

With Freyberg incapacitated by a shell splinter, temporary command of the division had passed to Brigadier Inglis. Only a break-out could save the division. In the early hours of 28 June, the troops of 4 Brigade's three battalions prepared for a desperate attack. They would open a path through the encircling enemy to allow the rest of the division to escape. The plan worked. Catching the enemy by surprise, the New Zealanders cut a swathe through them, the Maori infantrymen to the fore, in perhaps the most savage attack ever carried out by New Zealand troops. So ruthlessly did the troops use their bayonets that the Germans would later accuse the New Zealanders of failing to adhere to the rules of war by killing wounded and surrendering men — and there is little doubt that some unfortunate incidents occurred. Echoes of German bitterness could still be detected 60 years later when veterans gathered in Egypt for commemorative events.

As this breach was being made, the rest of the brigade drove through another gap, a ride that all present would never forget. Bumping across the desert, they finally got clear of the enemy fire, leaving many trucks blazing in their wake. In the confusion the rest of the division broke out through other points in the ring. About a thousand casualties were suffered in this episode — the New Zealand division's most dramatic moment of the whole campaign — and numerous vehicles were lost, but the division had escaped almost certain destruction by a narrow margin.

As the various units fell back eastwards to link up with the rest of 8th Army and gradually came together again, those who had been captured were left to bear the brunt of German wrath, made worse by the realisation that a golden opportunity to knock out one of the *Panzerarmee's* most feared enemies had been lost. One group of New Zealand POWs found themselves in imminent danger of being slaughtered by their captors until an officer intervened, apparently to save them from this fate.[98] German radio dubbed the New Zealanders 'Freyberg's butchers',[99] an epithet that only served to boost morale among troops pleased that they had struck a telling blow against the enemy.

Captain Charles Upham (centre) is congratulated by his platoon sergeant on the award of the first of his two VCs.

New Zealand gunner Lance Bombardier Bruce McKay Smith recalls the break-out from Minqar Qaim:

> *As it got dark all the guns that were serviceable were lined up behind their quads to pull them, and all personnel were allocated space in a vehicle of some kind to get out. Then … we set off going south. Now the Maori infantry put in an attack towards the Germans and all hell was let loose. The Germans, apparently, hadn't expected us to move at night; they weren't prepared, so they were firing blindly at anything. The vehicle I was in, we had quite a few machine-gun bullets through the canopy, but nobody got hurt. There was just utter confusion — flares, gun shots, machine-gun fire, mortars, anything that could make a noise seemed to be going. We got through the main line of German defences, or whatever they were — they were pretty scattered and ineffectual — and carried on in the vehicles. There were always some vehicles knocked out and some casualties, but not a great many.[100]*

As he drove further into Egypt, Rommel came up against the problem of geography — the Qattara Depression, jutting up towards the Mediterranean, greatly narrowed the usable terrain. Not only did this reduce his scope for manoeuvre but also it thickened up the depth of the defences confronting him. The defending divisions, New Zealand's among them, had a distance of only about 65 kilometres to cover. This area became known as the Alamein Line, after the small railway station at El Alamein.

In early July the New Zealanders took part in the first battle of El Alamein, which stopped Rommel in his tracks. On 3 July 1942 they showed great proficiency in effectively destroying the Italian Ariete Division. But when 8th Army commander, General Auckinleck, went over to the offensive in search of a decisive victory, poor planning and co-ordination led to a series of disasters for the New Zealand division, matching those of Sidi Rezegh and Belhamed.

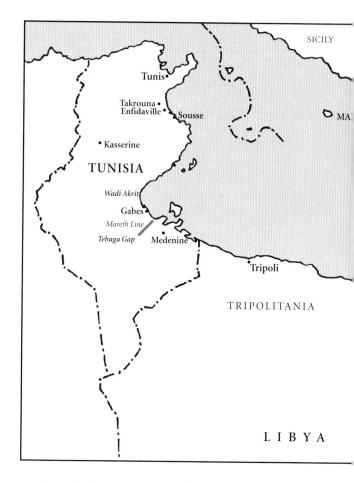

In a night attack on 14 July troops of both 4 and 5 Brigades had advanced onto Ruweisat Ridge, a low escarpment jutting into the Allied line. The rocky terrain made it difficult to dig in, but they expected to be supported by British tanks next morning, when an enemy counter-attack could be expected. But poor planning led to confusion. At dawn it was German, not British, tanks that appeared. They overran 5 Brigade's 22 Battalion, and later in the day two battalions in 4 Brigade suffered a similar fate. The unwillingness of nearby British armoured units to move onto the ridge without orders to assist the hapless New Zealanders left 5 Brigade commander Brigadier Howard Kippenberger beside himself with rage. He would later describe the battle as 'a tragedy of misdirection and

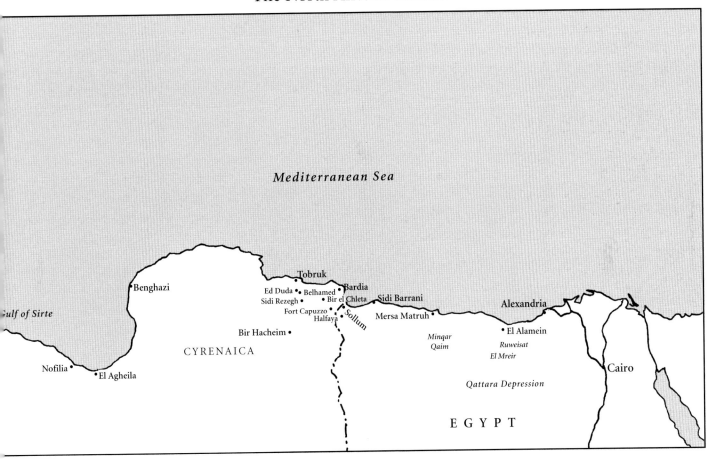

mismanagement'.[101] His complaint, in a letter intercepted by the censor, that his wife could have run the battle better than his corps commander caused some embarrassment when it eventually reached General Auckinleck in Cairo. As a result of the débâcle nearly a thousand men went into the bag — men who would be sorely missed because of the hiatus in the flow of reinforcements. Among them was a wounded Charles Upham, whose courageous efforts here and earlier at Minqar Qaim would earn him a bar to his VC, the only time a combat soldier has achieved this feat. Sergeant Keith Elliott also won a VC at Ruweisat Ridge for his inspirational leadership; although wounded three times, he led his men in overcoming a series of enemy posts to break-out and avoid captivity.

Yet another disaster a week later further soured the New Zealand mood. As part of an Allied attack, the New Zealanders were given the task of capturing the El Mreir Depression. According to the plan, British armour would then use the position to thrust deep into enemy territory. This time 6 Brigade made the attack. Once again the troops advanced successfully at night to secure their objectives. But at first light on 22 July the only armour in sight was German, the tanks of 21 Panzer Division. Two more battalions suffered a severe mauling, and another 500 New Zealanders went into captivity, most eventually joining their compatriots in camps in northern Italy.

The constant failure of co-ordination between armour and infantry left the New Zealanders frustrated and angry;

Kippenberger would later write of 'a most intense distrust, almost hatred, of our armour'.[102] Convinced that having tanks under command was the only practical solution to this problem, Freyberg decided to convert the battered 4 Brigade to an armoured unit. Withdrawn to base, it would play no further part in the campaign.

A lull now developed on the Alamein Line. As both sides settled in behind minefields that sweating sappers steadily extended, a 'drowsy lethargy' descended on the front. 'Heat waves shimmered off the burning sand and boredom and discomfort almost drove us crazy,' recalled infantry NCO Pat Kane.[103] Myriads of flies made life all but unbearable for the troops holding the forward positions. 'They were always with you — in countless millions,' a divisional cavalryman later recorded, 'God knows what rotten corpse or foul latrine they'd fed on before drowning in your tea, or becoming transfixed to your bread and jam. It was better to fish them out and not think.'[104] The men could combat the flies by, where possible, eating after sundown, but they had no such defences against dysentery and desert sores. Occasional sand storms added to the misery, leaving 'every body orifice … choked and choked with sand'.[105]

The enemy added to the men's discomfiture. Enemy gunners harassed them, while the *Luftwaffe* continued to make its presence felt. The soldier lying in his slit trench could only pray as Stukas screamed down towards them and released their bombs. 'What a night,' Gunner Struan MacGibbon wrote after enduring a particularly strong attack. 'Enemy planes were over us all night, dropping bombs, butterfly bombs, parachute and ground flares. Looked like city lights at times and the butterfly bombs go off like giant strings of crackers.'[106] A steady trickle of casualties reminded the troops of their mortality.

Hurricane pilots prepare for a mission at a desert airfield. In all, 750 New Zealanders would serve with the RAF in the Mediterranean theatre prior to mid-1943; 115 of them lost their lives.

RNZAF Museum, MUSO20843

Breaking the stalemate

As a stalemate developed along the Alamein Line, Rommel knew that time was not on his side. He faced huge difficulties in keeping his force supplied. Many of the ships failed to make it across the Mediterranean, and the supplies that did arrive had often to be trucked in from as far west as Benghazi, for Tobruk proved unable to cope with the flow. Nor was he receiving enough reinforcements to sustain his force's strength. On the other hand, his opponent only grew stronger, as the influx of American resources began to tip the balance the Allied way.

In a last attempt to force the issue before it was too late, the Italo-German forces attacked on 30 August, 'a night of flame and noise' as the Allied artillery responded.[107] Rommel had little hope of success, and his pessimism soon proved justified. Now under a new commander, Lieutenant-General Sir Bernard Montgomery, 8th Army countered the thrust with little difficulty. Even if ULTRA intelligence counted for more than his tactical skill in this engagement, Montgomery's reputation soared, both within the army and beyond.

These operations highlighted another Allied advantage: the growing power of the Western Desert Air Force, which harried the exposed enemy forces mercilessly. Under the command of yet another New Zealand RAF officer, Air Vice-Marshal Arthur Coningham, its airmen had perfected air-ground support tactics that would greatly assist Allied operations for the rest of the war.

Like Freyberg, Coningham was not by birth a New Zealander but had been brought up in Wellington. He took part in the occupation of German Samoa in 1914 and later served at Gallipoli before being invalided home. In 1916 he made his own way to England to join the Royal Flying Corps, beginning a highly successful career as a fighter pilot. His New Zealand origins earned him the nickname 'Maori', which later became corrupted

New Zealand troops dig slit trenches.

Sir Arthur Coningham.

to 'Mary'. Like many of his compatriots, he took a permanent commission in the RAF following the war. In the early stages of the Second World War, he had commanded a bomber group before being despatched to the Middle East in July 1941.

Deployed in the so-called 'New Zealand Box', the New Zealanders observed with satisfaction the growing evidence of Allied air superiority. They became involved in the fighting only after the Axis forces faltered, taking part in a half-hearted counter-attack that left 80 of them dead by the time it ended early on 5 September. Despite this, Allied morale soared as both sides pulled back to their pre-attack positions. The Battle of Alam Halfa, as it was later designated, had been a considerable overall success.

Another lull developed on the battlefield as 8th Army prepared its own stalemate breaker. By now disposing twice as many men and tanks, and enjoying substantial superiority in aircraft and anti-tanks weapons, Montgomery intended to knock Rommel's army for six, as he put it to receptive troops. Determined that this time the enemy would be given no chance of a comeback, he resisted pressure from an impatient Churchill for early action. Not till all was ready would he launch his offensive.

The New Zealanders awaited the coming battle with anticipation, not least because Montgomery inspired confidence among them. Freyberg found his tactical approach more to his liking than those of previous commanders, for Montgomery was no supporter of the hated 'battle groups'; his belief in the concentration of force accorded well with Freyberg's own preference. The troops found Montgomery's emphasis on practising the attack reassuring. Moreover, their fears of again being left unsupported on their objectives, as at Ruweisat Ridge, lessened with the attachment of the British 9 Armoured Brigade to the division. The close links established with this unit boded well for the future.

Shortly before 10 p.m. on 23 October 1942, the flash of 900 guns heralded the opening of Montgomery's quest for a decisive victory. For the infantrymen waiting on their start lines, this artillery barrage was an unforgettable and reassuring sight. The plan provided for the troops of four infantry divisions — New Zealand, South African, Scottish and Australian — to 'break in' to the enemy's defences. Behind them sappers would rapidly clear corridors through the now extensive enemy minefields, not only to allow support weapons to reach the infantrymen but also to open the way for the tanks. Advancing through the infantry, the tankies would ensure the 'break-out' by defeating the enemy armour. The mobile New Zealand division would then form part of the thrust that would seek to encircle the beaten enemy.

Behind a carefully planned First World War-style creeping barrage, men of 5 and 6 Brigades moved rapidly forward in the darkness, made more impenetrable by the clouds of dust thrown up by the shelling. In an attack later described by 6 Brigade's commander as 'a model of its type',[108] they took all their objectives on Miteiriya Ridge except in one sector, where a misjudgement led the battalion concerned to pull up short. More than 1500 men had been killed or wounded.

Sir John White Collection

Freyberg with General Montgomery (left).

Although infantrymen carried out their part of the plan effectively, the battle did not develop as Montgomery had hoped. Congestion, poor co-ordination and a lack of drive prevented the British armoured units from getting forward with any momentum. Over the next two days a 'grinding sort of battle' developed that threatened to become a stalemate.[109] Montgomery turned his attention to the northern sector of the front.

For a week 9 Australian Division 'crumbled' the enemy defences, in savage fighting that eventually drew in the last of the Axis reserves. With a breakthrough seemingly impossible in this area, Montgomery planned a new thrust in the south. He looked to Freyberg and his efficient divisional staff to organise the break-in component of Operation Supercharge, even though the division itself no longer had the strength needed for the task after its losses in the initial attack and the fighting in the following four days. Two British infantry brigades attached to the division would provide the main assault element, with New Zealand infantry battalions being used to protect the flanks.

Opening at 1.05 a.m. on 2 November, the break-in attack followed a similar pattern to that of 10 days earlier. Once again infantrymen secured their objectives, but this time the armour got to grips with the enemy, with 9 Armoured Brigade to the fore. Hampered by fuel and ammunition shortages, Rommel's tank forces melted away. Within two days he had ordered a retreat — despite Hitler's unrealistic demand that he hold fast. The way was opened for the Allies to launch the break-out phase.

Trucks of 2 New Zealand Division advance through the desert. More than 1700 New Zealanders became casualties during the second Battle of El Alamein – about 12.5 per cent of 8th Army's total. Of these 379 had been killed or mortally wounded.

John White Collection

123

The New Zealand division took part in this pursuit, as planned. But Freyberg remained cautious about committing his weakened division — a tactical approach matched by Montgomery, who was determined to give Rommel no chance of turning the tables by some bold riposte. An untimely deluge helped to ensure the escape of the bulk of the German forces; but deprived of transport, many of the Italians had been forced to surrender. The New Zealanders pressed westward as far as Halfaya Pass near the Libyan-Egyptian border before being relieved on 10 November.[110]

The road to Tunis

By the time 2 Division pulled out of the line, the Axis outlook in North Africa had taken another turn for the worse. On 7–8 November Anglo-American forces landed in Morocco and Algeria. Limited opposition by Vichy French forces quickly came to an end, and an Allied force thrust eastwards into Tunisia, also a French colony. Only the rapid deployment of German and Italian forces there from Europe prevented the Allies from rapidly seizing Tunis. As the Germans responded to this new front by creating a new army, under General von Arnim, Rommel fell back before 8th Army's still cautious drive as Montgomery missed opportunities provided by ULTRA information to outflank and destroy his force. On 20 November Allied troops took Benghazi for the third and last time as Rommel retired behind defensive positions at El Agheila.

As 8th Army advanced into Tripolitania, the New Zealanders made a series of left hooks. While other forces attacked in the coastal sector, they moved inland in an attempt to get behind and cut off the enemy's line of retreat. At both El Agheila and Nofilia in December, however, Rommel's force slipped away before the noose could be tightened. Abandoning Tripolitania, Rommel awaited the oncoming Allied force on the Mareth Line on the Tunisian-Libyan border — always on the lookout to deliver a counterpunch. Turning away from 8th Army

temporarily, he inflicted a sharp defeat on American forces approaching from the west at Kasserine Pass in mid-February 1943. The end of this action coincided with his elevation to command all Axis forces in Tunisia as Commander-in-Chief Army Group Africa, with General Messe taking over the *Panzerarmee* (now retitled 1 Italian Army). When Rommel attempted to turn the tide against Montgomery's force at Medenine on 6 March, however, New Zealand gunners helped beat him back. Three days later he handed over his command to von Arnim and departed for Germany on sick leave, ending his involvement in the campaign.

When Montgomery assaulted the Mareth Line on 20 March, the New Zealanders again had the task of delivering a left hook. Moving through rugged terrain at night — 'no lights, no smoking and vehicles nose to tail for visual contact'[111] — and lying up under camouflage during the day, they reached the Tebaga Gap, a defile opening into the rear of the enemy position. The New Zealand Corps stood poised to cut off the Italian-German forces now under attack on the Mareth Line. But temporary corps commander Freyberg hesitated just long enough to allow the enemy to hastily redeploy substantial forces into the area. He then became even more hesitant to commit his forces. Montgomery sent reinforcements, and a replacement corps commander. Hard fighting followed, culminating in an attack on 26 March that was notable for its co-ordination of air and ground forces.

In Operation Supercharge II the New Zealand infantrymen once again made the 'break-in' that opened the way for British armour. In this Allied blitzkrieg, the Maori battalion had a stiff fight for a key point on 26 March; in one sector 23-year-old platoon commander Moana-nui-a-kiwa Ngarimu, wounded in leg and shoulder, rallied his men throughout the night to throw back enemy counter-attacks before being killed next morning while still firing his sub-machine gun. His inspirational conduct earned him a posthumous VC — the first won by a Maori serving with the New Zealand forces.

For all its violence and proficiency, Operation Supercharge II failed to trap the enemy, who fell back deeper into Tunisia in some disorder. When they stood at Wadi Akarit, Montgomery planned another major assault to break through. New Zealand gunners toiled over their weapons as 8th Army unleashed a prolonged artillery bombardment of the enemy positions. 'The horizon was a mass of flashing lights and the rumble was like a thousand thunderstorms,' one of the gunners recorded.[112] This was enough to persuade the enemy commander to withdraw further northwards to more defensible positions at Enfidaville, obviating the need for a planned New Zealand attack.

With the enemy now confined to a limited area of northern Tunisia, the Allies planned an all-out assault. The main brunt would be borne by the 1st Army in the north, where the terrain was less formidable, but Montgomery was determined that the 8th Army should push forward as well. As part of its attack the New Zealanders had the task of assaulting the area west of the enemy strongpoint at Enfidaville. Their attack to clear the foothills between Takrouna and Enfidaville began during the night of 19–20 April. While 6 Brigade had little difficulty in gaining its objectives on the right, 5 Brigade found its advance hampered by minefields and suffered more than 500 casualties in the attack. The fight for the rocky outcrop of Takrouna itself culminated, on 21 April, in a spirited and successful attack by a 28 (Maori) Battalion platoon, in what was described by the British corps commander as 'the most gallant feat of arms' he saw in the whole war.[113] Sixty years later many still argue that one of the Maori soldiers should have won a VC for this exploit.

The Enfidaville operation proved to be the New Zealanders' last major action of the campaign. Despite the capture of Enfidaville, Montgomery's army could make no significant progress against the strong defensive positions held by its opponent, and for the New Zealanders the campaign faded away as events further north decided the issue. On 13 May 1943 Axis forces in North Africa capitulated. Temporary corps commander Freyberg took the surrender of newly promoted Marshal Messe and a German divisional commander. More than 200,000 men laid down their arms — in terms of numbers, though certainly not of psychological impact, a catastrophe matching that inflicted by the Russians at Stalingrad three months earlier. Although it delayed the outcome by six months, Hitler's belated decision to throw resources into North Africa had greatly magnified the scale of defeat.

New Zealand's contribution to the victory in North Africa had been substantial. Apart from the efforts of its seamen and airmen, its division had excelled in desert combat. During the course of the campaign a formidable

Second Lieutenant Moana-nui-a-kiwa Ngarimu VC.

New Zealand transport negotiates a canal after passing through Gabes, while locals repair the crossing destroyed by the retreating Axis forces in March 1943.

fighting machine had been honed, one that earned the respect of its adversaries for its fighting spirit and growing professionalism. Rommel certainly regarded it highly. After the Minqar Qaim escape, he described it as 'among the elite of the British Army' and rued the fact that it was still confronting him, not in captivity.[114] A less exalted enemy officer, who fought at El Alamein, recalled the New Zealanders as 'excellent troops, stern in defence, ready in attack, and most intelligent'.[115] Their effectiveness rested not merely on proficiency in the use of weapons or tactical agility; an esprit de corps had developed among men who had come through difficult situations, who had helped each other in innumerable scraps with the enemy, and who had shared common hardships. Pride in the exploits of 'the Div' provided a powerful motivating spring to action, as did small-group solidarity — nobody wanted to let their mates down. But the Div's success had come at a heavy price. Nearly 3000 men had lost their lives, 7000 had been injured, and another 4000 languished in POW camps in Italy, nearly half of them at Gruppignano in the north of the country.

Two days after the surrender in Tunisia the New Zealanders began the long journey back to their base at Maadi. The troops enjoyed the leisurely retracing of their steps, passing through the sites of earlier actions. By the end of the month they were settling back into the Egyptian environment. For 6000 of the longest serving, morale was soon enhanced by the prospect of seeing their loved ones. The government had decided to institute a furlough scheme whereby these men would be brought home for a three-month break. While those affected prepared to leave, the remainder of the division awaited their next assignment. Reorganisation became the order of the day. For the time being New Zealand's war would be sustained by the airmen and seamen spread throughout the European and Mediterranean theatres — and by New Zealand units operating much closer to home, in the Solomon Islands.

Aug 1942	Sep 1942	Oct 1942	Nov 1942	Dec 1942	Jan 1943	Feb 1943	Mar 1943

7 Aug – US Marines land on Guadalcanal

New Zealand soldiers land in New Caledonia

2 Dec – Enrico Fermi carries out first controlled nuclear chain reaction

5 Jan – Japanese bomb hits HMNZS *Achilles* at Guadalcanal

25 Feb – Japanese POWs charge guards at Featherston camp, 48 killed

10 Mar – forms 1 (Group in Santo

15 Dec – 25th Minesweeping Flotilla arrives in Solomon Islands

29 Jan – HMNZS *Kiwi* and *Moa* destroy submarine *I-1* near Guadalcanal

Harold Barrowclough (left) in his command post during the Solomons campaign.

– HMNZS *Moa* sunk by
nese bomb in Tulagi harbour

5 Aug – Munda airbase on
New Georgia Island
captured by US forces

'Battle of Manners Street' riot
NZ and US servicemen

18 Sep – 3 NZ Division
troops land on Vella Lavella

27 Oct – 3 NZ Division
troops make amphibious
assault on Mono

23 Nov – US Marines take
the island of Tarawa

1 Dec – Cairo Declaration on
disposal of the Japanese Empire
made by UK, US and China

The Solomons Campaign

Slipping easily through the sea north-west of Guadalcanal in the Solomon Islands late on 29 January 1943, the deck crew of the minesweeper HMNZS *Moa* enjoyed the warm tropical conditions. But they were far from relaxed. On the bridge, their commander, Peter Phipps, peered anxiously into the darkness, searching for signs of Japanese activity. A mile away Lieutenant-Commander Gordon Bridson in *Moa*'s sister ship, HMNZS *Kiwi*, did the same.

Shortly after 9 p.m., *Kiwi*'s ASDIC operator reported a contact, quickly identified as a submarine, a little less than 2 miles away. Bridson immediately altered course towards the object and, racing over the spot at full speed, dropped a pattern of six depth charges. These were followed by another six as *Kiwi* made her third pass over the area. Sufficient damage was caused to force the submarine to surface.

Spotting the submarine trying to make its escape in the darkness, the two corvettes raced towards it, their gunners firing for all their worth and scoring hits. The Japanese gunners responded with their more powerful weapon, narrowly missing both vessels as they approached. With the submarine beam-on, Bridson did not hesitate; he aimed his ship directly at it and prepared to ram. *Kiwi* struck it just behind the conning tower. Pulling off with difficulty, Bridson rammed it again, striking a glancing blow. All the while shells and machine-gun bullets were ravaging the submarine, on which landing craft had been set ablaze. A third ramming did further damage, and the damaged *Kiwi* now pulled back to allow *Moa* to carry on with the assault. A running battle ended when the submarine went aground on a submerged reef.

At the cost of one life, a seaman on *Kiwi*, the small craft had destroyed the submarine *I-1*. This startling victory provided an intelligence bonus — various code-books and other material were recovered from the wreckage.[116]

For the men of *Moa* and *Kiwi*, success had come early in their fight against Japan. Part of the RNZN's 25th Minesweeping Flotilla, they had arrived in the Solomon Islands from New Zealand just six weeks earlier. Their task was to support American forces that, since August, had been taking the fight to the enemy in a two-pronged counter-offensive aimed at ultimately destroying the major Japanese naval base in Rabaul, in New Britain. While MacArthur's South-West Pacific forces drove eastwards through New Guinea, Nimitz's Pacific forces were doing the same northwards through the Solomon Islands.

Guadalcanal landing

The southern prong of this offensive jumped off from New Zealand, where the commander of the South Pacific Area, American naval officer Vice-Admiral Robert Ghormley, had established his headquarters in Auckland in May. Under his direction, the plan for an amphibious landing on Guadalcanal was developed. The marines camped at Paekakariki would provide the core of the force to be used in the venture. During late July dock units worked feverishly to prepare transport and troopships to carry the marines and their equipment to the island. With everything ready Ghormley moved his headquarters forward to New Caledonia.

When the marines landed on Guadalcanal on 7 August 1942, all went well at first. Finding little opposition, they advanced rapidly inland from the beaches to seize a rudimentary airfield (soon to be christened Henderson). So easy had been the landing, and so limited the Japanese presence, that some were tempted to believe the enemy had decided not to fight for the island. But a series of Japanese counter-attacks quickly dispelled any such complacency. The marines were soon engaged in a life-and-death struggle with an enemy that fought with suicidal valour. As the ferocity of the battle increased, their hold on the vital airfield became tenuous.

In the days that followed, both sides threw more troops into the cauldron. In the waters off the island, savage naval battles erupted repeatedly as the Americans sought to halt the 'Tokyo Express' — small groups of Japanese destroyers, sometimes escorted by cruisers, that dashed down the New Georgia Sound ('The Slot') to Guadalcanal at night with men and supplies. Despite the best efforts of the Allied naval forces, the Japanese had by 12 November managed to build up a force on the island roughly comparable to that of the invaders.

Although no New Zealanders took part in the Guadalcanal landing itself, seamen of the RNZN were kept busy in the weeks preceding it. *Achilles* and *Leander* helped escort the troopships bringing men from the United States to the South Pacific, long-haul voyages that passed without incident. Not until September did *Leander* get close to the action: she spent a period on escort duties between Espiritu Santo in the New Hebrides (now Vanuatu) and Guadalcanal. After escorting a convoy from Fiji to Auckland and thence to Noumea in October, she joined the forces near Guadalcanal trying to halt the Tokyo Express. The discovery of hull damage forced her to withdraw almost immediately, however, and *Achilles* took her place in December in an American task force that included six American cruisers and five destroyers.

Meanwhile the RNZAF had also established a presence in the combat zone. Airmen of 9 Squadron RNZAF, a bomber reconnaissance unit equipped with Hudson bombers, began flying anti-submarine patrols from New Caledonia in July 1942, and three months later 3 Squadron joined it in the area, operating from Espiritu Santo. In late November some of 3 Squadron's aircraft went forward to Guadalcanal, where they flew search and patrol missions from Henderson Field. They ranged the surrounding seas at 1000 feet searching for enemy submarines, and for the Tokyo Express. Occasional brushes with enemy aircraft and bombing missions provided some relief from the monotony of these tiring flights.

A handful of New Zealand soldiers took part in the later stages of the fighting on Guadalcanal. Officers and NCOs of a small Fijian commando unit that went to the island in December 1942, they mounted reconnaissance patrols in the jungle. By this time, however, the tide had turned against the Japanese, now heavily outnumbered.

Accepting defeat at last, the Japanese command evacuated the remnants of the force in early 1943, but continued strongly to attack the Allied forces in the area from the air and the sea.

As the balance began to tip the American way, New Zealand's naval effort had been bolstered by the arrival of the minesweeper-trawlers *Matai*, *Tui*, *Kiwi* and *Moa* in mid-December 1942. They began the nightly anti-submarine patrols in the Guadalcanal-Tulagi area that would soon bring success. When, following the triumphant encounter with *I-1*, *Kiwi* was forced to return to New Zealand for repairs to her hull, the converted coastal vessel HMNZS *Gale* took her place in the flotilla.

Official war artist Russell Clark's depiction of *Kiwi* ramming the Japanese submarine *I-1*.

National War Art Collection, Archives New Zealand, AAAC898, NCWA311

All the Allied warships near Guadalcanal faced many dangers from the air. Japanese bombers struck repeatedly in an attempt to break up the formations supporting the troops ashore on the island. *Achilles* bore the brunt of one such attack on 5 January 1943. A bomb struck one of her turrets, killing or mortally wounding 13 men and doing such damage that she was forced to head for New Zealand. After a temporary patch-up in Auckland, she would go to the United Kingdom for extensive repairs, and it would be 16 months before she rejoined the RNZN after an accidental explosion delayed this work.

Bombing raids continued to threaten the New Zealand warships, as was brutally demonstrated on 7 April 1943 when more than 60 enemy bombers attacked Tulagi harbour, covered by a hundred fighters. A direct hit by a bomb sent *Moa* to the bottom. Five of her crew died.

New Zealand as a support base

While the contribution of New Zealand servicemen to the Guadalcanal effort was limited, New Zealand itself provided valuable assistance to the forces engaged in the Solomons campaign, whether as a staging point, as a

American troops take a break during a route march around Wellington's Oriental Bay in 1942.

place of recuperation or as a source of supply. The American presence in New Zealand greatly expanded — to more than 48,000 by mid-1943.

Fighting troops made up the bulk of this influx. By the end of 1942 the US Army's 43 Division had moved into the Auckland area, where it trained until moving forward to New Caledonia. In November, units of 2 Marine Division, engaged in Guadalcanal, had begun to fill up the camp facilities at Paekakariki, and following the end of the fighting on the island the whole division was concentrated there for reorganisation. The American marines became a familiar sight around Wellington: 'They would be taken for route-marches, miles and miles around Wellington,' one resident recalled. 'You could hear the echoes of their voices as they called in unison, "One, two, three, huh!" They would be in full battledress....'[117] Exercises took place at various places, and men occasionally lost their lives in accidents.

Apart from the fighting troops, who came, trained and left, many hundreds of support personnel bolstered the American presence, running naval bases and stores depots or operating hospitals and other facilities.[118] A constant stream of troops was soon returning to New Zealand from the forward area for hospital treatment and rest and recreation. In all, about 100,000 came to New Zealand for extended periods during the war, along with perhaps several hundred thousand more that made transient visits on ships or aircraft.

Most enjoyed the experience. Bemused by the conditions, one later described New Zealand, during the war, as 'the world's most beautiful small town'.[119] New Zealand hospitality greatly impressed the young American GIs and marines. They were welcomed into homes, and their stay provided a pleasant interlude away from the grim business of war. Although interactions were normally friendly several ugly incidents did occur. The most notable clash was the so-called 'Battle of Manners Street' in April 1943: a series of brawls that probably arose from a confrontation between American troops and New Zealand merchant seamen. A fracas in

Auckland between Maori and American seamen a month later left several in hospital.

The American presence had important economic consequences for New Zealand. The supply of food and other resources for the American forces in the South Pacific was lucrative, helping offset aid New Zealand received under the Lend Lease scheme. But meeting this commitment put a further strain on an economy already struggling to overcome the effects of the removal of so many men for the fighting forces. Mechanisation was one answer, and the United States supplied more than 7000 tractors under Lend Lease to increase the efficiency of New Zealand farms.

The Featherston incident

The Solomons campaign also brought another alien group to New Zealand — Japanese POWs. At American request, a POW camp was established near Featherston in September 1942. By early the following year more than 800 Japanese had been transported there from the Solomons. More than half of these men were civilian labourers, either Korean or Japanese, who had been used to construct airfields on Guadalcanal. A few score army and naval officers and several hundred naval personnel made up the balance.

The servicemen found captivity a great burden. The belief that they had failed in their duty to their Emperor not to surrender left many of them in a state of suicidal depression. Grievances against the camp authorities further fanned their resentment at their dishonourable predicament. This explosive mix detonated on 25 February 1943. The trigger was a refusal by the servicemen to work — putting POWs to work was sanctioned by the Geneva Convention (which the Japanese had, however, never ratified).

A tense situation developed, with the POWs sitting on the ground surrounded by guards. For two hours, the camp adjutant, Lieutenant James Malcolm, negotiated with a Japanese officer. In the end he determined to remove this officer (and another), who retreated among the POWs. With his revolver, Malcolm attempted to coerce him into submission, and when ignored fired two shots, one of which hit the officer in the shoulder.

At this the POWs leapt to their feet and charged the guards, hurling stones and improvised weapons. With only seconds to react if they were not to be overwhelmed, the guards opened fire with their rifles. They managed to stop the assault, but close-range fire into a mass of advancing men had caused great carnage: 48 POWs lay dead or dying and more than 60 were wounded.[120] Caught in the crossfire, one guard suffered a fatal wound — the first (and only) person killed on New Zealand soil by enemy action in either world war. Ten guards suffered minor injuries.

New Caledonia

In November 1942 New Zealand soldiers began landing on the French island of New Caledonia. The vanguard of a new expeditionary force, they moved into hastily prepared camps and settled down to await the arrival of

John Pascoe Collection, Alexander Turnbull Library, F-770-¼

Japanese POWs from the camp at Featherston clearing roadsides in the Wairarapa in November 1943.

the rest of 2NZEF (Pacific Section). Four months later their numbers had risen to 17,000.

For the men of the force's main fighting element, 3 Division, it was not their first experience of island conditions. They had spent the first half of the year garrisoning Fiji, only returning to New Zealand in August after being relieved by American troops. Determined that New Zealand should take part in the Solomons land fighting to enhance its credentials as an ally, the government agreed to make 3 Division available to Ghormley. The American commander envisaged the division taking over Guadalcanal and other areas captured by his forces.

A combat role demanded a fully manned division of three infantry brigades. But in Fiji 3 Division had had only two. Finding another proved impossible because of the numerous commitments already undertaken. Quite apart from the need to provide reinforcements for

2NZEF in the Mediterranean, many New Zealand troops were scattered throughout the South Pacific area. In Fiji more than 1500 had, by the end of 1942, been seconded to the Fiji Defence Force, which had begun forming a brigade group under a New Zealand officer's command. In October 1942 an infantry battalion and a fighter squadron deployed to Tonga to replace American forces needed for Guadalcanal; although the squadron withdrew in February 1943, troop numbers there rose to 1700 over the next nine months. Yet another 1500 infantrymen and gunners helped protect the important cable station on Norfolk Island.

Responsibility for preparing the force for the Solomons fell to Major-General Harold Barrowclough, a lawyer by profession and a leading Territorial Force officer who had gone overseas with 2NZEF as a brigade commander in 1940. He had proved his competence during 2 Division's early battles in the Mediterranean

A 3 Division unit trains in New Caledonia.

before being sent home to New Zealand to assume command of the troops in Fiji prior to the outbreak of the Pacific War — an intention which, to Barrowclough's chagrin, was not fulfilled; he had to be content with commanding the Northern Division in New Zealand itself during the worrying early months of 1942. However, when 3 Division's commander, Major-General OH Mead, was killed in a plane crash en route from Fiji to Tonga (the highest ranked fatal casualty in any of New Zealand's wars), this finally opened the way for Barrowclough to take command of 3 Division.[121]

Under Barrowclough's direction, the troops embarked on a harsh training programme. A testing final exercise in the rugged Kaimai Range — the so-called 'Battle of the Kaimais' — was recalled by some as more severe than the experience they later had in the islands. In October deployment orders arrived at last — not to Guadalcanal, where the fighting continued, but to New Caledonia. Barrowclough established his headquarters at Bourail. His troops pressed on with their training, impatient for a more active role. Their frustration increased as the months passed without prospect of early action.

Jungle warfare in New Georgia

As the fighting on Guadalcanal wound down, the Americans began preparing for the next step in their drive towards Rabaul. In June 1943 American marines made the first of a series of landings on New Georgia Island, the site of an important Japanese airbase at Munda. Although they again got ashore without difficulty, the fighting bogged down. The American forces' drive on Munda was likened to 'a gigantic but timid snail approaching an ant hill'.[122] Three American divisions eventually had to be committed before Munda was taken on 5 August, and it was well into September before all resistance ended on the island.

More than 40 New Zealanders took part in this struggle. Members of 1 Commando Fiji Guerrillas, which had been despatched to the theatre under the command of Canterbury farmer Charles Tripp, they entered the thick jungle to reconnoitre Japanese positions, enduring the sapping damp heat, malaria, insects and snakes, and the constant fear of a sudden clash with the enemy in the cloying undergrowth. 'Jungle warfare,' one of the commandos wrote later, 'becomes a very personal affair between yourself and the enemy, who is so close at times that you can almost see the whites of his eyes.'[123]

Major DG Kennedy, a coastwatcher in the Australian forces, was another New Zealander to fight behind the lines on New Georgia. He had been a civil administrator in the Solomons when the Japanese arrived in 1942, and had taken to the hills. He carried out a mini-guerrilla campaign against the enemy and assisted downed Allied airmen.

Once again New Zealand seamen helped support the force ashore. They included the crew of *Leander*, which had returned to the area after repairs in March 1943, been frustrated by inactivity at first, then spent dreary weeks escorting convoys between Hawaii and New Caledonia. Once the fighting began on New Georgia, the prospect of action beckoned as she moved into the operational area.

Naval operations again focused on stopping the Tokyo Express — still very much in business bringing reinforcements and supplies to the Japanese fighting on New Georgia. This was the objective of a task force, including *Leander*, which headed into the strait between New Georgia and Kolombangara on the night of 12–13 July.

Making contact with a Japanese force in the darkness, the Allied warships were quickly in action. The flash and crash of gunfire filled the air, but it was the silent menace of the torpedo that proved more lethal. *Leander* was hit by one of a salvo launched by four Japanese destroyers shortly after 1 a.m. Within an hour, two American cruisers and a destroyer had suffered the same fate.

The Solomons Theatre

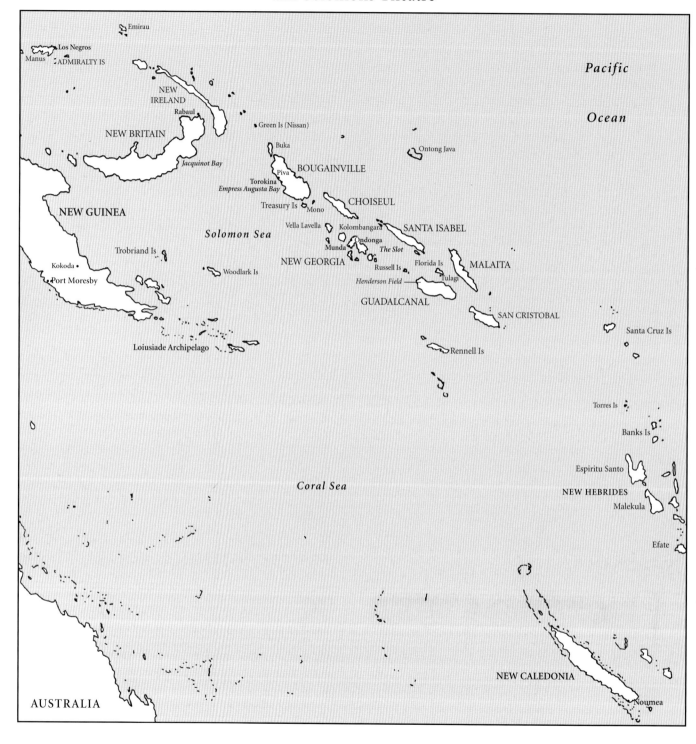

The torpedo that hit *Leander* killed or swept overboard 28 of her crew and left her in imminent danger of sinking. The surviving crew performed miracles to keep her afloat as she crept back to refuge in Tulagi harbour. The damage spelt the end of her participation in the Solomons campaign. After temporary repairs, she set off for Auckland. Repairs in the American port of Boston followed, and she then reverted to the Royal Navy.

With *Leander*'s departure, the four small craft of the minesweeping flotilla — converted coastal vessel HMNZS *Breeze* had replaced the ill-fated *Moa* — carried the New Zealand naval flag. They performed their escort and patrol duties effectively, with only occasional brushes with the enemy. One occurred on 19 August 1943 when *Tui* detected a submarine, later identified as *I-17*, between New Caledonia and Espiritu Santo. After making a depth-charge attack, she lost contact. She was heading away from the scene when an aircraft reported a submarine on the surface. Quickly reversing course, *Tui* soon had it under shellfire from her gun and kept up the attack until it sank.

New Zealand's naval contribution to the Solomons campaign was not made at sea alone. In 1943 several hundred personnel were provided to operate New Zealand-made radars supplied to the American forces operating in the islands. Some RNZAF personnel were also deployed to operate British-made radars. Later Radio Development Laboratory scientists would join them in the theatre.[124]

New Zealand airmen also made an increasingly important contribution to the campaign. The growing scale of RNZAF participation led to the establishment of base facilities at Espiritu Santo. A repair unit deployed there in January 1943, and two months later 1 (Islands) Group Headquarters took control of RNZAF activities in the area. A newly formed transport squadron provided a link between Espiritu Santo and New Zealand.

Guadalcanal provided the operational focus of the New Zealand air campaign. Patrols by 3 Squadron's Hudson bombers continued. The search for enemy forces was unending, with the monotony broken only by occasional bombing missions. On 2 April 1943 one of the Hudsons shot down an enemy floatplane — the RNZAF's first air-combat victory of the Solomons campaign.

Within weeks New Zealand involvement in the battle for air supremacy in the Solomons became more direct. An RNZAF fighter unit arrived at Kukum airstrip on Guadalcanal. Commanded by Battle of Britain veteran

asualties of the Kolombangara naval action of 12–13 July 1943 are buried at sea.

RNZN Museum, AAG0022

The hole made by the torpedo that struck *Leander* during the action at Kolombangara.

137

Michael Herrick, 15 Squadron joined the American units providing air cover over the landing areas. Fourteen Squadron relieved it in June 1943. Three more squadrons, numbered 16 to 18, would follow. They maintained a deployment that, from mid-September 1943, involved a second squadron operating out of Guadalcanal.

The Japanese air force remained strong, and dogfights were common. Once again New Zealanders fought at a disadvantage, for the Japanese Zeros out-performed their Kittyhawks (or Warhawks, as the variant used by them was known). Although a New Zealand RAF pilot would later describe the Kittyhawk as having 'the flying characteristics of a brick',[125] it represented a big improvement on the ponderous Buffalo for men who had fought at Singapore. One of them, 14 Squadron's Geoffrey Fisken, in a plane dubbed the 'Wairarapa Wildcat', added to his reputation with a series of 'kills' — he would end the war as the Commonwealth's leading ace in the Pacific theatre.

The fighter planes escorted bombers on missions to attack airfields on New Georgia and later Bougainville. Bob Spurdle, another New Zealand Battle of Britain veteran who flew with 16 Squadron in mid-1943, was less than impressed by the ill-directed and unaggressive performance of the bombers that he helped escort, describing early missions as 'a farce and a monumental cock-up' and 'a silly waste of time'.[126]

The fighters also escorted Catalina flying-boats on 'Dumbo' missions — picking up downed pilots from the sea or off islands. Such operations could become an endurance test, as on 3 August 1943 when Spurdle provided cover for a Catalina that had more than 60 native canoes surrounding it as it picked up three Europeans. 'Around and around we went gritting our teeth and sweating in our hot cockpits. A four hour and twenty-five minute flight!'[127] Strafing enemy barges and positions provided some exhilarating relief.

RNZAF Warhawks being serviced at an airfield in the islands.

Archives New Zealand, AIR118,

For the pilots it was a frenetic six weeks — the length of their squadron's tour — before heading back to New Zealand, their places taken by the pilots of another squadron that rotated into the combat area from Espiritu Santo. The five fighter squadrons took part in a revolving deployment, with some airmen doing as many as six tours over the next two years. Although the pilots spent only relatively short periods in the islands, the men who serviced their aircraft were not so fortunate; they had to endure the heat and isolation for a year.

Pacific versus Mediterranean revisited

While the fighting raged in the central Solomons, the troops in New Caledonia chafed at their inaction. They would have been even less happy had they known that the fate of their division hung in the balance, as the War Cabinet in Wellington grappled with the endemic problem of finding enough men to fulfil all the country's commitments. The shortages demanded the establishment of priorities between the needs of the Mediterranean and the Pacific theatres.

The possibility of bringing home 2 Division had been considered at various stages of the North African campaign. When after the victory at El Alamein Australia recalled its remaining division from the Middle East, New Zealand had declined to follow suit — and had been reassured when the American authorities soon after stated that leaving 2 Division in the Mediterranean was their preference too. But when, early in 1943, Churchill sought the use of 2 Division in the planned invasion of Sicily, Fraser firmly rebuffed him. With the end of the campaign in North Africa looming, it seemed time for a reassessment in Wellington of where New Zealand could best make its contribution.

When the question was taken up following the Axis surrender in Tunisia, no reasons of home defence demanded the return of 2NZEF from the Middle East; the enemy no longer stood at the gates. But 2 Division's presence in New Zealand would allow a wholehearted effort to be made in the Solomons, either by replacing 3 Division with 2 Division, or by using 2 Division's personnel to bring 3 Division up to full strength. Ensuring a larger British Commonwealth presence in the fighting seemed important, if only to enhance the 'British' voice in any eventual settlement with Japan. Australia would also be pleased — its Prime Minister, John Curtin, made no secret of his distaste for New Zealand's failure to follow Australia's lead and pull out 2 Division from the Mediterranean.

On the other hand, there were good reasons for leaving 2 Division in the Mediterranean. It was now a highly trained, mobile division suitable for operations in a theatre very different to the South Pacific. Before moving to the islands, 2 Division troops would need a substantial period of retraining, taking them out of the fight for an indefinite period. Both British and American leaders favoured 2 Division's retention in the Mediterranean, and its continued presence there was in

Hard driving American naval officer Vice-Admiral William ('Bull') Halsey, the commander of the South Pacific Area, is greeted on arrival in New Zealand by Air Vice-Marshal Leonard Isitt, the Chief of the Air Staff.

RNZAF, 3348

139

line with agreed Allied strategy to beat Hitler first. Moreover, the American commander in the South Pacific, now Vice-Admiral Halsey, had revealed no great interest in bolstering New Zealand's ground effort, or even using the existing force in any active role. Indeed, it soon transpired that the Americans regarded New Zealand's air force contribution as the most important, with New Zealand's army only a distant third after its navy.

With the arguments for and against bringing 2 Division home finely balanced, the personal initiative of New Zealand's Prime Minister proved decisive. Fraser persuaded his colleagues, the majority of whom had at first been inclined to bring the division home, to leave it in the Mediterranean. By the end of the year it would be in Italy.

Secretary of External Affairs Alister McIntosh describes Fraser's persuasion of his colleagues to leave 2 Division in the Mediterranean:

> *I leave to your imagination War Cabinet's discussions on this matter and the halts and shifts which were devised for protracting the time at which a decision would have to be made and Cabinet, Caucus and Parliament informed. When this point did arrive the Prime Minister was at his 150 per cent best. He decided on rush tactics and kept the matter entirely confined to the War Cabinet. After being on the point of taking the Cabinet into his confidence for about a week he broke the news to them on a Wednesday afternoon following a short Session in the House. All the telegrams were read and the Prime Minister was at his most impartial, calm and judicial best. He called for an individual expression of opinion, paid deference to all the views which were opposed to the retention of the Division [in the Middle East], restated their opinions and gave a comment on the alternative. He ended up the meeting with five noes, four ayes and two neutrals. In the evening he had the Chiefs of Staff up and*

> *[the Director of] National Service, and declared an open slather. As a result of the cross talk and the expression of the opinions of the Chiefs of Staff, three noes became three ayes, the neutrals disappeared and he was left with two dissentients. Again, after the Chiefs of Staff withdrew, he went out of his way in summing up to pay special attention to the opponents' views and almost wept over the distress which this policy was likely to inflict upon Curtin....*
>
> *Although the decision was arrived at with such unanimity, the result was entirely due to the Prime Minister's skill....[128]*

So pressing were the manpower problems that this outcome seemed to spell the end for 3 Division. When he was called home for discussions in June, Barrowclough begged the War Cabinet to allow his men an opportunity to participate in the Solomons campaign. 'All he asked for was one campaign', claiming that the American commander had already earmarked his division for an active role.[129] After receiving an affirmative response, Barrowclough hurried back to New Caledonia to prepare his troops. By August they had moved forward to Guadalcanal, and were training with new zest for the coming test of their skills and courage.

Vella Lavella

The island of Vella Lavella provided the setting for the division's first combat assignment. US Marines had invaded the island in mid-August 1943 in preparation for a move against Bougainville. Within a few weeks they had established a firm foothold, though many Japanese remained in the island's jungles. It was the New Zealanders' task to root out these defenders to complete the occupation of the island.

Landing on 18 September 1943, the men of 14 Brigade spent the next 12 days pressing back the Japanese. The air support provided from Guadalcanal included aircraft of the two New Zealand fighter squadrons now based there. The troops endured the horrors of jungle fighting, the fear of being ambushed or shot by a sniper hidden among the foliage. Thirty-two men were killed in the operation, which ended with the night-time evacuation by the Japanese Navy of the remnants of the Japanese garrison.

The admittedly limited task assigned to the New Zealanders had been carried out very efficiently, despite the unfamiliar framework. For the first time in the war they had operated alongside American troops. Several thousand of the latter on the island had come under Barrowclough's command, the first occasion that American troops in the South Pacific served under a non-American officer.

'Treasury Islands landing

Within a few weeks, 8 Brigade got its chance to enter the fray. As a further preliminary to the intended landing on Bougainville, the Treasury Islands to the south were to be invaded by a mixed New Zealand-American force. The principal landing would take place on the southern coast of the main island, Mono. At the same time, a small force would go ashore on the northern coast with the technical personnel needed to establish a radar station there.

On 27 October 1943 New Zealand troops stormed ashore on Mono — the first amphibious assault mounted by New Zealand troops since Gallipoli. The Japanese defenders could not prevent the landing, and were soon being pushed back by the New Zealanders and Americans. The northern group also got ashore without problems, but the risks involved in this isolated action were brought home in early November when the troops had to beat off a strong counter-attack. In little over a fortnight the island was cleared, at a cost of 40 New Zealand lives.

The preparations for Bougainville also affected the deployment of New Zealand's two fighter squadrons. In October they moved forward to an airstrip at Ondonga in New Georgia. With the Japanese air forces now largely gone from the area, they mainly provided a deterrent to any interference with Allied shipping. 'We flew cover over the shipping supplying the area for countless hours to guard against possible enemy air attack,' one pilot later recalled. 'The monotony of these trips was rarely broken.'[130]

On 1 November, the US 3 Marine Division, which had been camped near Auckland since the previous March, landed on Bougainville. Once a foothold had been secured, several airstrips were rapidly built. In January 1944 New Zealand's fighter pilots flew in to set up base at one of them, Torokina.

Shifting focus

By this time, Nimitz had launched a new thrust against the Japanese. While the marines landed on Bougainville, another US marine division (the 2nd) was preparing to do the same far to the north on the small island of Tarawa in the Gilbert Islands (now Kiribati). Once again New Zealand provided the springboard; the marines had

Troops of 3 Division take a break for a meal in the jungle of Vella Lavella.

spent 10 months at Paekakariki recovering from their ordeal on Guadalcanal and planning the new operation.

The invasion of Tarawa was a bloody affair. It was made worse by the failure of the American commander to heed the warnings of a New Zealand liaison officer, Major Frank Holland — who had a long history of colonial government service in the islands before the war — that the tide would be too low at the crucial moment. More than a thousand Americans died in securing the island.

This central Pacific drive rendered the operation against Rabaul a backwater, at least in Nimitz's eyes. His forces had in any case been fighting in MacArthur's area, for the drive through the Solomons chain to Bougainville had taken them over the boundary between the two command areas (on the 159° East longitude line). While MacArthur continued his push eastwards in New Guinea towards Rabaul, Nimitz's emphasis shifted to containment and neutralisation, rather than capture, of the Japanese base. In the interests of tightening the noose still further, his forces would later capture islands north of Bougainville suitable for naval or air bases.

A new amphibious assault beckoned for Barrow-clough's men. This time the target would be the Green Islands. Although again only a brigade-sized operation for the division — 14 Brigade did the honours — this operation was more extensive than those previously conducted by the division, involving as it did the landing of more than 6000 New Zealanders and Americans on the first day. After careful preparations by the divisional headquarters and with the Americans, the force went ashore on the group's largest island, Nissan (usually called Green Island by the air force), on 15 February 1944 and had little difficulty in quickly disposing of the limited Japanese forces they found. Once again New Zealand fighters formed part of the air cover for the operation. Sappers were quickly in action building airfields and they had the first finished well ahead of schedule. The build-up of forces on the island meant that Barrowclough found himself commanding more than 10,000 Americans, in addition to the 6000 New Zealanders ashore, in what was a model of New Zealand-American co-operation in the field.

The Solomons was the only wartime campaign fought by New Zealanders in which UK forces did not take part. Operating with American forces proved difficult at times for Barrowclough, not only in terms of logistics but also in dealing with men from a very

New Zealand troops on Vella Lavella prepare for the invasion of Nissan Island.

A New Zealand anti-aircraft gun crew sets up on Nissan Island.

different military culture. He personally found the change refreshing, warming to the more straightforward approach of the Americans and contrasting it with that of some British officers he had dealt with in the Middle East earlier in the war. The men of his division could take satisfaction from the competent fashion in which they had undertaken the tasks allotted to them.

The Solomons campaign has one other distinction. It is the only campaign in which all three New Zealand armed services have been involved in a combat role. (Although New Zealanders fought in all three elements in the Mediterranean campaigns, airmen and naval personnel did so as part of British services.)

New Zealand's participation in the Solomons campaign had been partly designed to bolster its credentials as a belligerent in the Pacific War. But it soon became apparent that the co-operative and friendly approach of American officers in the field was not replicated in Washington. The needs and sensibilities of small allies counted for little. Even Australia, which had committed far more troops than New Zealand to the Pacific fighting, found itself sidelined. This was starkly revealed on 1 December 1943, when the British, American and Chinese leaders, meeting in Cairo, announced their plans for the disposition of the Japanese Empire following the war. Neither Australia nor New Zealand, much to their dismay, had been consulted about the terms of the Cairo Declaration. They learned of them only in the press.

This slight upset Australasian leaders already uneasy about American post-war intentions in the South Pacific. They responded by meeting in Canberra in January 1944 and boldly asserting their views on post-war settlement issues. Along with much about future regional co-operation of the two countries, the Anzac (or Canberra) Agreement — one New Zealand official later irreverently described it as the 'ANZAXIS'[131] — proclaimed their view that wartime usage gave no rights over the post-war sovereignty of islands. Obviously aimed at the United States, this angered the American Secretary of the Navy and other influential policymakers in Washington.

Looking towards a situation in which Japanese power had been finally broken, the agreement addressed problems of the future. For most New Zealanders, however, the present was of more pressing moment, as they struggled to meet the commitments undertaken by the government, to adjust their private lives to public needs and to overcome feelings of war-weariness.

Jul 1943 | Aug 1943 | Sep 1943 | Oct 1943 | Nov 1943 | Dec 1943 | Jan 1944 | Feb

6000 2NZEF men arrive
home to begin their
three-month furlough

25 Sep – General Election
leaves Labour still in power

28 Oct – Butter rationing begins,
8 oz per person per week

15 Dec – 25th
Minesweeping Flotilla
arrives in Solomon Islands

21 Jan – ANZAC Agreement
signed in Canberra

NZ Freelance Collection, Alexander Turnbull Library, C-24431-½

Members of the Women's War Service Auxiliary parade through Dunedin on 18 March 1942.

10 Mar – RNZAF forms 1
(Islands) Group in Espiritu Santo

1 Jul – Five NZ scientists leave
for North America to work on
atomic bomb projects

1 Sep – New Zealand Air
Task Force formed

6 Mar – Meat is rationed in
NZ on a value basis

9 Sep – New Zealand agrees to
participate in the United Nations
Relief and Rehabilitation Agency

The Home Front

Shivering in the cool of an August evening in 1943, Taradale teenager Doreen Hunt peered through binoculars from the observation post overlooking the entrance to Wellington harbour. The beam of a powerful searchlight, mounted nearer the beach below her, stretched across the narrow strait to the rocky coastline opposite. Her orders were clear — to keep her eyes fixed on the lighted water and to ensure that nothing passed through it unnoticed. With her in the post were two soldiers and Floris McDougall, from Dannevirke, who would shortly take over the vigil at the binoculars. In a nearby hut, two other young women slept; at midnight they would relieve Hunt and McDougall.

These women were attached to 10 Heavy Regiment, which manned the heavy guns mounted at Fort Dorset and Palmer Head to protect the harbour. Some weeks before, the women had arrived in the capital by train, having enlisted in the army. They suffered the indignity of having their hair washed in kerosene and cut above the shoulders, before donning the heavy khaki uniforms issued to them. For most, communal living in the barracks was a new experience that took some getting used to. On the plus side the food was tasteless but plentiful, and was supplemented by crayfish and paua taken from the rocky foreshore by the soldiers manning the searchlights. And there was much camaraderie among women who suddenly found themselves living in the city for the first time.

During the day the women practised pulling the searchlights to bits, and cleaned them. At night they manned the observation post when rostered on duty. The arrival or departure of ships broke the monotony of the observation duties. Alert to the possibility of an enemy submarine attempting to sneak in under cover of a 'friendly', the observers were especially vigilant at these times. Occasionally a ship failed to identify itself properly. When this happened 'all hell broke loose in the camp'. Alarms sounded, and men rushed to man the guns as searchlights exposed the vessel. 'After one more warning had been given, if it still did not give the right signal the guns boomed away,' one woman soldier recalled. 'Fortunately the guns missed by a country mile — bad shooting — but some fishing boat must have nearly died of fright after giving the wrong signal.'[132]

Hunt and her companions were part of the many-faceted 'home front'. In one sense, that front denoted the experience of war of the 1.6 million New Zealanders who remained in New Zealand — of how they reacted to the developing situation and lived their lives in circumstances far from normal.

But it also encompassed the war effort of New Zealand, which was not purely overseas in nature, even if the battlefields were. New Zealand, for a time, needed to enhance its local defence preparations against the possibility of an attack by Japan that never eventuated. Filling the ranks while also meeting reinforcement commitments for the forces fighting outside New Zealand disrupted New Zealand society and the economy in an unprecedented fashion.

An important element in New Zealand's contribution to the war effort lay in maintaining the flow of produce to Britain while meeting new commitments arising from

The searchlight observation post at Wellington harbour entrance in 1943. Flanking Captain EL Mathers are WAACs Joan Edwards (left) and Shirley Gunning, with an unidentified WAAC at the binoculars.

Faye Honnor Collec

the war. This economic home front demanded effective utilisation of all the country's resources. State controls greatly affected the lives of a large proportion of the population, determining where they might work, how much they might eat, even what they might say in public. Sustaining this effort in turn depended on maintaining the people's willingness to accept the many restrictions and impositions.

Mobilising women

Shortages of manpower for both military and industry placed the spotlight on the reservoir of labour existing among the women of New Zealand. In the previous war their uniformed participation had been confined to nursing, and similar work soon engaged a substantial number of women in the present conflict. Initially hopes for a wider role received little encouragement, other than the chance to don the uniform of the Women's War Service Auxiliary, which proved popular; at its peak, in 1942, the auxiliary boasted 75,000 members. The picture changed in early 1941 when the services, unable to find sufficient men for all their purposes, began to recruit women for a variety of roles. The invasion threat in 1942 accentuated this process as the need to free up men for service in combat units became acute.

The air force was the first out of the blocks. The first WAAFs — derived from the title Women's Auxiliary Air Force — donned their uniforms in January 1941. They were soon followed by WAACs, the army equivalent. The navy also got into the act, recruiting a far smaller number of Wrens. By mid-1943, 8500 women were in uniform, slightly more than half of them WAACs.[133]

Women took over many clerical functions in service headquarters and units. Napier teenager Faye Honnor, who arrived in Wellington with Doreen Hunt, found herself shuffling paper in the master gunner's office in 10 Heavy Regiment's headquarters at Fort Dorset — though sometimes she had more exciting duties. After

one poor display of shooting by the gunners, she was ordered to report to the *Jane Seddon*, a small craft that would pull a target up and down the harbour entrance to give them practice. 'I was part of the team recording Fall of Shot,' she later recalled. 'Knowing what inexperienced and poor shooters were to man the guns, my, and many others fear was that they would miss the target and hit the *Jane Seddon.…* I need not have worried, they hit neither the target nor the boat towing it, the shells finishing over near Baring Head or thereabouts.' The night's work ended with a rum ration at 5 a.m., 'a welcome drink after a cold and shaky night'.[134]

The searchlights were just one aspect of the defence system in which women became involved. Driving was another important task undertaken by them.

Women also played a part in secret intelligence work. One such was Marguerite Boxer, a Wren who found herself sequestered in a Marlborough house with a handful of companions, engaged in a hush-hush project to track enemy submarines by radio fingerprinting. Others worked in army intelligence units in Wellington.

Marguerite Scott (née Boxer) recalls her involvement in radio fingerprinting work while serving in the navy:

> Our station was under the command of the Resident Naval Officer, Picton.… We were housed in an old wooden farmhouse at the end of a no-exit road, with Lombardy poplars and big walnut trees for sentries.…
>
> Here we would remain for the duration, apparently just growing scarlet runner beans up the 8-foot barbed wire fence. In reality, we were on a war footing 24 hours a day, listening out over the infinite sweep of the South Pacific, watched over by a Vital Points contingent, all over 60, camped in Army Huts in the front paddock. In the initial stages at least, we were all … enchanted with our adventure and our surroundings, enthusiastic about our assignment and utterly loyal and tight-lipped.

This cartoon on the effect of women joining the Women's War Service Auxiliary appeared in the *New Zealand Freelance* in October 1940.

There were eight of us in the 'crew,' under the supervision of a Wren Petty Officer.... Four were Wren-telegraphists, hand-picked with extra training in Japanese Morse code and communication procedures. The other four were University graduates in various subjects and they were called 'Classifiers' for identification purposes....

We quickly settled into a routine, governed by the requirement of having a telegraphist on duty 24 hours a day and a classifier on duty from 7 a.m. till 10 p.m. If there was any kind of a 'flap', we simply remained on duty as needed....

Results of our work were telephoned by direct 'scrambler' line to Naval Intelligence in Wellington, but the traffic was one way. They wanted our information, but how we obtained it was known to very few, if any, of them.[135]

Not all women served in New Zealand. Nurses formed a substantial group in hospitals overseas and in hospital ships. Just under a fifth of the WAACs served overseas, mainly in the Middle East. Some also went to the Pacific islands, as did 135 WAAFs. The first to go were women recruited by the Women's War Service Auxiliary to run clubs for 2NZEF; known as the 'Tuis', they later became part of the WAAC. Their task, according to Freyberg, was to provide a 'home touch' for the troops in these facilities. Others served as hospital orderlies or assistants; or carried out a variety of clerical tasks. Although none lost their lives to enemy action, a few died as a result of accidents or illness. Several New Zealand women also made their way to the United Kingdom to serve in the Air Transport Auxiliary, piloting new aircraft from factories to operational units; one was killed in an air accident.

'Manpowering'

Although women became a valuable part of the armed services during the war, they also made a large contribution to the other strand of New Zealand's war effort — the flow of produce and goods to Britain and other destinations. Single women had moved into the workforce well before the Second World War, but society frowned on those who tried to continue working after marriage, and especially after bearing children. A married woman's place was firmly in the home; her role was nurturing her family.

In the first two years of the war, labour had been controlled only to the extent that some industries were deemed essential. This restricted the options of those men working in them to enlist in the forces. But in the main, conditions remained similar to those pertaining before 1939. However, all that changed with the entry of Japan to the war and the mobilisation of large numbers of working men for the home defence forces. Gaps appeared even in essential industries, threatening New Zealand's capacity to maintain production targets. Longer hours of work provided only so much additional capacity. Only by tapping the reservoir of non-working single women and married women with no children or older children could this problem be overcome.

To meet this situation, the government took drastic action in January 1942. The services of all men of military age — between 18 and 49 — now became at the disposal of the National Service Department. When called up, they could be directed into essential industries if not taken by the services. Women also became liable to such direction — or 'manpowering' as it became known from the terminology of the regulations. Initially only those aged 20 and 21 were affected. All women in those ages had to register with the department and go where directed. As the number of essential industries grew (by the end of 1942 they employed about a third of the workforce), more and more age categories of women found themselves subject to the 'manpower' regulations. In the end all those between 18 and 40 — just under 150,000 women — were liable to be 'manpowered' unless they had children under 16 years of age.

Many women sought to forestall being 'manpowered'. Some essential industries were better than others.

Two Wrens service the engine of the Commodore's barge in Auckland harbour.

WAACs are trained in the use of a machine tool. By June 1942, 5000 men and women had been 'manpowered' into essential industry. This figure quadrupled in the next six months and by the end of the war had reached 176,000, of whom 37,500 were women.

Those less attractive ones that had traditionally been a female worker's domain suffered the most serious labour shortages, not least because they paid less than some others that were traditionally male domains but were now more open to female workers. 'Manpowering' was common in these traditional female areas. But it was not just the level of pay that made some jobs unattractive. The nature and conditions of some did not appeal. The prospect of being manpowered into a psychiatric hospital or freezing works spurred many women to seek alternative employment. They either found a position in a more congenial essential industry of their own volition or joined the women's services.

Numerous women were directed into factories. Alister Street recalled being one of six in a Wellington munitions factory 'sorting and sifting the pins for hand grenades and doing a bit of welding'. She also helped produce mortar bomb tails: 'We would take it in turns to work this tremendous machine. It was about a 70-ton press, it breathed fire and dust and heat.... It was an *enormous* thing, almost frightening, but we girls learnt and we managed.'[136]

Aileen Andrew describes her experience as a munitions worker in Wellington:

We were taken to the factory in buses, which lined up outside the hostels every morning. For those under 21 there was routine machine work of a light nature. As I was over 21 I was selected for the 'powder room'. Naive, I thought that the 'powder room' was the toilet block and I reluctantly followed a rather bossy lady, thinking that I was going to spend the rest of the war cleaning toilets. But we were soon enlightened. Down to the back of the factory to a guarded area where a soldier stood in the sentry box. We were relieved of matches and cigarettes. Then into the building where the gun powder was used. Here we removed our clothes and were given a towel.... We stepped over a barrier from the area that was henceforth to be known as the 'dirty' area into the 'clean' area. No-one could cross the barrier without discarding everything she wore. In the clean area we were handed shapeless calico undies (probably made from flour bags and soon known as flour-bag undies), battledress, turban, socks and sandshoes. Sandshoes were to avoid sparks being created.... When we left our work we removed our clothes into a bin and took a shower. Then in our birthday suits stepped into the dirty area where our own clothes were, dressed and made a screaming run for the buses.

WOMEN!
—— OVER 17 YEARS OF AGE ——
For a HEALTHY, VITAL WAR JOB
Join the WOMEN'S LAND SERVICE
APPLY NOW AT YOUR LOCAL W.W.S.A.
OR DISTRICT MANPOWER OFFICE

A poster seeking women for work on farms.

John Pascoe Collection, Alexander Turnbull Library, F-858-¼

Women load rounds into clips at the Colonial Ammunition Company's factory in Hamilton in January 1944.

The precautions were in the interests of our own health. The powder we worked with caused some really horrible allergy effects on some girls, even with all the precautions. Swollen faces, streaming eyes, a rash like measles and general misery. Fortunately I escaped, but the powder turned me gradually yellow — around my eyes, my hands up to my elbows, all a bilious yellow.... [137]

As with the armed services, women moved into hitherto male-dominated areas of the economy. They became herd testers and tram conductors. Some worked on farms. Many farmers remained reluctant to accept compulsory labour. They feared that unenthusiastic or inexperienced labourers would not care well for farm animals. Farmer's wives and children often helped maintain farm output. But some men and women were compelled to work on farms. Doreen Foss was one sent into the country against her inclination. 'I would be 18 and I'm on a farm — and of course I'm floored — I didn't know how to milk a cow. And as for chasing bulls into bull paddocks I didn't know anything about that either.' [138]

Following a similar development in the United Kingdom, a Women's Land Corps was formed in 1941 (and later renamed the Women's Land Service). It did not exactly catch fire, as women were slow to join. Only 146 had come forward by June 1942, but numbers more than quadrupled in the following year. By March 1944, 1900 women were wearing the uniform of the corps (though more than half were farmer's daughters, who might have provided farm labour even without the scheme).

Ensuring sufficient labour to meet farming requirements posed problems. Here soldiers assist with the harvest.

The Maori war effort

If women made a big contribution to the home front effort, so too did Maori. When Japan entered the war, all those in the Territorial Force, and men who had volunteered for 2NZEF, were called up. Assigned to units near their homes, they became part of the defences against a possible Japanese attack. Another Maori battalion made an appearance, formed from men who had volunteered to serve overseas. As in 28 (Maori) Battalion's formation, Maori officers were in short supply — the Territorial Force had only three. Efforts were made to increase this number, along with the overall number of Maori soldiers. By 1943, 15 per cent of all Maori, all volunteers, were under arms and many more were making a non-military contribution to the war effort.

While not liable to be conscripted (see 'Conscription', page 49), Maori could, from January 1942, be directed into essential industries. This contribution to the home defence effort was co-ordinated by the Maori War Effort Organisation (MWEO), which had been formed in 1941 primarily to find reinforcements for 28 (Maori) Battalion. Based on a committee of Maori MPs chaired by Paraire Paikea, this organisation co-ordinated the efforts of more than 300 tribal committees throughout the country. It helped prepare registers of Maori men of working age and young women from whom workers could be drawn for essential industries, advised the National Service Department on the locality and type of industry suitable for particular workers being manpowered, and found volunteers for particular vacancies in areas where labour shortages became acute,

Maori soldiers parade on a Ruatoria marae during the hui for the posthumous award of the VC to Lieutenant Moana-nui-a-kiwa Ngarimu. In October 1941, 559 Maori were serving with 2NZEF, 741 in the Territorial Force and 487 in the Home Guard. By late 1943 the number of men sent overseas had topped 4000 with another 740 in the pipeline. At the same time, more than 2000 Maori were serving in home defence units. More than 7000 served as home guardsmen.

War History Collection, Alexander Turnbull Library, PA1-q-292-23-505 such as freezing works or dairy factories. In rural areas it encouraged Maori to grow crops.

By late 1943, just less than 11,000 Maori worked in essential industries. For many it was a time of big adjustment. For the first time they were away from their tribal support framework. They endured unfamiliar surroundings and long hours at tasks that were often difficult and tiring. They also found themselves in much closer association with Pakeha than they had been before the war, when Maori had tended, except in some rural areas, to live in informal segregation. Numerous young Maori women lived in hostels in cities, and by residing and working together, people of both races gained a new appreciation of the other. Wartime experience tended to break down previous barriers, but not completely. In some areas Pakeha prejudice still made everyday living difficult for many Maori. Because of landlord resistance to renting to Maori, they often struggled to find suitable accommodation. The resulting substandard lodgings many had to endure merely reinforced negative perceptions by some Pakeha. Although the MWEO extended its scope to address these problems, it could not completely overcome them.

The economy expands

Maori and women helped New Zealand expand its productive capacity to meet war needs. With overseas sources cut off, greatly reduced or uncertain, local manufacture became more important. The invasion danger in 1942 gave new impetus to the process. Once it had passed, New Zealand's capacity could be directed to meeting orders from overseas for specific products. Allied co-ordinating bodies oversaw the application of New Zealand's output, both pastoral and industrial, to the war effort. Particularly important in this respect was the Eastern Group Supply Council, sitting in India.

New Zealand industries produced a range of new products. Shipbuilding firms turned out more than 500 small craft both for local use and for the British and Americans. Thousands of radios were manufactured to meet an order from the supply council in India, and radars were made for the American forces in the South Pacific. But the biggest expansion lay in the field of armaments, especially to meet local needs in 1941–42.

A Ford Motor Company advertisement proclaims the company's contribution to the war effort.

With little in the way of heavy industry, New Zealand had no capacity to produce tanks or artillery pieces, although some attempt was made to improvise. Inventors demonstrated considerable ingenuity in coming up with imaginative designs for improvised weapons. Some showed promise, but were not put into mass production. The Semple tank, developed at the instigation of Cabinet Minister Robert Semple, proved the most notable of these improvisations — it was perhaps fortunate for those who might have had to operate this lumbering armoured vehicle that it never faced the enemy. The army decided that it was too ponderous to be worth promoting, but it was used to boost public morale.

New Zealand's greatly expanded munitions industry focused on small arms. Apart from long-standing ammunition production, factories made hand grenades and shell fuses for use by British forces, along with steel helmets and other items of equipment.

Economic stability is threatened

If most people of working age were hemmed in by the manpower regulations, they also faced a range of other controls designed to maintain economic stability. The nature of New Zealand's economy, heavily dependent on imports, left it vulnerable to inflation in wartime. New Zealand, through the bulk-purchase arrangements, suffered no fall-off of money flowing into the country; but because of shipping and supply difficulties, fewer goods were available in shops. Competition for what did arrive pushed up prices. War loans, which soaked up some of the excess money in people's pockets, only partially alleviated the problem.

Inflation emerged as the most serious threat to New Zealand's economic war effort. As prices rose, so too did demands for higher wages. Workers who downed tools in support of such demands not only undermined New Zealand's productive capacity but also presented Labour

Two of eight towboats built by an Auckland shipyard for the US forces are launched on 21 August 1943. Nearest the camera is the *Korokai*.

A Semple tank.

John Pascoe Collection, Alexander Turnbull Library, F-603-¼

War History Collection, Alexander Turnbull Library, C-14276-½ ministers with a difficult challenge, given their acceptance of the right of workers to withdraw their labour. Because of the strategic importance in New Zealand's economy of freezing works and wharves, strikes in these areas could have a crippling effect.

The government's response to this danger was a wage-price clamp. In December 1942, it froze workers' wages and forced farmers to deposit a proportion of their returns in special accounts. This latter measure ensured that the burden was shared equitably while easing inflationary pressure by limiting the flow of money into the economy. More than a hundred important items had their prices set at their existing levels. The prices at which farmers could sell produce locally were also fixed. An Economic Stabilisation Commission oversaw this

system, which worked effectively albeit without entirely preventing strikes.[139]

Apart from its inflationary danger, the shortage of goods introduced another problem — hoarding. People naturally tried to insure against future uncertainties of supply by laying in extra stocks. This applied especially to goods brought in from overseas, but later in the war it extended to New Zealand's own produce. Increased exports of food to Britain rendered it necessary to control people's access to the available supplies. Food rationing in a land of plenty became another wartime imposition, one that affected every person in the country.

Rationing began immediately after the war broke out for some products, notably petrol. But in 1942 its range greatly extended, partly to prevent hoarding and to

A poster urging investment in a Victory Loan. Apart from providing funds for the war effort, war-related loans, by soaking up excess cash in the economy, helped to reduce inflationary pressures.

ensure equitable distribution of available goods as supplies dried up, but mainly to maximise the amount of food being sent overseas. With the need to supply American forces in the South Pacific from 1942, British requests for increased supplies posed problems. Nonetheless, few objected to making this contribution, even though it meant cutting consumption within New Zealand because poor seasons had depressed production.

From April 1942 people had to make do with 12 ounces of sugar a week, and from June tea was rationed to 2 ounces a week per person over nine years of age. Clothing, footwear, and household linen were rationed from May 1942. During 1943, the population felt the bite of food rationing. From May it became impossible to obtain fresh pork, which was reserved for American troops. After October 1943, to meet British butter needs, each person in New Zealand could obtain only 8 ounces of butter a week; the rate fell to 6 ounces in June 1945, though this was still considerably above the 2 ounces available to people in Britain. From March 1944 meat was rationed on a value basis. Most New Zealanders accepted these limitations on their diet without complaint. Compared with their British counterparts, they knew that they had it easy. Sympathetic feelings were enhanced when a new and frightening blitz began on Britain in 1944, as the Germans launched flying-bombs ('doodlebugs') at London, to be followed by the more frightening V2 rockets, whose speed gave little warning of their approach.

Controlling dissent

Controls were not confined to the economy. In the interests of maintaining social harmony, New Zealanders also faced significant restrictions on their freedom of speech. The government's approach was broad. Apart from the need to maintain operational security and prevent the enemy gaining information of value (which everyone accepted), it was determined to prevent the broadcasting or publishing of anything that might undermine the war effort. This applied in particular to the expression of pacifist or communist views.

SERGEANT WORK

As the war situation in the Pacific improved and war-weariness grew, many workers slackened the intensity of their effort. Here a cartoonist reminds New Zealanders that the Christmas-New Year break was only a temporary relief.

Ensuring that the enemy does not obtain sensitive miliary information is always important in war. Here members of the Women's War Service Auxiliary advertise the 'Don't Talk' campaign urging New Zealanders to be careful about what they conveyed to other members of the public.

The director of publicity, JT Paul, oversaw the censorship of newspapers, a function that often verged on political control, as criticism of government actions was suppressed. More draconian than that instituted in the United Kingdom, New Zealand's censorship system left the public in the dark about numerous important aspects of the war effort and often led to intriguing press reports of cases in the courts in which the nature of the offence could not be spelt out. A committee oversaw the censorship of publications arriving from overseas. Numerous books, especially those relating to communism (despite the alliance with the Soviet Union from 1941), were banned.

Behind the scenes, the Police Special Branch carried out security surveillance. In February 1941 a specially formed security intelligence organisation took over this task. But its credibility suffered fatal damage when its director, a British officer on secondment, allowed himself to be convinced by a con man that a Japanese invasion of Taranaki was imminent. In the aftermath of this farcical incident, the police resumed control of security activities.

Making do

Controls and shortages dominated wartime life in New Zealand. But most accepted them as a temporary imposition in an emergency. They got on with life, adjusting to the situation as best they could in the hope that victory would soon release them from the annoying constraints. It was a time of making do.

New Zealanders faced severe problems in running their homes. Goods and services hitherto taken for

A group of war brides prepare to leave for the United States in June 1945.

War Effort Collection, Alexander Turnbull Library, C139

granted now became unavailable. Home deliveries, a feature of life before the war, dried up as petrol rationing and labour shortages bit. People had to endure overcrowded public transport to go to poorly stocked shops to obtain necessary supplies. Ration books had to be presented for more and more purchases as the war progressed. Queuing became a constant irritation.

At home, cooking became an exercise in ingenuity. Without ample supplies of butter and sugar, in particular, cooks had no choice but to experiment. They discovered new ways of producing meals and stretched out what they had. Shortages of cloth also caused many difficulties, and required much revamping of old garments.

Combining homemaking and work responsibilities confronted many women with big problems. If they had children under the age of 16, they were not liable to be 'manpowered', but many still had to work to make ends meet. Some crèches and daycare centres were provided by the authorities in Wellington for workers in essential industries, but elsewhere such facilities were rare. Working mothers struggled to find suitable minders for their children, often having to rely on relatives.

There was a never-ending search for ways to get round shortages. Some looked to avenues outside the law. A black market existed, though not on a large scale. Most just tried to make existing resources go further. Those with cars faced the problem of stretching the miles their cars could run on the ration. Coasting down hills became a universal practice. Some looked to substitutes for petrol, and cumbersome gas engines made an appearance on the roads. The horse and cart once again became a familiar sight.

New Zealand served as a refuge for civilians from war-torn Europe. Refugees included British children. In September 1940 two batches, numbering 202, arrived under an official scheme; a few others arrived as individuals, sent by their parents to the apparent safety of the South Pacific. But the biggest influx occurred in 1944, when more than 800 Polish children and accompanying adults arrived and were housed in a camp at Pahiatua. Prime Minister Peter Fraser, seen here with Countess Wodzicka, the wife of the Polish Consul-General in Wellington, and some of the children, was there to greet them on their arrival in New Zealand in the *General Randall*.

People sought to maintain elements of normality, especially in recreational activities. Dances, parties and other social occasions brought some relief from the daily grind. Race meetings continued, as did sporting competitions. Golfers still frequented their courses, though petrol rationing eventually forced many country clubs to close for the duration.

Marital relationships

Apart from the many controls and impositions, wartime life in New Zealand was also hugely affected by the absence overseas of so many men. The war drastically affected relationships. Many marriages had been contracted hastily before the husband embarked for overseas service, and women could find themselves waiting up to four years before seeing their loved one again. These were years of loneliness. For many it meant uncomfortable accommodation with in-laws and struggling to bring up young children with few resources. Letter writing did much for the morale of those serving in distant theatres.

Bob Anderson, a member of the first furlough draft, greets Audrey Gilmore on his arrival at Wellington.

For many women, the separation proved no hindrance to the sustenance of strong relationships with their spouses, and the marriages would emerge from the war as strong as ever. For others, however, the death of their spouse shattered dreams of long-lasting marriage. All those with husbands, sons or brothers overseas had to live with the nagging fear of the telegram boy, the harbinger of tragic tidings. Some began to feel remote from husbands they realised they barely knew, and were unable to bear the separation. Some drifted into relationships with more accessible men, often causing great heartache to their loved ones overseas as news of infidelities percolated through to them.

The presence of Americans in New Zealand from 1942 provided a new element on the social scene — and temptations. The Americans' manners, different dating habits and affluence appealed to many women, despite a certain community disapproval of such liaisons (and much resentment among 2NZEF troops). One woman recalled being 'treated like queens'. 'They never called for their partner without candy in one hand and flowers in the other,' she said.[140] Often no more than friendship was involved, but there were also more serious relationships. These often ended with the American soldier's death on some Pacific battlefield, indicated by a sudden cessation of letters. But a proportion survived, and about 1400 New Zealand women became war brides, joining their husbands in the United States following the war.

Maintaining unity

The invasion threat in 1942 had a unifying effect on New Zealanders. But once the immediate danger had passed, old divisions began to reassert themselves. As the war dragged on, war-weariness also permeated society, and a degree of resistance to the continuing controls developed.

At the political level, unity had not survived long. The War Administration collapsed in October 1942, when its National members walked out after disagreeing with

War History Collection, Alexander Turnbull Library, F-2234-35mm-DA

Fraser's approach to a strike. The effect was offset, however, by the continuation of the War Cabinet, albeit in a slightly different form, with two National members Gordon Coates and Adam Hamilton serving on it as private individuals. (When Coates died in 1943, Sir William Perry, the President of the RSA, took his place.) The co-operation achieved in overcoming the many problems confronting New Zealand's war effort left one of its Labour members convinced that the War Cabinet was a 'political miracle'; he saw existing in it 'something deeper than co-operation and understanding'.[141]

Despite the War Cabinet's survival, party politicking revived with a vengeance in 1943. With the demise of the War Administration, the agreement to defer the general election for the duration lapsed. The country therefore faced the disruption of a general election campaign in 1943 — though the extent, nature or direction of the war effort did not become an issue. At the poll, on 25 September, Labour again prevailed with 47 per cent of the vote. Although it lost some seats, it remained comfortably in power with 45 of the 80 seats, and took the result to be an endorsement of the existing arrangements for conducting the war effort.

The furlough mutiny

Even as New Zealanders prepared to exercise their delayed democratic right to vote, a major threat to harmony arose. In July 1943, the first draft of the 6000 2NZEF men had arrived home to begin their three-month furlough. Many quickly became disaffected when they found that numerous fit men were still being held back in essential jobs. Such feelings were encouraged when National's leader, Sidney Holland, during the election campaign, maintained that nobody should be forced to go overseas twice before all had gone once. When politics and shipping problems extended the furlough period, men began to take up civilian jobs, determined not to return to the Middle East.

By early 1944, when the return of the first furlough draft to the Middle East at last became practicable, its numbers had been whittled down. In deference to the Maori community, Maori soldiers had been discharged. So too had married soldiers with children and many on medical grounds. Just over 1600 remained to enter camp pending re-embarkation on 12 January. Nearly a thousand of these men obeyed all orders except that to go aboard ship. The government faced a dilemma; discipline demanded that the men be forced to embark, but as the war situation was now less threatening, the public would not easily accept such a situation, given that many sympathised with the defaulters' viewpoint.

Some of the defaulters eventually agreed to re-embark. Most did not, and they duly faced courts martial. Found guilty of desertion (later quashed on appeal), they were dismissed from 2NZEF and lost all privileges and benefits — at least until the end of the war (when these privileges were restored). They were joined by a small number of men from the second furlough draft, which had arrived home in February 1944. In all, 550 men were penalised for refusing to re-embark.[142] Strict censorship prevented the public from receiving full details of the affair, though rumours circulated.

By late 1943, the progress of the Allied war effort had rendered the likelihood of defeat increasingly remote. The huge productive power of the United States and the immense manpower resources of the Soviet Union had begun to have their effect on the Axis powers. Maintaining the home front effort at a high pitch became less easy in such circumstances. Most people stoically endured the ongoing restrictions in the fervent hope that the war might be brought to an early conclusion. This hope was encouraged by evidence that Germany was beginning to falter as it was assailed from three sides and from the sky — a hammering in which many New Zealanders continued to play their part with considerable distinction.

2 Feb – Germany suffers
first major defeat at
Stalingrad

13 May – Axis forces in
North Africa surrender

5 Jul – Battle of
Kursk begins

8 Sep – Italy
surrenders

9 Oct – First 2 NZ Div
troops land in Italy

3 Sep – Allied forces land
on Italian mainland

25 Jul – Mussolini deposed and
placed under arrest

17 Aug – Allied leaders meet
at Quebec Conference to
discuss strategy

War History Collection, Alexander Turnbull Library, F-794-53mm-DA

New Zealand soldiers approach a downed bridge over the Lamone River.

22 Jan – Allies
land at Anzio

17 Feb – 2 NZ Division
attacks Cassino town

23 Mar – Freyberg
closes down NZ
operation at Cassino

6 Jun – Allied forces
land at Normandy

11 Sep – War Cabinet
agrees that 2 NZ Division
will remain in Italy

15 Feb – Monastery
at Cassino bombed

4 Jun – Rome
falls to Allies

4 Aug – Florence
falls to the Allies

18 May – Allies finally
take Cassino

Italian Setbacks

As darkness fell on 28 November 1943, Sergeant Pat Kane began preparing himself for action. In a few hours' time he and his platoon would move forward to the forming-up point for an assault that would take them over the nearby shallow river and onto the high ground opposite. Some of his men made their peace with God; others checked their weapons or equipment, ensuring that shovel and pick were firmly attached; the rest just tried to compose themselves. Some reflected on previous battles fought in very different conditions. Many others wondered how they would fare in their debut, their baptism of fire; for the division now had a solid leavening of newly arrived men, replacing those who by now were enjoying their furlough in New Zealand.

For a week now they had been waiting for the chance to attack. Held up by the rain-swollen stream, they had cursed the cold, rain and mud that added to their misery. But the prospect of action at last pushed these discomforts into the background. As they approached the river, the shells could be heard bursting on the high ground ahead — a normal harassing pattern designed to persuade the enemy that nothing was amiss. Reaching the water, Kane and his men waded into it up to their chests. The freezing cold left them gasping, for the river flowed directly from snow-covered heights not far away. On the other side they formed up, shivering, to await the barrage that would

163

herald the battalion's push for the objectives on the higher ground.

Precisely on schedule at 2.45 a.m., the darkness was rent by gun flashes as the gunners opened the barrage. Scores of shells whined over the infantrymen to burst on the ground ahead. The troops began to advance, undeterred by the tracers that floated towards them as enemy machine-gunners opened up in their direction. Kane's platoon soon reached its objective, a village. The newly arrived officer had been killed, and Kane, now in command, ordered them to take cover. Numbingly cold, they took shelter where they could to await the dawn.[143]

Kane's platoon had successfully crossed the Sangro River, as part of 2 Division's first major action of a new campaign. The New Zealanders had returned to the European mainland from which they had been ejected so ignominiously in 1941. This time they would do battle in the homeland of their old North African adversary — Italy.

Allied plans

The Allied decision to invade Italy arose from a combination of opportunism, improvisation, misplaced hopes and coalition compromise. It was made possible by the Allied victory in North Africa in May 1943, which had opened up the soft underbelly of Hitler's Europe at a time when the Italians were demoralised by the loss of their empire and the realisation of the cost of throwing in their lot with the Nazis.

When Anglo-American forces invaded Sicily on 10 July 1943, the Italians lost their appetite for war. Mussolini was deposed 13 days later, and the new government under General Badoglio began secretly negotiating an armistice with the Allies.

The British were keen to invade mainland Italy. Not only would this precipitate the exit from the war of one of Germany's major allies but also it offered the prospect of Allied forces rapidly moving up the peninsula to the line of the Alps. If the Germans fell back to these defensible positions, the Allies would have gained jumping-off points for attacks throughout the Balkans, to say nothing of the advantages that airbases in Italy would bring for extending the reach of Allied bombing operations against German territory.

American strategists were less impressed by the potential advantages. They feared that an Italian campaign would detract from preparations for the real showdown with Germany, which would come in north-west Europe with the opening of the long-awaited Second Front. The Americans favoured the direct approach, rather than the indirect one suggested by the British government. But in the end they reluctantly went along with the plan for an invasion of Italy. By the time the Axis forces had surrendered in Tunisia, it had become clear that the invasion of north-west Europe could not occur until 1944 anyway. The scale of the preparations required ruled out an attempt to land in the summer of 1943. At the Quebec Conference in August 1943, a compromise emerged: Italy would be invaded to knock Italy out of the war and establish airbases in the Rome area, from which the air campaign against Hitler's Europe could be intensified. Two major formations, Montgomery's 8th Army and the Anglo-American 5th Army commanded by American General Mark Clark, would be committed to the task.

Italy surrenders

The first objective of the campaign was achieved almost before it began. Within five days of the first Allied troops landing at Reggio di Calabria on 3 September 1943, Italy surrendered — a major blow to the Nazi cause politically and militarily. Although Italian fighting capacity had proved to be limited, Italian troops had garrisoned many parts of the Balkans. The need to take over these Balkan tasks left Germany still further stretched at a time when additional resources had to be found to defend German-held territory in Italy.

Although wavering at first, Hitler confounded British hopes by resolving to defend as far south as possible, using the 18 German divisions in the country at the time of the armistice. The geography of the peninsula lent itself to a defensive strategy. German forces in Italy were determined and competent, and commanded by one of the more effective German commanders, Field Marshal Kesselring. They were well disposed in good defensive positions on what was termed the Gustav Line, blocking the way to Rome at the narrowest point on the peninsula. The implications of this German approach were not at first apparent; in November, Allied leaders meeting in Tehran agreed that the objective in Italy should be to secure all of the peninsula south of a line running from Pisa to Rimini, well to the north of Rome.

In a daring operation German special forces rescued Mussolini from captivity. He now became ruler of a fascist republic established in the German-occupied part of Italy. The Italian government, for its part, declared war on Germany, and Italian troops in due course took their place in the front line, fighting alongside their erstwhile enemies. In Mussolini's domain, many Italians joined partisan units, which operated with increasing effectiveness against German lines of communication. A vicious civil war began.

The rapid German response to the Italian surrender also forestalled Allied hopes to recover 70,000 of their POWs being held in Italian camps, including 3600 New Zealanders. Ordered by the Allied authorities to wait in their camps until Allied forces arrived, most soon found themselves in German custody. Taken north by train, they ended up in German POW camps, mainly in Austria. More than 400 New Zealanders were among those who got away before German units arrived to take control of their camps. About a quarter made it across the border into Switzerland; most of the rest made their way south through Italy or Yugoslavia to eventually reach Allied lines. Some stayed in the hills and operated with partisan bands.

Dodecanese fiasco

Following Italy's surrender, opportunities for action in Italian overseas territories also opened up, especially now that the Allies held full control of the sea throughout the Mediterranean. The Germans were alive to this danger, and moved rapidly to establish control over Italian-held islands, sometimes with extreme brutality towards their former allies.

Churchill urged action against the Italian Dodecanese Islands, lying off the south-west coast of Turkey and on the periphery of the enemy perimeter. Seizing them, he believed, would bolster the Allied position in the eastern Aegean and perhaps influence Turkey to enter the war on the Allied side.

The Long Range Desert Group (LRDG) was given the task of occupying the islands. This ensured that several hundred New Zealanders would be involved, for they still formed an important element of the LRDG. By September 1943 they were on the island of Calino, one of eight islands occupied. But the Germans reacted so strongly that the LRDG soon moved to Leros, where a British infantry brigade had been landed to form the garrison.

News that New Zealanders were in action in the Dodecanese came as a shock to the government in Wellington, which had never been consulted about the operation. Fraser angrily demanded their withdrawal. By this time the decision had been taken, in light of the loss of the island of Levitia with heavy casualties, to withdraw the whole LRDG from the Aegean.

Before this could be done the Germans launched a fierce attack against Leros, and defeated the British troops holding it. Most of the New Zealanders managed to escape by caiques or rowboats, but four were killed. Those taken prisoner soon began the long journey north to POW camps in Germany.[144] After this fiasco, all but a handful of the New Zealanders serving in the LRDG were pulled out and reassigned to 2 Division's Divisional Cavalry.

New Zealanders enter the fray

The first New Zealanders involved in Italy arrived with the Desert Air Force. Dozens of New Zealand pilots helped man the RAF fighter squadrons that supported the Allied ground effort, and five commanded squadrons. Before long others arrived with bomber squadrons; these squadrons were soon using Italian bases to seek out targets in South-East Europe that had previously been largely invulnerable to the bomber campaign mounted from the United Kingdom. During the following 18 months, 90 New Zealanders served as aircrew in these strategically important operations.

By the end of 1943 New Zealand troops were also in action on the peninsula. For a time there had been talk of sending them to Britain to prepare for the planned landing in France. A mobile force with an armoured regiment, the division was well fitted for fighting on the plains of north-western Europe. A shift to this theatre would, however, have entailed developing new lines of

communication and a new base, whereas the existing Egyptian base could support a deployment in Italy. Once the uncertainties about 2 Division's next assignment had been resolved in October, the troops moved to Alexandria, where they embarked on ships that would convey them across the Mediterranean to the Italian port of Taranto.[145]

As they landed and settled into temporary camps, the New Zealanders, militarily at least, found themselves back in a familiar environment. They would operate in Italy, as in North Africa, as part of 8th Army with the Desert Air Force in support. As previously, they formed part of a multi-national force.

Though the context remained the same, much had changed in the six months since the end of the fighting in Africa. The division had lost a third of its most experienced members, men whose skills and character had been honed in surmounting early disasters. Those who remained had been wearied by their experience, a situation that could only be partially alleviated by rest and recuperation in the Egyptian heat. A large number of untried reinforcements now fleshed out many units. It would clearly take time for the division to regain its former efficiency.

The division also faced new and very different conditions to those they had experienced in North Africa, as became evident as soon as they began to move forward to the front line in November. The rugged hills could not have been more different to the generally flat desert. The troops admiring the precipitous ridges they drove slowly over and the ravines with rushing torrents below them had few illusions about the difficulties attacking troops would face in such conditions. After the freedom of the desert, the slow progress of columns winding into the hills along a single road seemed 'unnatural and tedious', as one soldier recalled. 'The terrain became more rugged and difficult as we moved into the higher country. We passed village after village perched on almost inaccessible heights, frequently surrounded by walls or sheer rock faces.'[146]

War History Collection, Alexander Turnbull Library, F-4695-¼-DA

New Zealand gunners manhandle vehicles through a muddy road on the Sangro River front in December 1943.

The Italian Theatre

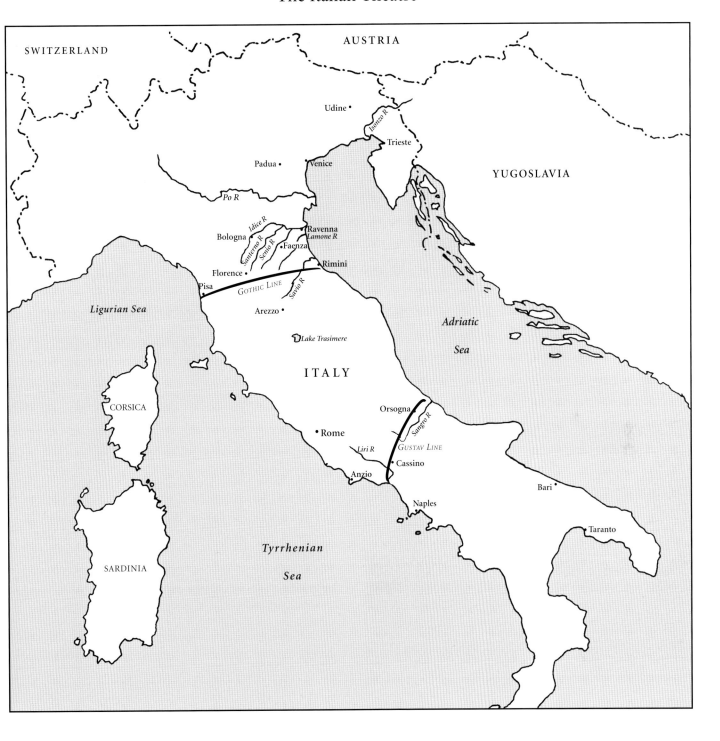

The soldiers soon became aware of another difference — the weather. Snow, hail and rain came as 'a shock to the system' after three years in the arid desert.[147] They played havoc with communications and made travel anywhere in winter difficult. In these conditions, the weather lined up with the enemy to make soldiering a test of endurance. Freezing in their slit trenches soldiers thought nostalgically of the desert heat. But it was not just the cold that made conditions unpleasant; clinging mud also tried men's patience.

Another difference from the desert campaign was immediately apparent — the presence of civilians, both in the combat zone and behind the lines. Although they were former enemies, few Italian civilians seemed hostile to the presence of the Allied troops. Indeed many now saw them as liberators from the fascist or German yoke. Many lived in very deprived conditions. The sight of starving women and children left few troops unmoved.

War History Collection, Alexander Turnbull Library, F-4600-½-DA

The Italian campaign made huge demands on 2 New Zealand Division's field engineers, especially in keeping communications open in the face of both enemy action and adverse weather. Here sappers work on a deviation in the Sangro River area in November 1943, with a bridge demolished by the retreating enemy in the background.

At the same time the presence of civilians also introduced temptations not present in the desert. Discipline suffered as men took opportunities to loot civilian property or engage in black market dealings.

Orsogna

The New Zealanders' first operations in Italy quickly dispelled any notion that this might not be a difficult campaign. Deployed on the eastern side of the peninsula, they were ordered to cross the Sangro River and push north through the Gustav Line positions as part of an 8th Army drive that, it was hoped, would turn the German defences and allow the Allies to descend on Rome through the Apennines.

The New Zealanders' attack, which began before dawn on 28 November 1943, went well enough at first. Both 5 and 6 Brigades crossed the river with relatively limited casualties, leading the commander of the former to reflect later that generally 'it was a satisfactory and surprisingly easy affair'.[148] As several hundred German POWs trudged back, sappers were hard at work bridging the Sangro to allow supporting arms to get forward to assist the infantry. Using the new Bailey bridge that they would become masters at laying in the next year and a half, they quickly had the link established, despite enemy gunfire. The Maori battalion came up to resume the attack, but the advance continued so aggressively that no formal assault was necessary. Enemy minefields and mortar fire harried the troops as they pressed forward, cursing the mud that impeded them at every turn. 'At times we had to stop and cut the mud off our heels with our bayonets,' one soldier recalled, 'but it accumulated again before we had progressed much further.'[149] Despite these hindrances the New Zealanders had secured the tactically important village of Castelfrentano by 2 December, and looked to grab the nearby strongpoint of Orsogna.

Although some infantry managed to enter Orsogna next day, the Germans were determined not to lose this key feature in their next line of defence. The New Zealanders were quickly thrown out. Over the next three weeks they made a series of attacks, about a week apart, in an effort to take the town or, later, to outflank it. Up against effective defenders who made good use of the terrain, they achieved no significant progress. As stalemate set in, morale dropped. In an unprecedented incident, there was even a minor mutiny, when most of one platoon refused to obey an order to attack on Christmas Eve.[150]

In the end, the weather put an end to further attempts to force the German line. As the winter set in proper, fighting took second place to finding shelter. The intense cold, the continuing mortaring, sniping and shelling, and their consciousness of failure left the troops in a despondent mood. Orsogna lay like a tempting but unreachable morsel and the men 'were tired of looking at it all day and every day'.[151] Few were sorry when in mid-January orders came to hand over the positions to relieving troops and pull back.

The New Zealand division's first taste of Italian campaigning had been costly. More than 1600 men had been killed or wounded. These initial operations had made it clear that the division, with only two infantry brigades, lacked the infantrymen needed for fighting in such rugged conditions. To overcome this problem, divisional cavalrymen and machine-gunners would eventually be transformed into infantrymen to help man another infantry brigade (9 Brigade).

Cassino

After moving or obscuring their badges and markings to hinder enemy spies, the New Zealanders began a move that would take them to the other side of the peninsula. Painful memories of the Orsogna fighting were soon obscured by the dangers of the mid-winter trek. As they ground their way up and down mountains, the sight of rushing torrents in great chasms below them did nothing

for the mood of troops aware of the icy roads on which they were proceeding. After a brief rest period they moved forward to their destination near the town of Cassino.

Just as 8th Army's drive up the Adriatic coast had been blunted, so too had the 5th Army offensive in the west. The only feasible route north to Rome in this sector lay through the Liri Valley, the entrance to which, at Cassino, was only 12 kilometres wide. The route north passed through Cassino, a small town of about 5000 inhabitants that was overlooked by a monastery on Monte Cassino. By blowing the stopbanks on the Rapido and Gari rivers, the Germans had created wide marshy bogs that greatly narrowed lines of approach to the town

Alexander Turnbull Library, Eph-A-WAR-WII-German-propaganda-1944-01

A damned hard nut, just the right job for our New Zealand pals

A German propaganda leaflet designed to undermine the morale of New Zealand troops fighting at Cassino.

and made outflanking it more difficult. All this combined to make Cassino 'as strong as any position could be without being impregnable', in the opinion of the officer who found himself facing the unenviable task of organising a New Zealand attack on it.[152]

Initially this had not been the New Zealanders' task. As part of the New Zealand Corps, which included their old desert allies 4 Indian Division, they had expected to drive through a gap that American forces would open and, linking with other forces landed at Anzio to the north of Cassino, to drive on Rome. But the attack foundered. Failing to act with sufficient boldness, the Anzio force was soon bottled up by the quickly reacting Germans, while further south American attempts to cross the Rapido and enter Liri Valley were repelled with heavy losses.

Anzio, far from threatening the enemy position, now became a liability; 5th Army was forced to keep attacking in an attempt to relieve it. This brought the New Zealand Corps into the fray. Its commander was Freyberg. (In his absence Kippenberger had taken over command of 2 Division.) Freyberg approached the task with foreboding. With the bloody lesson of the futile American attacks before him, he saw the danger of the New Zealand division being bled white in an attempt to secure the breakthrough, and was determined to prevent this from happening.

But the nature of the battlefield ensured that any success would be dearly bought. Freyberg planned a two-prong attack. While the Indian division attacked to the north of the town where the Americans had made some gains, the New Zealanders would seize its railway station and two other nearby points. They would then cover the crossing of the Gari River by American units further west to outflank the town and drive into the Liri Valley.

In the New Zealand part of the operation, the Maori battalion drew the short straw. Two of its companies would have the daunting task of attacking well dug-in defenders on a very narrow front. To get to a position to mount their attack on the railway station, they would have to use the only dry approach route through the flooded,

marshy area — the railway causeway. So too would the tanks and other supporting weapons needed if the Maori companies were to hold off the inevitable German counter-attacks. But this latter movement could be made only after sappers repaired a dozen demolitions in the causeway — a difficult task to complete before daylight.

As the sappers prepared for their monumental task, Freyberg was taking care of another perceived problem. The troops believed that the Germans were using the monastery as an observation point. When the Indian divisional commander requested its destruction, Freyberg agreed, and permission was eventually granted at a higher level. As a consequence, on 15 February, the waiting troops watched in awe as the monastery disappeared under massive bomb blasts. While few disagreed with the decision, they would soon have cause to wonder if the bombing had gained them anything other than a temporary psychological boost. Whether or not they had been using the monastery before the bombing, the Germans now certainly made use of the rubble to create a strongpoint.

As soon as darkness fell on 17 February, several hundred Maori infantrymen moved forward along the causeway. Deploying on a start line on the other side of the marsh and shivering in the frosty air, they waited for the attack to begin at 9.30 p.m. Precisely on time they moved silently forward towards the railway stations and the two flanking objectives. No shells crashed comfortingly ahead of them. A barrage had not been laid on in the hope that surprise could be achieved.

Hopes of a sudden coup were quickly dashed. As flares went up, machine guns stuttered into life. The troops had to battle their way forward. It was not until 2 a.m., well behind schedule, that the station was in Maori hands. The other two objectives, which would have provided flanking cover for this point, remained out of reach. Meanwhile, on the causeway, sappers were frantically trying to overcome the demolitions. Problems had been experienced getting bulldozers along the causeway, and when the moon rose at 3 a.m. enemy mortar fire hindered

New Zealand troops fight inside Cassino town.

the work. Despite valiant efforts, the sappers could not complete their task before daybreak.

The Maori troops holding the railway station were left out on a limb. Only if they could hold out till darkness fell again could they be properly supported. Smoke was laid down to obscure them, but they spent uncomfortable hours under mortar fire as they waited. Late in the afternoon, their position became untenable as German tanks and infantry pressed in on them in a concerted counter-attack. When the Maori were forced to pull out of the station and back across the causeway, all hope of saving the operation passed.

The New Zealand division's first foray into Cassino had failed, but the problem of relieving Anzio remained.

Freyberg prepared to make another push, using a different approach. The Indian and New Zealand divisions would attack side by side from the north, the former on Castle Hill below the monastery, the latter on the town itself and the slopes above it.

The narrow fronts on which the divisions would have to attack remained a major disadvantage. Troops fed into the attack would find it difficult to dislodge determined defenders, among whom were now the New Zealanders' old Crete adversaries, the paratroopers. It was hoped, however, that these defenders could be so disoriented by a massive bombing attack on the town that rapid progress would be possible. But bad weather intervened. And before the plan could be implemented 2 Division suffered the loss of its temporary commander; while descending from an observation point in early March, Kippenberger stood on a mine, suffering wounds that led to a double amputation of his legs. Brigadier 'Ike' Parkinson took over.

Not until 14 March did the operation begin. Once again the troops watched spellbound as 500 bombers unloaded their lethal cargoes on the town. Once they had finished, 600 guns added to the destruction. The town was smashed. In the words of one soldier present, it was 'an indescribable jumble of churned masonry'.[153] But, not for the first time, expectations that heavy bombardment would leave defenders incapacitated went unrealised. Enough of the enemy had survived to put up fierce resistance to the New Zealand troops moving into the devastated town. The bombardment had proved counter-productive, for it hindered the movement not only of the attacking troops but also of tanks and other support weapons. Innumerable strongpoints now existed among the rubble from which the defenders could keep up a withering fire on any groups advancing towards them. The conditions were ideal for snipers, and their presence added to the stress on the attacking troops. Defining the front line became impossible as enemy parties constantly infiltrated behind the New Zealanders, reoccupying shattered buildings already captured.

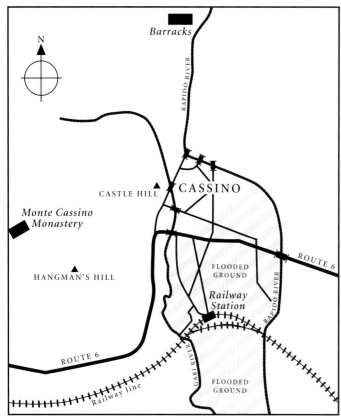

Cassino, Italy.

For the first time New Zealanders came to experience something of the street fighting that had become a feature of the struggle on the Eastern Front. Cassino was a mini-Stalingrad. Many years later John Waititi, an officer in 28 Battalion, described the ordeal: 'Oh man, it was pathetic.... All you did was move down one hole and up and down into another hole. You could drive a truck into one of these holes and it would disappear. Some had so much water in them you couldn't touch the bottom.'[154]

Sergeant Roger Smith describes his platoon's return to the combat zone in Cassino town after a brief respite from the fighting:

> *From then on we were back in the environment of primitive man, lurking stealthily among the ruins, nerves taut with a constant watchfulness. We went up the track beside the highway as quietly as possible....*
>
> *We were once more in that familiar ghost world that lacked all colour; a world sometimes lit for minutes by a brilliant flare which made the ensuing darkness seem all the blacker. A world of crumbling ruins, twisted concrete and gaunt tentacles of exposed reinforcing iron. A world of dust and water, of insecure footholds and rattling rocks; a world where a Spandau [machine gun] lashed at your every mistake. Crossing that area, we were forced on to our faces while bullets cracked and sung above us.... At last we reached the shadow of the shattered walls that were to be our home. It was a queer post, an isolated prominence of walls that the bombing had not flattened, in an area where barely one brick still rested on another. We climbed into the shell of a building that had no roof and two gaping holes in the front wall. These holes looked onto what had been a small courtyard, now blocked off on its open side by a collapsed building. The only exit left in the yard was a small wrought-iron wicket gate across a little passage in the far corner. On the other side of this lurked the enemy....*[155]

New Zealand infantrymen on manoeuvres on the Cassino front in April 1944.

Bren gunners of 23 Battalion firing on targets from a strongpoint in a house that had received more than 50 hits by enemy shells.

173

Once again the New Zealanders found the task beyond them. Although both infantry brigades were eventually committed to the fighting, only marginal gains could be made. Freyberg fought with what one senior British general complained was a 'casualty conscious mind' that led him to avoid risking the New Zealand infantry.[156] By 23 March 1944, as the division's total casualties neared a thousand, he had had enough. He closed down the operation. A little over two weeks later the weary troops were pulled out. The battle had taken the lives of 340 of their number.

Cassino finally fell in May 1944 when British and Polish troops occupied the town and the ruins of the monastery. By this time the defenders had realised they were being outflanked, and most had been pulled back. With the coming of spring, the Allied armies had launched a co-ordinated offensive that at last broke the Gustav Line. Among the units that entered the smashed town in this final drive were the tanks of 19 NZ Armoured Regiment.

The fall of Rome

The Allied offensive placed the German forces in extreme jeopardy. The chance existed to cut them off before they could get back to a new defensible position. But they were saved by the egotism of 5th Army commander Clark, who placed the glory of seizing Rome before the interests of the Allies' campaign in Italy as a whole. His troops entered the Italian capital on 4 June.

By extricating their forces from a perilous position, the Germans confronted the Allies with the need for more costly attacks on good defensive positions. Their task was helped, moreover, by developments elsewhere. The Allied landing at Normandy, two days after the fall of Rome, underlined the secondary nature of the fighting in Italy. This was soon driven home by the removal of seven divisions from Italy for an Allied landing in southern France in August 1944. The Italian campaign would continue, but only to draw off German resources from the vital theatre in France, a not unimportant role.

New Zealand infantrymen crouch in the depression formed by a ditch and wait the order to advance on German-held Faenza in December 1944.

War History Collection, Alexander Turnbull Library, F-7953-35mm-

The fall of Rome had also brought into question New Zealand's continued participation in the campaign. There was talk in London of forming a British-led force to operate against the Japanese from Australia. The idea appealed to Fraser.[157] By committing 2 Division to such a force, New Zealand could not only resolve its Pacific versus Mediterranean conundrum but also ensure that its troops served in the preferred familiar British command framework. But nothing came of the proposal. At the same time, the success of the D-Day landings and huge Soviet gains on the Eastern Front seemed to foreshadow an early end to the war. This expectation reduced the urgency of a decision. Not till 11 September 1944 did the War Cabinet in Wellington resolve that the division should remain in Italy until the end of the campaign.

Advance to the Senio

With the Germans still resisting strongly, backed by strong positions on the so-called Gothic Line running from Pisa to Rimini in the northern Apennines, the Allied armies faced the task of continuing the slog up the peninsula. When the New Zealanders returned to the front in July, they took part in the drive on the city of Florence. Once again the troops faced the problems of dislodging well dug-in enemy troops. In the summer heat, they sweated their way forward to capture the town of Arezzo on the sixteenth. But the path to Florence was blocked in the hills to its south. For a week the New Zealanders hammered away before finally overcoming the resistance. By 4 August 1944, the city was in Allied hands. These operations had cost the division more than 1000 casualties.

In their next advance, the New Zealanders found the going made more difficult by the number of rivers and canals in the area. Bad weather also caused problems. But they drove back determined opponents, and by 20 October stood on the Savio River.

Private Norcott Hornibrook, 24 Battalion, describes an attack on the night of 24–25 September 1944:

At 8 o'clock barrage lifted 100 yards and we started forward: Shells falling short and bursting all around us. So dark couldn't see 10 feet. I was sending out a call trying to contact control — had the earphones on and couldn't hear the near ones coming in — something hit me! Felt like a railway train! Could feel left arm broken and something seemed to be pushing my lungs in. Dropped in my tracks. Orders were not to stop for casualties so they put on Shell Dressings and left me lying in an open ploughed field — covered me over. Managed to breath somehow but had to fight for every breath. Then some minnies [rockets] and mortars came over pretty close so got up and struggled to a Jerry trench. Was bleeding badly and couldn't stand up without blackout. Jerry mortaring all around — nearly hit my trench several times. Could hear the attack going ahead. Streams of Jerry tracer.

25 September 1944 Dawn — very weak from loss of blood — area deserted — chewed a few old grapes I had found to keep down the thirst! Jerry still sending mortars over — further back. About 9 o'clock my bacon was saved. An Italian snooping past my trench saw me and jumped in with me and kissed me on both cheeks. Sent him for help. Returned some time later with Pongos [British] in a tank. Got me on the front of it and took me back. Jeep took me to R.A.P. [Regimental Aid Post] — Much Morphine — memory pretty hazy from then on.[158]

As the troops contemplated the unwelcome prospect of another Italian winter, they launched a new drive in late November. The immediate goal was the Senio River. Crossing the Lamone River, they took Faenza on 14 December. By Christmas, the Senio had been reached. The division took up defensive positions.

The troops settled down to endure the miseries of the Italian winter. 'The ground was frozen over and was frequently covered in snow,' one soldier recalled. 'It was far

New Zealand and the Second World War

too cold to occupy the slit trenches which had been dug about the buildings. More often than not they were half full of water with a thick coating of ice on top. The war had come to a standstill …'[159] But patrols had to be mounted. In the freezing conditions and darkness, a listening patrol was invariably a trying experience for the troops.

A small group of New Zealand escaped POWs found the winter close-down especially frustrating. Expecting the Allied advance to overrun them, they now faced a long wait in uncomfortable conditions. Some hid with Italian families; a few became actively involved in organising the POW pipeline, or in sabotage operations against enemy facilities or transport. In the Udine area Frank Gardner — dubbed 'Franco' by the locals — gathered together a group of Italian partisans and blew up a train; he subsequently carried out numerous other operations, including the blowing up of an important railway near Germona. Another escapee, David Russell,

organised Allied POWs in hiding. A Crete veteran, he had been captured at Ruweisat Ridge in 1942 but escaped from a POW camp after Italy's capitulation. When recaptured, Russell courageously withstood torture to avoid incriminating an Italian peasant taken with him. He refused to give any information about underground activities in the area. Shot by a German firing squad at Ponte de Piave on 28 February 1945, he was later posthumously awarded a George Cross, the first New Zealander to earn this decoration.

As they endured the winter on the Senio, frustrated and impatient troops grew disillusioned with the campaign. With all eyes on the fighting in north-west Europe, Italy had become 'not only a disappointing front but also a forgotten front'.[160] The results of the campaign in Italy had certainly not matched early British hopes. The skill and determination of the German forces in the peninsula had seen to that. Even when, after much hard

Members of 28 (Maori) Battalion prepare for action later in 1944.

Alexander Turnbull Library, F-8057-½-D

176

fighting, an opportunity for a decisive victory had emerged, incompetent and lacklustre generalship had allowed it to slip through the grasp.

But, even if secondary and frustrating, the Italian campaign was not unimportant, quite apart from the bases it provided for extending the strategic bombing campaign against Germany. Even before the Allies landed, Hitler had been forced to divert significant resources to the peninsula. Between 19 and 23 divisions — 15 per cent of the German total — had to be supplied with reinforcements, equipment and munitions at a time when Germany could ill afford to spare anything from either the main front in Russia or the West Wall in France. The attrition rate in Italy significantly favoured the Allies. More than half a million Germans became casualties in the fighting — twice the Allied figure — and the *Luftwaffe* suffered heavy losses, especially in 1943. The campaign tied down men who could have been used elsewhere.

While the Allies also had to maintain forces in Italy, they were better placed to do so by 1943. The commitment in Italy did not detract from the Allied effort elsewhere.[161]

The New Zealand division represented only a tiny part of the huge forces that bore down on Germany in 1944–45, and its absence would not have made any difference to the outcome. But its performance had upheld New Zealand's reputation as a valuable coalition member — albeit at a heavy cost. Two thousand New Zealanders lay in Italian graves, and another 7000 had been wounded or taken POW. The efforts of its division, and of its airmen and seamen in the British forces, had contributed to the whittling away of German strength that had now made possible the decisive thrust against Hitler's Europe from the west. While the New Zealanders did their bit in the Mediterranean, others of their countrymen were making an equally valuable contribution at sea and in the air in north-west Europe.

New Zealand troops, moving forward at Gambettola, pass a divisional sign.

177

22 Jun – Massive Soviet
summer offensive opens

20 Jul – Hitler narrowly
avoids assassination by
group of army officers

12 Sep – Second Quebec
Conference opens

12 Nov – *Tirpitz* su

13 Jun – First German
V-1 lands in UK

8 Sep – First German V-2
lands in UK

24 Oct – Battle of
Leyte Gulf begins

25 Aug – Paris is liberated

New Zealand Fleet Air Arm pilots after an attack on the German battleship *Tirpitz*.

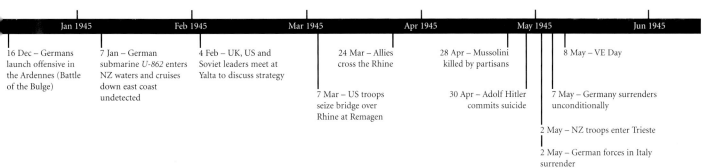

Jan 1945	Feb 1945	Mar 1945	Apr 1945	May 1945	Jun 1945

16 Dec – Germans launch offensive in the Ardennes (Battle of the Bulge)

7 Jan – German submarine *U-862* enters NZ waters and cruises down east coast undetected

4 Feb – UK, US and Soviet leaders meet at Yalta to discuss strategy

24 Mar – Allies cross the Rhine

7 Mar – US troops seize bridge over Rhine at Remagen

28 Apr – Mussolini killed by partisans

30 Apr – Adolf Hitler commits suicide

8 May – VE Day

7 May – Germany surrenders unconditionally

2 May – NZ troops enter Trieste

2 May – German forces in Italy surrender

Victory in Europe

As *U-468* ploughed through the Atlantic off West Africa on the morning of 11 August 1943, her 26-year-old commander remained uneasy. Too many of his fellow submariners had already fallen victim to sudden attack from the air for him to be other than watchful. Approaching at speed, an aircraft could release a lethal shower of depth charges, blowing in plates even with near misses. Even if the submarine crash-dived, the depth charges could follow it into the deep.

Because of the depth-charge danger U-boat commanders had been ordered to stay on the surface and fight it out with attacking aircraft. This was *U-468's* response when an aircraft was spotted dropping down below the clouds and approaching fast. Swinging their weapons, including a quad 20-mm, towards the distant target, her gunners opened a rapid and accurate fire. Hits could be seen on the aircraft, now clearly a Liberator. But it pressed on relentlessly, never deviating from its course straight for the submarine.

As the stricken Liberator passed overhead, the crew on deck watched in horror as half a dozen canisters came hurtling down towards them. These exploded with a thunderous roar on both sides of the U-boat's hull, a perfect straddle that inflicted fatal damage. Within seconds, the Liberator ploughed into the sea several hundred yards away, and quickly sank. Aboard the U-boat there was no time to dwell on this spectacle.

179

New Zealand trainee airmen inspect the cockpit of a Spitfire at a training school in Canada.

Flying Officer Lloyd Trigg VC.

Most, trapped inside, went down with their ship, but the captain and six others on the deck were left floundering in the sea. They managed to get into a dinghy that had floated free of the Liberator before it disappeared.

The captain of the Liberator, 29-year-old Lloyd Trigg, never knew that his attack had succeeded, for neither he nor any of his crew survived the crash. A New Zealander, his path to the encounter with *U-468* was typical of that of more than 7000 of his countrymen. It had started with his call-up in 1941. Leaving his job as a salesman in Whangarei, he entered the RNZAF, which sent him to Canada for training as a pilot — one of the stream of Commonwealth aircrew channelled into the RAF through the air training scheme. Posted to Coastal Command's 200 Squadron, he began flying anti-submarine patrols from its West African base. By the time of his encounter with *U-468* he was an experienced campaigner, having flown more than 40 missions.

Trigg's bravery did not go unrecognised. Picked up by a British warship, the *U-468* survivors praised the determination with which the Liberator had pressed home the attack, even after being badly damaged. In an unprecedented step, the authorities awarded Trigg a posthumous Victoria Cross on the testimony of an enemy officer.[162]

Battle of the Atlantic

Trigg and his crew lost their lives in perhaps the most crucial confrontation of the whole war — the Battle of the Atlantic. Few in New Zealand doubted the importance of the struggle to keep open the sea lanes to Britain. The British population depended on the inflow of food for their sustenance; their continued war effort demanded the steady supply of raw materials and munitions, especially from the United States. The outcome of the war depended on maintaining Britain as the base for operations against Germany and for the supply of the Soviet Union. And New Zealand's own economic survival rested on continued access to British markets.

This struggle, which began on the first day of the war and mounted steadily in intensity, involved many New Zealanders. While New Zealand troops grappled with the enemy in the Mediterranean theatre, others of their countrymen, including Trigg, were heavily engaged in the various facets of the battle for control of the sea lanes to Britain. Some served as merchant seamen or as naval personnel manning defensive weapons on the merchant ships that carried the vital cargoes. Some helped crew the escort vessels that tried to shepherd these ships through the dangerous approaches to British ports. Others flew the planes that patrolled the sky above the sea lanes.

It was not the first time that Britain had faced such a threat. During the First World War, German U-boats had almost brought it to its knees before effective tactics were adopted to counter the menace. Convoys — groups of merchant ships escorted by warships — had saved the day, and the system was immediately adopted in 1939. But the Royal Navy did not have sufficient escort ships to fully protect the convoys. Moreover, during 1940 the Germans found means of nullifying some of the tactical advantages of the convoy system. Screens of U-boats were used to locate convoys, which were then attacked by 'wolf packs' of U-boats directed to the area. Many ships fell victim to these predators. Nor was the danger confined to submarines. German surface warships also made forays into the Atlantic, armed merchant raiders preyed on isolated vessels, and motor torpedo boats and aircraft threatened ships as they neared their destination.

Among the ships in most convoys would be one or more associated with New Zealand, vessels of the New Zealand Shipping Company or the Union Steam Ship Company. Passing through the Panama Canal, they moved up the North American coast to Halifax (and later American ports) to begin the crossing of the Atlantic. At first they would set off individually, joining a convoy in mid-ocean to be escorted through the dangerous Western Approaches; but as more escort ships became available the convoys were formed before setting out from American or African ports.

Even in a convoy, the merchant crews endured long days of tension as they steamed steadily towards Britain, zigzagging to make it more difficult for U-boats to gain attack positions. Would they get through safely? Or would they find themselves fighting for their lives as their ship slipped below the waves, the victim of a well-aimed torpedo? Only prompt rescue could save them from the freezing waters of the North Atlantic, and even if they got into a lifeboat or raft the chances of dying remained high. All knew that ships stopping to pick up survivors put themselves at severe risk of being sunk as well. More than a hundred New Zealand merchant seamen lost their lives during the war.

A recruitment poster for the RNZAF.

Alexander Turnbull Library, Eph-B-VARIETY-1944-01-p2

The North-West Europe Theatre

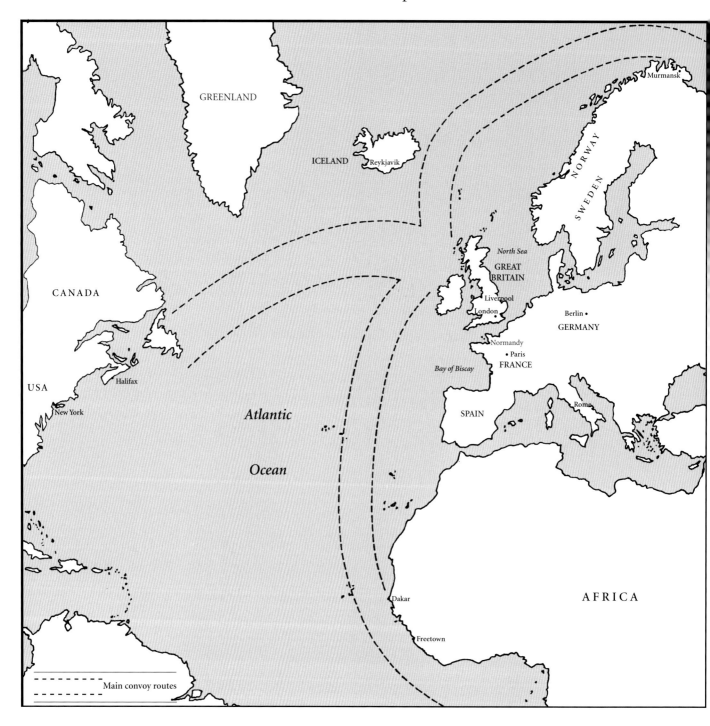

GREENLAND

ICELAND
Reykjavik

NORWAY

SWEDEN

Murmansk

CANADA

North Sea

GREAT
BRITAIN

Liverpool
London

Berlin •
GERMANY

Normandy
• Paris
FRANCE

USA

Halifax

Bay of Biscay

New York

Atlantic

Ocean

SPAIN

Rome

Dakar

AFRICA

Freetown

------ Main convoy routes
- - - -

A New Zealand merchant marine officer, RH Keyworth, describes the sinking of his ship, the Canadian Star, *on 18 March 1943 while on passage from New Zealand to Britain, an attack that cost the lives of 30 of the 87 men aboard:*

> *I was watching a Liberty ship at the head of the next column to port when it appeared to be struck by a heavy sea throwing spray over the entire ship as high as the funnel but, when it lost way, I realized that it had been torpedoed. I rang the alarm bells and the men came up to action stations. The gunner on the port wing of the bridge was tearing the cover off his Oerlikon gun when I suddenly spotted, coming up between our ship and the next column to port, a periscope about a yard clear of the water…. The captain and I called out at the same time and gunner started to swing his Oerlikon onto it, but, almost at once, we were hit. It felt as though the whole ship had blown up underneath me. There was a tremendous amount of cordite, I can still almost taste it. The captain ordered Abandon Ship. I dashed into the chart house to get my little 'get-away bag' with my sextant and some of my navigation books. I had ideas of a long voyage in an open boat.[163]*

Numerous New Zealanders were among those who took part in the unrelenting struggle to protect the merchant ships. John Holm, a merchant marine officer in civilian life, was in the thick of the battle as commander of the corvette HMS *Crocus*. Among his exploits was the ramming of a U-boat. Although the sea war could erupt into dramatic action, for the most part it was a frustrating contest with an unseen enemy. 'Far more often than not,' he recalled, 'the results were inconclusive.'

While the New Zealanders were attacking at El Alamein in October 1942, Holm was battling to protect a convoy of more than 40 merchant ships that had set out from the Sierra Leone port of Freetown for Liverpool.

Ten days out, submarine attacks began. 'Our drama continued for five weary days and five awful nights. It was an uneven battle that became a bizarre game, with the lives of men and ships as the stakes.' Nightly attacks by U-boats whittled down the convoy despite the desperate efforts of the outnumbered naval escorts.

John Holm describes a typical scene on the escort ships:

> *… the operators crouched over their sets watching and listening, as the ping went out on this bearing and then on the next one, two degrees further on, and intent on hearing an echo coming back or seeing a high thin line of light if anything got in its way. If it did, 'Contact, Sir', in a clear voice just short of anxious. And then the careful routine, sweeping back and forth across the suspicious bearing to find if it was a solid object that might be a U-boat and, if it was, to get its bearing, distance and movements, if possible.*

Guided by sonar, the corvettes dropped depth charges where enemy submarines seemed likely to be lurking. As the convoy neared Britain, a new danger appeared: aircraft flying out from France bombed the ships, albeit with less success than the U-boats had had. By the time it reached the safe haven of Liverpool on 9 November, 16 ships had been lost.[164]

Another New Zealander to command a corvette in the battle was Auckland-born civil engineer Alfred Miller in HMS *Puffin*. But most New Zealand personnel served relatively anonymously, part of the team that is a ship's company, doing their job to the best of their ability. They included two (later three) of Holm's seven officers on HMS *Crocus*. Stanley Jervis, for example, as anti-submarine control officer on the destroyer HMS *Oribi*, had a demanding and hectic job.

Although most New Zealanders involved in the Battle of the Atlantic were on British warships, New Zealand's own warships occasionally took part. New warships built in Britain for the New Zealand navy joined the escorts on their journey to New Zealand. One convoy, in March 1942, had *Tui* and four other New Zealand minesweepers among its escorts across the Atlantic.

The embattled seamen had two allies of increasing importance in their fight. The first was the growing ability of code-breakers in Britain to read radio traffic between the U-boats and their headquarters, helped by the seizure of important intelligence materials from a captured U-boat in May 1941. Decoded messages gave the whereabouts of the U-boat screens, allowing the British naval authorities to redirect convoys away from them. Losses fell dramatically in 1941. But all depended on the ability to read the German messages, and this was lost for most of 1942. The fact that the Germans had breached the British naval codes exacerbated the situation. Losses soared to frightening levels.

By this time, the other ally was assuming increasing importance. In the early stages of the battle, the effectiveness of aircraft had been hindered by their limited range, lack of bases, and lack of effective weapons. U-boats could operate with impunity in the so-called Atlantic Gap in mid-ocean. But by 1943 longer-range aircraft had become available, capable of covering this area. With bombs having given way to the more effective depth charges, aircraft became much more dangerous to submarines. Improved radar increased the chances of interceptions. The possibility of being attacked from the air forced U-boats to remained submerged, thereby reducing their mobility. U-boat losses mounted rapidly. During 1943, 90 fell victim to air attack, three times as many as had in the previous year.

The New Zealand High Commissioner, William Jordan, inspects newly arrived naval ratings in the United Kingdom in 1940. Lieutenant-Commander PG Connolly (a later Minister of Defence) introduces Lieutenant-Commander AC Swanson. The number of New Zealanders attached to the Royal Navy would peak in September 1944 at 4901 — 47 per cent of the RNZN's strength at that time. In all theatres, 454 New Zealand naval personnel — 41 per cent of them officers — lost their lives during the war, and 63 were taken POW, roughly one in seven of those involved. Many of these casualties were suffered in the Mediterranean, including 150 lost in the sinking of one ship alone (*Neptune*).

War History Collection, Alexander Turnbull Library, PA1-q-285-06

Lloyd Trigg was just one of many New Zealand airmen who took part in these operations. In Coastal Command, 490 (New Zealand) Squadron provided a 'New Zealand' presence. Formed in March 1943, it operated from Jui near Freetown in Sierra Leone from July, its Catalina and Sunderland flying-boats reaching out over the eastern Atlantic in constant search of U-boats.

For several months in 1942, 489 (New Zealand) Squadron joined the struggle; it sent out aircraft from southern England to patrol the Bay of Biscay, across which U-boats passed en route to and from their bases.

But, as in other commands, most New Zealand airmen flew in ordinary RAF squadrons, often in mixed crews of various Commonwealth nationalities. Patrolling was an arduous task. The numbing cold, the monotony of flying over a featureless expanse and the need for continual vigilance to spot U-boats all tested the aircrew. Weather conditions provided an additional hazard. Storms and navigational difficulties could bring disaster.

As the battle progressed, many airmen found themselves at sea as the Fleet Air Arm expanded its role. There were numerous New Zealanders among the aircrew aboard the light escort carriers that began to form part of convoy escorts. Others flew biplanes off rudimentary decks laid on merchant ships.

From March 1943 the German U-boat campaign began to falter. Once the code-breakers could read enemy messages again, the effectiveness of air cover increased markedly. So many U-boats were being sunk that the German naval high command eventually conceded defeat. In mid-1943, it withdrew the U-boats from the mid-Atlantic; an attempt to revive the campaign later in the year, using new acoustic homing torpedoes to attack escort vessels, failed to turn the tide. Men and *matériel* continued to flow into Britain — with dire consequences for the Nazi cause.

German U-boats operated in the waters around Britain until the end of the war and sank numerous ships. But increasingly the German high command sought greener fields outside this well-defended area, especially in the Indian Ocean. In 1944 long-range U-boats were sent to operate from Penang in Japanese-occupied Malaya. One that survived the dangerous journey to this theatre would eventually make the last German incursion into New Zealand waters of the war. *U-862* cruised down the east coast of New Zealand in January 1945 without being detected — she maintained strict radio silence — but also without inflicting any damage.[165]

Arctic convoys

After June 1941, the need to sustain the Soviet Union provided an important adjunct to the Battle of the Atlantic. With Germany controlling the Baltic Sea, supplies could only be channelled to northern Russia through the Arctic Sea to the port of Murmansk. As the slow-moving convoys of merchant ships skirted the coast of Norway, they suffered heavy attacks by German air and naval forces based there and by U-boats.

As in the wider Atlantic battle, New Zealanders served in all facets of the Arctic convoys. They endured the dangers of being the target of attack, made worse if the ship carried oil or ammunition; they struggled against the elements on the escort ships; and they crewed aircraft that sought to provide cover. Denis Glover, a seaman on an escort vessel, recalled weather that 'could change from flat calm to an 80-knot gale in five minutes', the extreme cold of the winter, the frustration of acting as 'a sheepdog on the flanks of a vast mob of vessels belching smoke … and the holding-paddock far away', the enemy aircraft that shadowed the convoy during the long summer days, the 'nicely planned' attacks. 'Suddenly would come attack by high level bombers, dive bombers, torpedo bombers and the submarines, often all together. The ship would erupt into a shattering, sinister symphony of gunfire.'[166]

As in other theatres, New Zealanders percolated into even the most unlikely spots. In September 1941 Petoneborn former test pilot Group Captain Henry Ramsbottom-Isherwood found himself commanding an RAF fighter wing in Murmansk. Although his squadrons were charged with training Russian pilots for the defence of the port, they also intercepted German bombers operating in the vicinity.

Other New Zealand airmen made their contribution to the Arctic battle by attacking the German forces in Norway. Archibald Richardson was one of numerous Fleet Air Arm pilots who flew into Norwegian fiords to attack German warships, dangerous operations because of the amount of anti-aircraft fire that could be brought to bear from both ships and land. RAF squadrons also mounted raids on targets in Norway.

A de Havilland Mosquito launches a rocket attack on a German ship. Coastal Command accounted for most of the 366 enemy ships sunk by 1945, roughly 73 per cent of the merchant ships available to Germany. Of the 366, 11 were sunk by 489 (New Zealand) Squadron aircraft.

The battleship *Tirpitz*, lying in an arm of Alten fiord, received particular attention. A midget submarine attack damaged her, but she remained a major threat to all convoys passing up the coast. When in April 1944 squadrons from six aircraft carriers attacked her in two waves, 60 New Zealanders, including one squadron leader, took part. By the time the last of the planes left, the battleship was on fire, having been hit a number of times. Further attacks were made in July and August. During the latter, the Hellcats of Archibald Richardson's squadron played a prominent part. In his third attack on the ship, Richardson held his course with utter determination, as flak smashed into his plane and destroyed it. So inspiring was his leadership that his superior recommended him, unsuccessfully, for a posthumous VC. These Fleet Air Arm attacks helped keep *Tirpitz* out of action for long periods, and heavy bombers of Bomber Command finally sank her in November 1944.

The blockade of Germany

While many New Zealanders fought in the defensive struggle in the Atlantic, others were taking the war to the enemy. The blockade of Germany aimed to undermine its economy by strangling the flow of raw materials from Scandinavia and Spain to German and Dutch ports. Iron ore supplies from Scandinavia provided a particularly important target. Although it got off to a slow start, the campaign became increasingly effective, especially as code-breaking enhanced the ability to intercept convoys.

Of the New Zealanders engaged in such operations at sea, Wellingtonian Jim Macdonald excelled as a motor torpedo boat officer. These small boats would dash among enemy shipping at high speed, unleashing torpedoes. By 1944, 22-year-old Macdonald was commanding a flotilla of them. During the night of 4–5 July 1944, his flotilla had notable success when it got in among an enemy convoy and sank two ships and damaged two others.

But, notwithstanding these naval successes, the RAF became the main enforcer of the blockade. The Coastal Command squadrons that took part in this campaign included 489 (New Zealand) Squadron, which, with UK and Australian squadrons, became part of an Anzac Wing. From the second half of 1942 its Bristol Beaufighters ranged over the North Sea and along the Norwegian coast. The substantial flak protection enjoyed by the enemy ships made this dangerous work. The ratio of planes shot down to ship kills remained very much in enemy favour until 1943. But the tide then turned. Allied airmen found that massed attacks lessened the flak effectiveness. Better intelligence and aircraft also helped.[167]

By 1945 ceaseless RAF attacks had brought Germany's seaborne trade virtually to a standstill. Had the war continued, the effects on the German war effort would have been severe. But the campaign had also brought short-term benefits. It had forced the Germans to divert much needed resources from other fronts to provide anti-aircraft protection for convoys.[168]

Bombing Germany

While Coastal Command sought to strangle Germany's economy, Bomber Command aimed to bludgeon it by striking the factories, installations and workers that sustained the enemy war effort. Maori pilot Johnny Pohe, a farmer at Taihape before his enlistment, was typical of many. Arriving in Britain in 1941 after pilot training, he was posted to 51 Squadron, and flew more than 20 missions with a mixed crew of Commonwealth airmen in 1941–42 before being posted as an instructor at a training unit.

The operations that Pohe and his fellow aircrew embarked on had as their objectives the destruction of industrial and military facilities and the de-housing of the workforce that operated them. With precision bombing ruled out at first by lack of capability, Bomber Command resorted to area bombing, an approach that would later arouse controversy. Some questioned the morality of deliberately attacking civilians, claiming that the Allies were descending to the same level as the Nazis. But area bombing advocates argued that it was the only way that Britain could take the war to the enemy, that the dislocation of the German infrastructure would undermine German war production, and even that it could force a German surrender by breaking the will of the population.

Although post-war investigation would later determine that German production actually rose despite the increasing devastation from the air, the bombing campaign had a severe effect on German war-making

RNZAF Museum, PR9194A

Sergeant James Ward VC standing in the cockpit of his Vickers Wellington bomber.

potential, and eventually on German morale. Without it war production would have soared even higher as the German economy was belatedly geared for total war. Moreover the bombing campaign, which from 1942 was greatly boosted by daylight raids undertaken by American bombers, forced the Germans to devote huge resources to providing anti-aircraft defences and fighter aircraft, all of which were badly needed elsewhere.

The German anti-aircraft defences took a heavy toll of Allied airmen, rendering service in Bomber Command far more costly in terms of New Zealand lives lost than in other RAF commands. All those who flew in the growing formations — the first 1000-bomber raid attacked Cologne in March 1943 — knew that a proportion of their bombers would fall victim to flak or night-fighters on the long flight to or from the target or during the bombing run. Nervous tension greatly added to extreme cold in making bombing missions a test of endurance. Mathematical odds suggested an airman was unlikely to complete a tour of 30 missions — though some lasted much longer. Wing Commander James Barron, the 23-year-old commander of 7 Squadron, was on his 77th mission when he died during a raid on 20 May 1944.

Sometimes extraordinary demands were made on the aircrews. A memorable incident involved Sergeant James Ward, a Wanganui-born schoolteacher in civilian life serving with 75 (New Zealand) Squadron. Following a raid on the German city of Munster on 7 July 1941, the Wellington bomber in which he was second pilot was heading for home when attacked by a night-fighter. The attack set fire to the aircraft's wing near its starboard engine — too far from the fuselage for the crew to attack it with fire extinguishers. Exiting through a hatch and kicking holes in the fuselage, Ward managed to get out onto the wing. Buffeted by the slipstream — he would later describe it as 'worse than any gale I've ever known'[169] — he crawled to the seat of the fire. Using an engine cover, he tried to smother the flames where a leaking petrol pipe was feeding them until the cover was blown away. Exhausted, he painfully retraced his path

Airmen returning from a mission pass one of 75 Squadron's Wellingtons. The squadron would later be equipped with Lancasters. New Zealand's long air war against Germany took a heavy toll. Losses began even before the men joined the RAF — over 500 were killed in accidents in New Zealand or in Canada. Of the more than 10,000 New Zealanders who served in the RAF, 3285 lost their lives, at one in three a much higher fatal casualty rate than experienced in either of the other services. More than 1800 — 60 per cent of New Zealand fatalities in the RAF — died serving with Bomber Command.

back into the aircraft. The fire had been contained and eventually burned itself out, allowing the crew to nurse the damaged plane back to base. Ward won a VC for this exploit — but he did not long survive it. On the following 15 September, his plane was set on fire by flak over Hamburg. He was still at the controls of the blazing plane when the last of his crew baled out.

Not all New Zealanders in Bomber Command served in heavy bombers. By mid-1943, 70 were involved in light bomber operations, the majority in 487 (New Zealand) Squadron. Their Venturas attacked targets in France and the Low Countries. A daylight raid the squadron made on the power station at Amsterdam on 3 May 1943 brutally demonstrated the dangers of such operations. New Zealanders captained eight of the 11 Venturas that, escorted by Spitfires, swept towards the target. One of them, Leonard Trent, led the formation. A Nelsonian, he had gained a commission in the RAF a year before the war began and had been posted to the squadron the previous August.

Over Holland more than 70 German fighter planes swooped on the formation in 'an aerial ambush'.[170] After dispersing the escorting fighters, they picked off Ventura after Ventura. Seven New Zealanders were among those killed. Only Trent's aircraft managed to reach the target, and drop its bombs. Trent, who had the satisfaction of shooting down one of the enemy planes when it crossed his bow, had pressed on with such determination that he would later be awarded a VC. But his bomber soon suffered fatal damage, and he was forced to bail out.

Squadron-Leader Trent describes the raid on the Amsterdam power station in which he won his VC:

> *As we approached Amsterdam the anti-aircraft guns joined the fighters in a race to see who would get us first. I was surprised that the fighters continued their attacks and as the power-house came into sight my observer had to direct me.*

> *'Bombs Gone' he called, and I looked up from the instruments to see that we were alone. At the same moment we were hit and I found that all controls had gone, but no fire and engines going perfectly. This continued for ten seconds or so, which seemed an age, and then suddenly the aircraft reared up, stalled upside down and went into a spin. Had ordered 'Abandon aircraft' before the zoom and now tried to get out from the roof hatch myself. However, the spin was so rapid that I was not getting anywhere until at about 7000 feet the machine suddenly broke up and I found myself outside. My navigator was also thrown out but unfortunately the others were trapped in a portion of the wreckage.[171]*

The POW experience

When Trent and his navigator — the only survivors from his crew — reached ground, they joined more than 500 other New Zealand airmen in captivity. A steady stream entered the POW cages, with occasional surges — as for example in March 1942 when 29 went into the bag. Their experience was similar to that of the 7500 2NZEF POWs that were also being held in Germany by the end of 1943. Boredom, deprivation and hunger were their lot.

Some made strenuous attempts to escape. A few got away, secreting themselves on freighters and making the sanctuary of neutral Sweden. Most merely had the satisfaction of causing trouble for their captors. VC winner Captain Charles Upham, for example, proved a thorn in the German side after being transferred to Germany with the other POWs originally held in Italy. His numerous escape attempts finally earned him transfer to the notorious camp for difficult POWs at Colditz. Other POWs found themselves serving time in grim military prisons for attempted escapes.

Some were less fortunate. Trent took part in what would later be dubbed 'The Great Escape' from Stalag Luft III at Sagan in March 1944. He was recaptured almost immediately after emerging from the tunnel. But 76 men got clear of the camp; they included Johnny Pohe, whose career as a bomber pilot had come to an end when his Halifax bomber was shot down on the night of 22–23 September 1943. Thousands of German troops and police had to be mobilised to round up the escapees, only a couple of whom reached Allied territory. Pohe and two other New Zealand airmen suffered a terrible fate after being recaptured. In accordance with Hitler's order that 50 of the recaptured POWs should be killed to terrorise POWs into desisting from escape attempts, the Gestapo murdered them.

D-Day

As darkness fell on 5 June 1944 Denis Glover, now commissioned, set out on the most momentous journey of his life. In command of a landing ship crammed with commandos, he set course southwards from Southampton towards the Normandy coast, 90 miles away. 'We skirled out to sea past the packed and cheering troopships,' he later recalled.[172] His orders were to beach his craft 70 minutes after the initial assault on 6 June, offload his cargo of commandos and pull back out to sea.

POWs in Stalag 383, Germany.

Alexander Turnbull Library, F-3688-¼-C

When the flotilla of small craft reached their destination, they found a vast armada of warships standing off the coast. Against the backdrop of the flashing and booming big guns of the battleships and cruisers, it headed inshore. Lining up on the beach, the flotilla roared in right on time, Glover's craft in the van.

Landing craft commander Denis Glover describes the approach to the beach on 6 June 1944:

Now eyes for everything, eyes for nothing. The beach looms close, maybe a mile. There are people running up and down it. There are fires, and the bursting of shells. Yes, and wrecked landing craft everywhere, a flurry of propellers in the savage surf and among those wicked obstructions....

We are on those bristling stakes. They stretch before us in rows. The mines on them look as big as planets. And those graze-nose ones pointing towards us on some of them look like beer bottles. Oh God I WOULD be blown up on a mine like a beer bottle! Now for speed and skill and concentration. Whang, here it comes — those whizzing ones will be mortars — and the stuff is falling all round us. Can't avoid them, but the mines and collisions I can avoid. Speed, more speed. Put them off by speed, weave in and out of these bloody spikes, avoid the mines, avoid our friends, avoid the wrecked craft and vehicles in the rising water, and GET THESE TROOPS ASHORE. Good, the Commando officers have their men ready and waiting, crouched along the decks. Number One is for'ard with his ramp parties ready. Everything is working as we've exercised it for so long....

Don't jump, you fool. It was near, but you're not hit. Straddled. All right, keep on. And here's where I go in, that little bit of clear beach....

Slow ahead together. Slow down to steady the ship, point her as you want her, then half ahead together and on to the beach with a gathering rush. Put her ashore and be damned! She's touched down. One more good shove to wedge her firm. Out ramps.[173]

The Second Front had opened — the long-awaited Allied landing in France. Thanks to success in the Battle of the Atlantic, a huge American force had been assembled in Britain to undertake the operation with UK and Canadian forces. For months before D-Day many New Zealanders had been helping to prepare the way for the landing. Some had done so directly — those, like Glover, who would be involved in the landing itself. Innumerable exercises had honed their skills for the task ahead.

Most of the New Zealanders serving in the Royal Navy and RAF — there were 10,675 in June 1944, including more than 4000 officers — contributed in some way to the operation, albeit often indirectly. The fighter pilots of 485 and 486 (NZ) Squadrons and those serving in other RAF squadrons, who had spent the months preceding D-Day carrying out sweeps over France seeking combat with the *Luftwaffe*, helped achieve the essential air supremacy over the planned landing zones. Meanwhile the heavy bomber squadrons, including 75 (NZ) Squadron, temporarily shifted focus away from German cities to strike at installations in France. By disrupting communications leading to the crucial area they made it more difficult for the enemy to respond to the landings.

Once again a New Zealander had a key role. The master of air-ground support Sir Arthur Coningham commanded 2 Tactical Air Force, which provided direct support for Montgomery's 2nd Army. His force included 487 (NZ) Squadron, which spent months before D-Day blasting enemy airfields with its fast Mosquitoes. Scores of New Zealanders served in other squadrons. One, Desmond Scott, commanded a wing of Typhoons, which attacked radar stations on the French coast before D-Day — a dangerous task because of the amount of flak protection. Scott's Typhoons came into their own after the landing. They 'roamed far and wide, and everything that moved, whether on rail, road or river, was straffed, rocketed or bombed'[174] — a relentless campaign that greatly hindered the Germans from moving up forces to counter-attack the beachhead.

Others made their contribution in the various RAF commands operating from Britain. Among the fighter squadrons operating over the landing zone early on 6 June, New Zealand pilot Johnny Houlton had the distinction of shooting down the first two enemy aircraft on the day. Coastal Command aircraft, including those of 489 (NZ) Squadron, patrolled the flanks of the landing zone to prevent enemy interference with the shipping.

Many New Zealanders also served in the more than 1200 warships involved in the operation. These escorted the landing forces, provided fire support by bombarding shore positions and, with air support, protected the invasion zone from enemy interference.

The noose tightens

Although the Allies succeeded in establishing themselves ashore, they struggled to break out from Normandy. German forces resisted strongly. But once the breach came, the Allies advanced rapidly across France, annihilating many German units in a pocket that developed at Falaise. A new landing in southern France on 15 August 1944 hastened the German retreat. Paris was liberated 10 days later.

Wing Commander Desmond Scott describes an attack he led on a 1.6 kilometre-long German column in the Falaise pocket:

The convoy's lead vehicle was a large half-track. In my haste to cripple it and seal off the road, I let fly with all eight rockets in a single salvo: I missed but hit the truck that was following. It was thrown into the air along with several bodies, and fell back on its side. Two other trucks in close attendance piled into it. There was no escape. Typhoons were already attacking in deadly swoops at the other end of the column, and within seconds the whole stretch of road was

bursting and blazing under streams of rocket and cannon fire. Ammunition wagons exploded like multi-coloured volcanoes. A large long-barrelled tank standing in a field just off the road was hit by a rocket and overturned into a ditch. Several teams of horses stampeded and careered wildly across the fields, dragging their broken wagons behind them. Others fell in tangled, kicking heaps, or were caught up in the fences and hedges.

It was an awesome sight: flames, smoke, bursting rockets and showers of coloured tracer — an army in retreat, trapped and without air protection. The once proud ranks of Hitler's Third Reich were being massacred from the Normandy skies by the relentless and devastating fire power of our rocket-firing Typhoons.[175]

Hopes of an early end to the war rose. But these proved unjustified. An airborne operation at Arnhem failed, and in December 1944 Hitler struck back with a major offensive that would become known as the Battle of the Bulge. The Germans made some gains but then faltered in the face of resolute American defence of Bastogne and the application of Allied air power. This proved to be Hitler's last throw of the dice in the west, but a bitter winter stood between the Allies and victory as they converged on Germany from both sides. Air operations over Europe continued to take a toll of New Zealand lives — more than a hundred died while serving on the continent with 2 Tactical Air Force alone — while a smaller number were lost in warships at sea.

Other New Zealanders suffered through the winter within the shrinking Reich — the 8000 POWs. As the front approached in the east, and later to a lesser extent in the west, POWs had been ordered out of their camps and onto the road in long marches away from the front. Freezing conditions, inadequate accommodation and lack of food made these treks especially hard for men already weakened by their long imprisonment. Some were on the road for months, moving hundreds of kilometres westwards. Exposure and exhaustion claimed the lives of a few; Allied aircraft that mistakenly attacked the columns or bombed nearby installations proved lethal to others.

These painful odysseys ended when Allied forces, thrusting into Germany in the spring of 1945, overran the columns. Some, liberated by Soviet forces, had further adventures before reaching England, and several lost their lives in accidents while en route to the evacuation port at Odessa. Most were soon being processed at a repatriation centre in southern England commanded by Howard Kippenberger, who had by then recovered from his wounds suffered at Cassino.

Victory in Italy

With the Allies across the Rhine in March 1945 and powerful Russian armies pressing in from the east, Germany at last teetered on the brink of defeat. Meanwhile in Italy New Zealand troops prepared for the last act in their long and difficult campaign. The Allied armies in the peninsula planned to inflict a knockout blow on the stubborn, but now heavily outmatched,

forces that had held them up so effectively.

On 8 April thousands of New Zealand soldiers — among them men of the newly created 9 Infantry Brigade — waited near the Senio River for yet another attack. They watched in awe as more than 800 bombers plastered the area opposite. Then, after they had pulled back from the southern stopbank (captured in the days preceding), the artillery went to work. Over the next four hours, 600 guns laid down a series of pulverising bombardments on the far bank. During the intervals fighter-bombers swooped down to strafe the hapless enemy on the stopbank. For many of the recently arrived replacements who had joined the ranks of the division, this demonstration of Allied power was both illuminating and reassuring.

At 7.20 p.m. the infantrymen of four battalions, who had moved up as close as possible to the stopbank under cover of the last stages of the barrage, began their assault on a three-kilometre front. As they did so, flame-throwers hosed the opposite bank with fire. In their assault boats or using assault bridges, the New Zealanders crossed the narrow river within five minutes. The demoralised defenders — the flame-throwers had been the last straw — quickly gave up and surrendered.

Once this bridgehead had been secured, the infantry

New Zealand POWs wait for trucks that will take them from their camp in Germany, liberated by the British 2nd Army in early 1945, to a transit camp in Belgium, from where they will be repatriated to the United Kingdom.

A New Zealand Sherman tank advances alongside men of 26 Battalion in northern Italy.

War History Collection, Alexander Turnbull Library, F-9151-35mm-DA

Maori troops on the march near Trieste.

The Bishop of Wellington, Herbert St Barbe Holland, addresses the crowd at a victory event in the Basin Reserve, Wellington, in May 1945.

formed up and launched a set-piece attack behind a creeping barrage. By daybreak the battalions stood on their objective, roughly three kilometres from the Senio. Meanwhile, the engineers with great efficiency had built six Bailey bridges over the Senio, across which support weapons moved. During 10 April the division began to drive forward to exploit the success in the river crossing. With 25 and 28 Battalions in the forefront, the New Zealanders rapidly advanced to the Santerno River, where a bridgehead was seized. Not until the Gaiana River was reached did the impetus falter.

To overcome this obstacle a set-piece attack was prepared — as it transpired the last by the New Zealanders in the war. A deluge of fire was brought down on the defenders, the paratroopers, a situation regarded with grim satisfaction by many of the New Zealanders who had encountered these fanatically determined fighters in earlier Mediterranean battles. Once this obstacle of the Gaiana River had been overcome, the New Zealanders raced forward to the Idice and then the Po rivers against little resistance. By the time the division entered Padua on 28 April, partisans had already taken control, and it became evident that most points on the route ahead had also been seized. 'Then we were off again, for the maddest drive of all,' Geoffrey Cox recounted later. 'This time there were no pauses. We rolled on past the great oil refineries, past partisans who saluted or clenched their fists, up the concrete ramp of the autostrada leading towards Venice.'[176]

The division then crossed the Isonzo River, the site of heavy fighting in the First World War, and sped towards Trieste. It moved forward in a 'great column of vehicles … moving nose to tailboard like some immense railway train', stretching back over the Isonzo and round the curve of the coastline.[177] New Zealand units reached Trieste just as German forces in Italy, on 2 May, surrendered unconditionally. Yugoslav partisans had already entered the city, but pockets of German resistance remained; these were quickly overcome as the last acts of New Zealand's Italian campaign.

Divisional intelligence officer Geoffrey Cox describes the final stages of 2 Division's drive to Trieste:

> *It was the last time the Division would pass forward like this to battle. The General [Freyberg] must have thought this too, for he remained there for several minutes, his red cap-band towering above the villagers, and watched his force go by. First the tanks passed, starting up with a grinding roar and then thundering on at what seemed breakneck speed. Their crews in their black berets stood in the turrets waving to the crowds, and their commanders, earphones clamped on their heads, gathered in the bunches of flowers which were thrown to them. Then the lines of Bren carriers, tossing as if in a rough sea until they got up speed, each with its Italian flag, the gift of some village on our way, and each with its smiling troops. Then the three-tonners, with troops on the top of the cab, and the backs jammed with troops sitting among their gear, the lean, smiling, alert, unbluffed New Zealand infantry, enjoying it all but deluded by none of it, bedecked with flowers but with their rifles and Tommy-guns ready for what they knew lay still ahead. They waved and shouted back to the excited Italians, but their faces showed that they knew the job was not yet over. These were triumphal marches to the Italians, but to the troops they were still the road to further battle.[178]*

For the New Zealanders, the end of the fighting did not at first allow complete relaxation. Tito's regime coveted the port of Trieste and hoped to detach it from Italy, even though 90 per cent of the population in the area were Italian speaking. A tense stand-off between the New Zealanders and the Yugoslav partisans in the city developed. For a time hostilities between the erstwhile allies seemed possible, but to the New Zealanders' relief tensions eventually eased. The partisans pulled back. The New Zealanders enjoyed the remainder of their stay in the area, which ended when in July they set off southwards to the area of Lake Trasimere in central Italy. From here, they would begin the long journey home.

VE Day in New Zealand

On the other side of the globe New Zealanders had awaited with anticipation the final demise of Germany in May. Russian troops were already fighting inside Berlin, and the two fronts had first come into contact at Torgau on the Mulde River on 25 April. Reports on 2 May that Hitler had killed himself in the ruins of his capital some days earlier indicated that the end was in sight. Late on 8 May the impatiently awaited news arrived — Germany had capitulated unconditionally to the Allies.

Preparations had been under way for some time for an official party to mark the occasion. Dutifully heeding calls to wait for this event on 9 May, most New Zealanders delayed their celebration. After the formal ceremony, many let their hair down, singing and dancing in the streets.

But underlying the occasion was consciousness of unfinished business — even if many regarded the ongoing war in the Pacific as a postscript to the victory in Europe. New Zealanders were still in action, and there were fears that New Zealand might yet be involved in the hard fighting likely to be needed to bring Japan to its knees.

War History Collection, Alexander Turnbull Library, F-3390-35mm-DA

Two New Zealand soldiers survey the waterfront from their tank in Trieste following Germany's surrender.

17 Jan – NZ fighter
wing moves forward to
Torokina, Bougainville

15 Mar – Japanese forces
launch offensive at Imphal

19 Jun – Battle of the
Philippine Sea begins

26 Oct – US wins
Battle of Leyte Gulf

31 Jan – US forces land in
Marshall Islands

5 Mar – First of two NZ motor launch
flotillas arrives in the Solomon Islands

15 Feb – 3 NZ Division troops
land on Nissan Island

RNZAF

An RNZAF Lockheed Ventura bomber near the Japanese-held port of Rabaul in June 1945

19 Feb – US Marines land on Iwo Jima

1 Apr – US forces land on Okinawa

NZ naval flotillas return to New Zealand from Solomon Islands

6 Aug – Atomic bomb dropped on Hiroshima

2 Sep – Formal Japanese surrender on USS *Missouri*'s deck

12 Apr – Harry S Truman becomes US President

11 Jun – NZ butter allowance drops from 8 oz to 6 oz

8 Aug – Soviet Union declares war on Japan

15 Aug – Japan capitulates

26 Jun – Peter Fraser signs the Charter of the United Nations on behalf of New Zealand

9 Aug – Atomic bomb dropped on Nagasaki

The Defeat of Japan

With torrential rain beating against his Corsair's windshield and lightning flashes repeatedly punctuating the darkness, fighter pilot Bryan Cox feared that he was about to die on his 20th birthday. Completely lost in the murk, and unable to read most of his instruments, he had no idea in which direction he was flying or the whereabouts of the airfield he sought, on Nissan Island. He knew that other pilots were facing the same problem nearby. But the danger of collision was a less pressing concern than the state of his fuel tanks. He knew that he could only fly for a few more minutes.

Cox's predicament arose from a chain of events that had begun earlier in the day, 15 January 1945. In what had become something of a routine, New Zealand Corsairs operating out of both Nissan Island and Bougainville had raided Rabaul. During the attack one of the planes had been hit by flak, and its pilot, Flight Lieutenant FG Keefe, had bailed out over Rabaul Harbour. Once in the water, he immediately started swimming towards the harbour entrance, to get to a point where a Catalina could safely land to pick him up. Corsairs covered him to ensure that no Japanese craft put out to capture him. Meanwhile plans were set in motion to rescue him when he reached a suitable position, likely to be shortly before dark.

By 6 p.m. Keefe, now exhausted after nine hours in the water, still lay out of reach for the Catalina. After a Ventura

197

bomber dropped rafts near him, the 15 Corsairs then in the vicinity set off back to Nissan Island. But between them and safety lay a tropical front that had suddenly blown up, its forbidding darkness soon made worse by nightfall. Once in the storm, the pilots had to rely on radio signals to get them back to the vicinity of their tiny atoll, where they struggled to find the airfield in the murk. Flying blind not far above the sea, planes collided, went into the sea or crashed on the atoll. Seven pilots of 14 and 16 Squadrons died in what would be the RNZAF's worst day of the islands campaign.

Faced with the option of bailing out or attempting to ditch when his engine cut out, Cox had virtually resigned himself to 'the third option of just shutting my eyes until "it" happened — when in the first of a series of lightning flashes I saw trees and jungle and the curvature of the tiny atoll directly below!' He found the flare path, then lost it again as he doubled round to the other end, but 'found the runway again by guestimation, and finally made my worst landing ever'.[179]

The Japanese picked Keefe up next day. When he died several weeks later, apparently of infection of his wound, he became yet another casualty of New Zealand's substantial air campaign against the Japanese in the South-West Pacific. With Australian and American air forces, New Zealanders helped keep the pressure on Japanese holed up in Rabaul and Bougainville, but by 1945 the main focus of the Pacific War had shifted elsewhere — and Japan faced the bleak prospect of defeat.

Central Pacific drive

As the guns fell silent in Europe, American forces were closing in on Japan. Following the seizure of Tarawa in November 1943, the Pacific Command had continued its central Pacific drive by making landings in the Marshall Islands early the following year. Enemy strongpoints were bypassed and neutralised with air and sea power.

In a series of operations between February and August 1944, Nimitz's forces wrested the strategic Mariana Islands from the Japanese. Realising the danger of their loss — American bombers would be able to reach the whole of the Japanese mainland from these islands — the Japanese made a major effort to disrupt the invasion fleet. But the Battle of the Philippine Sea, on 19–20 June 1944, proved another disaster for the Japanese navy. In a one-sided encounter that became known as the Great Marianas Turkey Shoot, the remnants of Japanese naval air power were destroyed. American bombers flying out of bases in the islands soon reduced Japan's major cities to rubble. So complete was the destruction by late July 1945 that suitable targets had become difficult to find.

In the meantime MacArthur's command had launched a separate thrust through the Philippines. The invasion, in October 1944, prompted a do-or-die sortie by the Japanese fleet. At the Battle of Leyte Gulf the then overwhelmingly superior US Navy completed the annihilation of Japanese sea power. But the Philippines operation remained secondary to the main American drive towards the Japanese home islands, which continued with the invasion of Iwo Jima in February 1945. In an operation matching in scale that launched at Normandy the previous year, American troops stormed ashore on Okinawa in the Ryukyu Islands in April. The Japanese defenders fought with fanatical determination, and both sides suffered huge casualties before organised resistance ended in mid-June.

Pulling back 3 Division

In terms of ground forces New Zealand found itself shut out of this drive towards the Japanese homeland. Riled by the Anzac Agreement, American authorities in Washington determined to minimise New Zealand or Australian participation outside their immediate areas. Only a handful of New Zealand specialist personnel took part in the operations in the central Pacific. Three merchant marine officers who had sailed in the area accompanied the invasion force to Tarawa. Several radar scientists also went forward with American forces to operate radars supplied by New Zealand. Present at landings at Peleliu and Ulithi Atoll, they were close enough to the action for one to be wounded.

In the now bypassed South Pacific, New Zealand's role diminished. With the shift of emphasis in the American approach, New Zealand lay too far to the south to continue as a support base, especially as the South Pacific Command wound down. The American presence in New Zealand began to disappear. When 2 Marine Division left for Tarawa, it was not replaced. The Americans handed back control of facilities in the Wellington area in May 1944. Most of the remaining Americans, in 43 Infantry Division, left two months later, and the various facilities in the Auckland area that they had used were then progressively closed. Residual US

Army personnel left in January 1945, leaving only a small US Navy presence in Auckland.

Nimitz's shift of focus to the central Pacific had important implications for 3 Division. With the South Pacific Command having closed down its combat role, 3 Division would be reduced to a garrison role — unless it was made available to MacArthur's command. Faced with endemic manpower problems, the government not surprisingly opted to concentrate on sustaining 2 Division at the expense of 3 Division. However sensible in terms of strategy and practical requirements, this decision was bound to offend Pacific soldiers who believed that their contribution had been under-appreciated. With some bitterness 3 Division began to pull back to New Caledonia, completing the process by April 1944. Although Barrowclough had persuaded the War Cabinet to maintain it as a cadre unit in the hope of later rebuilding it, any hopes in this direction soon faded

"WHERE NOW?"

As this cartoon suggests, the government faced difficult decisions in 1944 in using New Zealand's scarce resources to the best effect.

Gordon Minhinnick Collection, *New Zealand Herald*, 4 January 1944 as more and more men were withdrawn to be returned to civilian occupations or to be despatched to Italy as reinforcements. Eventually, at American request, the division was pulled back to New Zealand in August 1944, and disbanded a couple of months later.

A similar fate threatened the RNZAF group in the islands. In April 1944, the authorities in Washington proposed a radical reduction in the RNZAF strength in the South Pacific; all fighter squadrons were to be disbanded, and only a few bomber-reconnaissance and flying-boat squadrons retained for garrison duties. New Zealand could have greatly improved its manpower situation by accepting this decision. But maintaining a fighting contribution in the theatre seemed important for political reasons. So it transferred a substantial RNZAF contingent to MacArthur's operational control for use in the ongoing campaign in the northern Solomons. The squadrons in question — four (later nine) fighter, two bomber-reconnaissance and one flying-boat — formed the New Zealand Air Task Force from September 1944.

As a result, the build-up of RNZAF personnel in the islands continued, to reach a peak of 8000 in February 1945. The task force headquarters on Bougainville controlled squadrons operating out of airfields on that island, Nissan (Green) Island, Los Negros, Emirau Island and, towards the end, Jacquinot Bay in New Britain.

The navy also maintained a presence in the Solomons. The small ships of the New Zealand minesweeper flotilla continued their mainly night-time anti-submarine patrols and escort duties, which took them as far north as the Admiralty Islands. In March 1944 they were joined by two flotillas of Fairmile motor launches, 12 in all. With the fighting now relatively confined in the area, the operations became generally routine, broken only occasionally by groundings, friendly fire incidents and, in one instance that led to serious damage to one of the launches, by the explosion of an ammunition ship nearby. This naval effort continued until June 1945, when all the flotillas returned to New Zealand.

The South Pacific air war

The air war in the South-West Pacific in 1944–45 differed markedly from that fought by the New Zealanders earlier in the campaign. Japanese Zekes and Zeros had then vigorously contested the skies, and dogfights were common. By early 1944, however, Allied pilots struggled to find opponents. Two enemy fighters shot down by 18 Squadron Kittyhawks on 13 February proved to be the last RNZAF victories of the campaign — bringing to 99 the tally of claimed certainties for the fighter squadrons. By the end of that month the Japanese had withdrawn the remnants of their air force to Truk, well to the north. Although the Japanese mounted several isolated air attacks in the region in early 1945, including one on Manus Island, no New Zealand pilots became involved in air combat in the last year and a half of the campaign. Now with complete air supremacy in the region, the Allied air forces concentrated on harassing the Japanese and providing support for forces fighting on the ground. Bomb racks were fitted to the Kittyhawks and to the Vought Corsairs that soon replaced them, and from March 1944 the New Zealand fighters became fighter-bombers.

Bougainville remained one major focus of air action. At first, action centred on the Empress Augusta Bay area, where the Americans had rapidly constructed a number of airfields. They had no intention of trying to take the whole island, and operations remained defensive in character. Some New Zealanders took part; these were officers and NCOs, including the commanding officer, serving with the Fijian forces' 1 Battalion, which deployed on the island in December 1943 and carried out reconnaissance patrols. Only after the Americans handed over to Australian troops in October 1944 did the emphasis change. By this time, however, the Fijians (another infantry battalion and a dock company, both also commanded by New Zealand officers, had been sent to Bougainville in March 1944) had been withdrawn. Over the next 10 months the Australians pushed the Japanese back into four enclaves.

Ground support provided an ongoing task for New Zealand airmen in both phases of the Bougainville fighting. For a time such action took place uncomfortably close to their airfields. Two RNZAF dive-bomber squadrons, which arrived on Bougainville in March 1944 in the midst of a strong Japanese attack on the Empress Augusta Bay perimeter, attacked Japanese troops so near their airfield at Piva that their ground crews could see their bombs exploding. Two fighter squadrons, having also moved forward to Bougainville, had to contend with the shelling of their airfield. Even after they had been driven back, Japanese remained in the hills overlooking the airfields until finally ousted by the Australians. Strafing and bombing enemy positions both in the front line and in rear areas occupied New Zealand airmen until the end of the war.

Their other main task was to harass the Japanese in and around the Rabaul base on New Britain. The bombers, dive-bombers (until withdrawn in July 1944) and fighter-bombers all made many raids on the area. For those stationed on Bougainville (after April 1945 this amounted to four fighter squadrons), these operations invariably involved long, tiring flights, using Nissan Island as a key intermediate stop to load bombs.

Fighter pilot Keith Mulligan, of 16 Squadron, describes operations over Rabaul:

> We usually flew to Rabaul at 12,000 feet, the bombing run would start at about that height and 6,000 feet was the recommended height of release. I often wondered about that. To select an accurate height to drop the bomb in a dive with the altimeter unravelling frantically and the speed increasing by the foot required a certain amount of mental agility. It was always prudent to commence the dive at a sensible level otherwise the speed factor got out of control and so possibly could the plane....
>
> The flack [sic] was always present. Some targets were lightly defended while in the more important areas the flack was intense. The bursts you saw all around were harmless enough and the height of these varied quite a bit, but the numerous jolts you felt raising the nose or tail or tilting a wing indicated near misses and that was a little disturbing. Personally, I always wondered how the hell we got through the wall of 20-mm tracer we usually ran into as we pulled out of the dive. We were rarely hit, thank God, which was hard to believe with the amount of crap flying around.[180]

Fairmile 'submarine chaser' built in Auckland for the navy.

A formation of Corsairs flies near Guadalcanal in 1944. In all, 15,000 New Zealanders served with the RNZAF in the South Pacific between 1942 and 1945; 350 of them lost their lives.

Evatt Collection, Alexander Turnbull Library, F-106417½

The pilots had to endure intense flak over Rabaul. Where possible, if hit they came down in the sea, either bailing out or ditching. Taking this risk in the hope of being rescued by a Catalina seemed preferable to falling into Japanese hands. Several captured pilots suffered ill-treatment at the hands of the enemy; others who came down on land but evaded capture often had epic adventures before being rescued. As the tragedy of 15 January 1945, after the attempted rescue of Keefe, brutally demonstrated, the rapidly changing weather conditions presented an ever-present danger to pilots operating in the tropics.

The airmen performed well in a campaign that had as its rationale political not strategic considerations. By early 1944 the Japanese in the region were impotent. Deprived of their air cover, and isolated by the destruction of Japanese naval power, they were virtually prisoners in the areas they still occupied. They no longer constituted military assets that could affect Japan's fortunes in the war, except that they tied down a proportion of Allied forces — forces that the Americans did not need or want to use in any case. The need, from Canberra's and Wellington's perspectives, to be seen to be still engaging the Japanese would cost many Australian and a lesser number of New Zealand lives until the end, without contributing in any material sense to the outcome of the war, which was being decided elsewhere.

South-East Asia operations

While the campaign in the South-West Pacific dragged on, a few New Zealanders fought the Japanese in South-East Asia, another bypassed area. They had been present on the Burma Front from the outset, and more than 250 New Zealanders were serving in the India Air Command by the end of 1942. Scattered in 15 squadrons, they took part in the operations that had achieved air superiority for the Allies on this front a year later. Eric Osboldstone flew Blenheims with the RAF's 27 Squadron over the border area between India and Burma in late 1944 before being shot down and captured. 'We were being shot at here and there, and we'd fire at anything that moved — including dugout canoes, because the Japanese used to commission them to ferry their troops across the river….,' he later recalled. 'I got a train once, and a railway station that blew up. We didn't have much air opposition.'[181] Seven New Zealand officers commanded squadrons in Burma, and from February 1945 New Zealander Air Marshal Sir Keith Park oversaw the whole Allied air effort in that theatre.

New Zealanders also served with the Indian Army. In 1942 2NZEF had made available 26 sapper officers with experience in railway operations, marine engineering and dock operations, and another 46 had gone from New Zealand in 1943–44. Some of these men found themselves improving communications on the Indo-Burmese border, facilities that helped defeat Japanese offensives at Imphal and Kohima in eastern India in mid-1944. Air re-supply proved of decisive importance in these defensive operations, and also when the 14th Army went over to the offensive, driving the Japanese southwards. Rangoon was retaken in May 1945.

Other New Zealanders took part in naval operations against Japanese targets in South-East Asia. In January 1945 more than 60 flew in Fleet Air Arm aircraft to attack petroleum-refining facilities on Sumatra, which supplied three-quarters of the fuel used by Japanese aircraft. Many planes failed to make it back to their carriers. Two New Zealand officers, Jack Haberfield and EJ Baxter, were among nine airmen captured by the Japanese. Taken to Singapore, these men suffered a terrible fate — on 31 July Japanese troops beheaded them all.

On the day of this atrocity, another New Zealand naval officer, Lanyon ('Kiwi') Smith, serving in the midget submarine *XE3*, took part in a daring attack on the Japanese heavy cruiser *Takao* in the Johore strait. After a diver had attached limpet mines to the cruiser's hull, the submarine made good its escape, despite nearly being trapped under the cruiser and then inadvertently popping to the surface (unseen by the Japanese). Two of Smith's three companions won VCs for this exploit, which severely damaged the cruiser. Another New Zealand submariner, Lieutenant HP Westmacott, commanding *XE5*, had shortly before penetrated Hong Kong harbour in an attempt to cut the Hong Kong–Singapore cable. Both these submarines formed part of a submarine flotilla commanded by yet another New Zealander.

A few score New Zealanders also operated behind the Japanese lines elsewhere in South-East Asia. They served in Z Special Unit, an offshoot of the Special Operations Executive (SOE) that had been formed in Australia in June 1942 to carry out commando incursions and organise guerrilla operations. Donald Stott, who had made a name for himself in the destruction of the Asopos viaduct and other clandestine operations in Greece in 1943–44, organised the New Zealand involvement. Some other veterans of SOE operations in Greece also served. New Zealanders were in the parties that were inserted by parachute or submarine, and these parties organised native guerrillas. Several lost their lives, including Stott and another New Zealand officer drowned while attempting to land from a submarine in difficult conditions at Balikpapan in Borneo in March 1945. The Japanese summarily executed one New Zealander whom they captured in Borneo.[182]

These clandestine operations foreshadowed the opening of a mopping-up campaign on the island by a series of Australian amphibious assaults from May 1945. This dubious undertaking, which cost the lives of more than 500 Australians in operations of no strategic value, affected the RNZAF task force in the South-West Pacific. Squadrons earmarked for the Borneo area began moving forward in June; they were still at Los Negros when the course of events removed the need for their redeployment.

Tightening the naval stranglehold

New Zealand made its main contribution to the drive against Japan itself at sea. When Allied leaders at the Quebec Conference in September 1944 agreed that the British Pacific Fleet (later renamed Eastern Fleet) should join the American naval onslaught against Japan, they ensured indirect New Zealand participation. For, as in the European theatre, many New Zealand naval personnel were spread throughout the fleet, which eventually disposed more than a hundred ships, including the fleet train. Most of these New Zealanders in the Royal Navy carried out their duties anonymously in the team atmospheres of their ships. But the New Zealand naval aviators on the aircraft carriers — a quarter of the total — were more conspicuous. Some commanded squadrons.

The New Zealand ensign was also to be seen in the fleet. Two New Zealand cruisers, HMNZS *Gambia* and *Achilles*, had joined it during 1944 and had taken part in operations against targets in the Dutch East Indies as it moved eastwards. The corvette HMNZS *Arbutus* later joined the fleet as a radio and radar maintenance ship. The fleet train included the hospital ship HMNZHS *Maunganui*.

With its main base at Sydney and its forward operating base at Manus Island in the Admiralty Islands, the fleet moved northwards to operate with American task forces. *Gambia* was one of several of its ships to take part in covering operations for the American landings on Iwo Jima and Okinawa. In preparation for the latter operation, New Zealand Fleet Air Arm pilots had a busy time bombing airfields in the nearby Sakishima group. The savagery of the fighting on Iwo Jima and Okinawa indicated that an attempt to invade the Japanese homeland would be a costly business — a prospect that the military-dominated government in Tokyo yet hoped would induce the Allies to seek a negotiated settlement.

Late in March 1945 *Gambia* was given a respite from the fray when detached to tow a destroyer damaged in a kamikaze attack 1200 kilometres back to Leyte Gulf in the Philippines. Joining the force in May, *Achilles* formed part of a task group that harassed Japanese forces in the Caroline Islands in the following month. The bypassed Japanese base on Truk came in for particular attention in mid-June. Aircraft from the carrier HMS *Implacable* struck docks, airfields and other facilities, while *Achilles* and other cruisers and destroyers bombarded a seaplane base.

New Zealand Fleet Air Arm navigator Sub-Lieutenant Lewis Martin (828 Squadron) describes the raid on Truk in June 1945:

> The C.O. [commanding officer] was, of course, going to lead the bombing strike; but he lost power on take-off and went into the drink with his ton of bombs (all crew survived). So Reggie [pilot Reggie Blake] and I had to lead. I was sweating slightly as it was one thing to make a navigation error when alone; altogether different when leading twenty-four aircraft. But adrenalin was flowing…. We had to fly to Moen nearly over Kuop and right over Eten and Dublon, all three of which had airfields and anti-aircraft guns…. As soon as the flak appeared, Reggie led the whole unwieldy gaggle in evasive manoeuvres, beautifully judged to be as confusing as possible to the gunners while still gentle and simple enough to avoid aircraft colliding in the close formation that preceded his ordering them into line astern; once in line astern, each pilot chose his own manoeuvres. We were the first to bomb and they threw everything at us. No evasion was possible, as Reggie lined his sight up on an 'Irving' on the runway; we seemed to hold steady course in the dive for ages! We dropped our ton on the Irving (a large clumsy transport aircraft) and it seemed we got it.
>
> Then Reggie jinked all over the sky as we circled the target, watching the bombs of the rest. We destroyed or

> damaged every aircraft and hangar we could see on the ground and left a line of big craters on the runway. The fighters dealt with everything in the air. More jinking at low level as Reggie got out of the atoll so the squadron could reform. None were missing, although we all had holes and rips….
>
> Altogether an effective strike. Almost nothing had gone wrong![183]

In July the British Fleet moved north to Japanese home waters. It attacked shore facilities on Honshu as part of a massive Allied onslaught that wreaked havoc on Japanese cities; *Gambia* bombarded targets on the mainland until 9 August. The only real challenge to these operations came from the desperate, terrifying, costly but ultimately ineffective kamikaze attacks mounted by Japanese aircraft.

Plans to invade Japan

While Japan reeled under mounting Allied assault, the possibility of New Zealanders also being involved in air and land operations against the Japanese mainland grew. Plans to redeploy RAF units from Europe to the Pacific would have affected many New Zealand airmen. These units included two 'New Zealand' squadrons — 75 and 489. The former would join the strategic bombing effort already being mounted by the US Air Force, while the latter would be used in its specialist anti-shipping operations.

As for the invasion of Japan, the government's fears that it would be a bloody affair had been increased by the ferocity of the battles on Iwo Jima and Okinawa and the evidence of suicidal resistance provided by the kamikazes. But to stand aside did not seem possible for a Pacific state anxious to take part in the post-war settlement. Providing a force would, as ever, be difficult, but could be based on 2 Division. On 7 August the War Cabinet approved plans for the provision of a two-brigade division and air units to a British Commonwealth force for operations against Japan.

The use of atomic bombs

The fundamental assumption behind such planning was that an invasion would be necessary. But even before the War Cabinet's decision, a momentous event had undermined this assumption. New Zealanders learned to their astonishment that, on 6 August, the US Army Air Force had used a new weapon, an atomic bomb, to obliterate the Japanese city of Hiroshima. This startling development had been long in the making, and New Zealand, characteristically, had played a small part in it.

As early as December 1943, New Zealand's chief scientist Ernest Marsden had become aware of work on an atom bomb through his scientific contacts. He offered some New Zealand scientists to work on the project. Five scientists left New Zealand for North America in July 1944. Two were to work in the United States on the Manhattan Project, as the atomic bomb programme was codenamed; these two joined an expatriate New Zealander there who had been sent from Britain. The other three were to work on an Anglo-Canadian atomic project in Montreal, which was less directly aimed at producing a usable atomic bomb. Two more New Zealanders joined the latter in April 1945. In a way that epitomised New Zealand's war effort generally, these men made a small contribution to the successful Anglo-American atomic team effort, which reached fruition with the explosion of a test bomb in the New Mexico desert on 16 July 1945.[184]

Roosevelt having died suddenly in April, the new

Gambia shells targets on the Japanese coast in August 1945. A Colony-class cruiser with a crew of 980 men, *Gambia* was commissioned in the RNZN in September 1943 to replace *Leander*. After a short period operating against blockade runners in the Bay of Biscay, she proceeded to the east in February 1944.

RNZN Museum, AAI0065

205

President, Harry S Truman, faced a fateful decision. He quickly approved the use of the weapon against Japan, believing that it would save Allied lives by obviating the need for an invasion. His assumption that the new weapon would prove decisive proved correct — though not before a second atomic bomb had been dropped on the city of Nagasaki, on 9 August. Truman hoped that a quick Japanese collapse might forestall the Russians, who were committed to renouncing their non-aggression pact with Japan and entering the war three months after the defeat of Germany. But the Soviet Union declared war on Japan on 8 August. Bursting into Manchuria, Soviet forces quickly shattered Japanese resistance. Coming on top of the atomic explosions, this massive blow finally persuaded the Japanese government to capitulate unconditionally. At 8 a.m. on 15 August Japanese for the first time heard their Emperor, as he urged them to endure the unendurable and suffer the insufferable by laying down their arms.

Japan surrenders

The news of the war's end reached New Zealand at 11 a.m. on 15 August. Sirens sounded immediately. The surrender was not entirely unexpected; the course of events had indicated that the end would come sooner rather than later. A formal ceremony was held, and New Zealanders then settled down to celebrate with an enthusiasm that was somewhat less marked than on VE Day, partly because of inclement weather in the North Island. During the ensuing two days' holiday there were ceremonies at various places throughout the country, marred in Auckland by ugly scenes as drunken youths turned to violence and vandalism. Most people rejoiced. One woman recalled an 'absolutely marvellous atmosphere' at a crowded dance in Wellington on the night of the surrender as the realisation that it was all over sank in: 'Everyone laughing and happy, saying what they were going to do as soon as the peace was fixed.'[185]

Air Vice-Marshal Isitt signs the Japanese surrender document on behalf of New Zealand. General Douglas MacArthur stands at the microphone.

Meanwhile in Japanese waters New Zealand's cruiser *Gambia*, which had taken part in the last action of the war as her gunners helped beat off an air attack shortly after the Emperor's broadcast, prepared to take part in the formal surrender. She formed part of the great array of naval power — some 400 ships — that assembled at the end of August and made a triumphal entry into Tokyo Bay on the twenty-seventh. A landing party from the ship participated in the occupation of Yokosuka naval base on 30 August. On 2 September the surrender ceremony took place on the deck of the battleship USS *Missouri*. When Air Vice-Marshal Leonard Isitt, Chief of the Air Staff, signed the surrender document on New Zealand's behalf, he brought to a close New Zealand's war effort, an effort that had lasted 2176 days and cost the lives of 11,600 New Zealanders. The last of them, like the first, was an airman — Fleet Air Arm Pilot Sub-Lieutenant TCG McBride had the misfortune of being killed shortly before the Emperor's submission.

There remained the task of taking the surrender of the various Japanese garrisons still dotted around the periphery of their now defunct empire, including at Singapore, where Sir Keith Park was present at the formal surrender on 12 September. Six days earlier New Zealand officers had taken part in the ceremony in which the 139,000 Japanese troops in the South Pacific formally surrendered on the deck of a British aircraft carrier near Rabaul. On 8 September, at Torokina, the Japanese on Bougainville laid down their arms. At both ceremonies the senior New Zealand air officer in the South-West Pacific, Air Commodore GN Roberts, represented New Zealand. The commander of the 25th Minesweeping Flotilla, Commander Peter Phipps, performed the same role at the surrender of the Japanese troops on Nauru and Ocean Islands on 13 September and 1 October respectively. The withdrawal of RNZAF squadrons from the islands began immediately, the last leaving Bougainville at the end of October. Most were

New Zealand soldiers supervise a customs search of repatriated Japanese soldiers.

disbanded when they arrived in New Zealand. By December, 90 per cent of the RNZAF personnel serving in the islands, including Fiji, at the time of the surrender had been repatriated.

A second urgent requirement was to recover the several hundred New Zealand POWs and internees of the Japanese. The limited numbers meant that this was a relatively straightforward task, though the prisoners were spread over a wide area. For some who had been taken to Japan as early as December 1941, the air and naval bombardments of the final stages of the war were just the last of many tribulations, and a few had the misfortune to be killed by this Allied fire. But most POWs were held in South-East Asia. A flight of RNZAF transport aircraft, fitted out as air ambulances, was sent to Singapore in

September. As reports of POWs were received, these aircraft flew to other points in South-East Asia. Within two months 156 POWs and civilian internees, many of them emaciated, had been brought back to New Zealand.

Revelations of what the POWs had been through horrified those at home. They seemed further proof of Japanese barbarity. But only a few New Zealanders had been involved. Indeed, thanks to the Featherston incident, more Japanese POWs had lost their lives in New Zealand hands than vice versa, even though there was no comparison between the treatment of the two groups. No Japanese POW in New Zealand had had to fear summary execution — the fate of several New Zealand POWs — or the insidious and sometimes lethal effects of malnourishment and imperfectly treated disease.

A Jayforce patrol passes through a Japanese village. In all, 12,000 New Zealanders served in the occupation force in Japan. They included several hundred women who undertook nursing and welfare duties. Fifteen men lost their lives to disease or accidents.

War History Collection, Alexander Turnbull Library F-261-¹/₄

By comparison with Australia, New Zealand had got off relatively lightly. Whereas New Zealand had lost only 5 per cent of its POWs, mainly in Europe, Australia's POW death toll amounted to roughly a third — 8000 men. Most died in Japanese camps. Although the bitterness in New Zealand was correspondingly less, an undercurrent could still be detected 50 years later. It had been bolstered by significant numbers of former Dutch prisoners of the Japanese who came to New Zealand to settle in the late 1940s.

Bringing to account those who had committed war crimes provided another important post-war task. Since no atrocities had been committed within New Zealand's territories, it did not convene any courts martial for this purpose, but Australian and British courts condemned several Japanese for wartime acts against New Zealanders. Though it took no part in the trials of German war criminals, New Zealand did help to try the major Japanese war criminals in Tokyo. Sir Erina Northcroft sat on the 11-nation International Military Tribunal for the Far East, which condemned wartime Japanese Prime Minister Tojo and others to death.

Occupation of Japan

New Zealand also took part in the Allied occupation of Japan. Initially *Gambia* then *Achilles* provided a naval presence, but New Zealand also made available an infantry brigade and a fighter squadron for a British Commonwealth Occupation Force. On arrival both units deployed in Yamaguchi prefecture on the southern tip of Honshu, an area with about 1.4 million inhabitants, and quickly set about their occupation tasks. Because this had not been an area of large Japanese military activity, demilitarisation did not prove a difficult task. The New Zealanders oversaw the return of Japanese military personnel from overseas and the repatriation of Koreans to their country, now under Soviet and American occupation. Policing duties did not prove onerous. For most of the troops, boredom soon became a problem.

Unhappy with their fate, and influenced by wartime anti-Japanese propaganda, many of the troops arrived with a very negative perception of Japan and the Japanese. Under orders not to fraternise, they maintained their distance from the Japanese, carried out their duties and awaited their relief. For many a visit to Hiroshima would be the most memorable event of their time in Japan, which proved to be only a matter of months. The government had set about raising a volunteer force to replace them. Jayforce, as it was termed, arrived in the middle of 1946 to begin a one-year stay.[186]

The Jayforce experience, which came to an end in 1948 with the government's decision to end New Zealand's participation in the occupation, was New Zealand's first contact with Asia on any substantial scale. The initially negative perceptions of the Japanese had soon been superseded by more positive attitudes, as non-fraternisation rules broke down and men and women became acquainted with Japanese on a personal basis.[187] Many of the New Zealanders returned from Japan with their propaganda-inspired preconceptions of the country long since dispelled. But their numbers were too small to effect any major change in New Zealand perceptions, and Japan remained for the time being a source of fear and loathing amongst a large segment of the population.

20 Nov – Nazi war
crimes trial begins

15 Aug – India and Pakistan
gain independence

12 Nov – Japane
leaders convicte
of war crimes

5 Mar – Churchill warns of iron
curtain descending on Europe

1 Oct – 21 Nazi leaders
convicted of war crimes

14 May – State of
Israel established

3 May – Japanese war
crimes trial begins

29 Nov – UN General Assembly
approves partition of Palestine

Communists seize power
in Czechoslovakia

4 Apr – North Atla
Treaty sig

New Zealand food aid is loaded onto a truck in Auckland in January 1948 prior to being taken to a wharf for despatch to Britain where it is destined for the town of Finsbury.

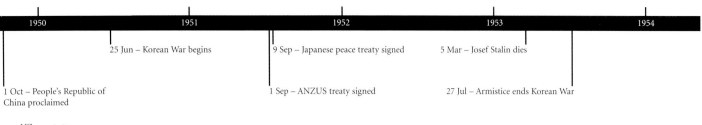

| 1950 | 1951 | 1952 | 1953 | 1954 |

25 Jun – Korean War begins

9 Sep – Japanese peace treaty signed

5 Mar – Josef Stalin dies

1 Oct – People's Republic of
China proclaimed

1 Sep – ANZUS treaty signed

27 Jul – Armistice ends Korean War

Aug – NZers vote to
introduce compulsory
military training

The Legacy

The Second World War cost New Zealand dearly in both blood and treasure. Every day of its duration five New Zealand servicemen or women, on average, lost their lives. On a population basis, this was more than the United Kingdom's 147 but roughly eight times less than the Soviet Union's appalling 8000, admittedly over a shorter period.[188] The butcher's bill, 11,600 New Zealanders in all, was mercifully lighter than that exacted by the First World War, when nearly 18,000 had fallen: one in twelve of those sent overseas had been lost, compared with one in six in 1914–18.

Within the Commonwealth, New Zealand held the dubious distinction of having lost the highest proportion of its population — 6684 per million (compared with the United Kingdom's 5123 and Australia's 3232). To these fatalities must, of course, be added the many thousands of men who were maimed in mind or body by their experiences at the front. New Zealand's ratio of wounded was roughly a third higher than those of both the United Kingdom and Australia.[189] These figures reflected the nature of New Zealand's contribution — the concentration in the naval and air spheres on combat rather than support personnel and the prolonged involvement of 2NZEF in active operations in the Mediterranean theatre.

In terms of resources devoted to the war, New Zealand's contribution also stood up well in comparison to those of its

211

allies. Only the Soviet Union and Britain did more. Overall New Zealand devoted nearly a third of its national income to the war effort and from 1942 to 1944 the figure was over half, peaking at 53 per cent in 1943.[190] As it had pledged in the Atlantic Declaration, New Zealand had devoted all its resources to the common cause.

This represented a big sacrifice. But in other respects New Zealand had been fortunate in not suffering the full impact of war. It did not experience the horrors of enemy occupation, with all the uncertainties and moral dilemmas inherent in such situations. Its resources were not deployed in support of a hated invader, which was the experience of so many smaller countries in Europe. Its population was not starved, beaten and subjected to summary execution, deportation and other tribulations. Nor did it suffer the horrors of aerial bombardment. Only for a brief period did there seem a possibility that such a fate might be in store for New Zealanders, though their fears of invasion were inevitably exaggerated. In the event, the soil of New Zealand, if not its territorial waters, remained unviolated (except for the fracas involving Japanese POWs at Featherston in 1943).

New Zealand, then, escaped from the war relatively unscathed. No problem of reconstruction of war-damaged property or factories confronted New Zealanders. In fact the New Zealand economy emerged from the war in better shape than it had entered it. Traditional primary production had been sustained, and productive capacity increased. New industries had been developed, pointing the way to a more diversified farming product range in future. Manufacturing capacity had been expanded to meet war demands. Many of the wartime industries, such as munitions factories, had only short-term significance. But an increased workforce had been trained in a range of skills that could be applied to peacetime production, lessening New Zealand's dependence on imported goods and meeting the pent-up demand for consumer goods in a population with considerable savings. The war had also further enhanced the trend towards greater state control of the economy that had been apparent in the late 1930s. The regulatory framework provided the instrument for the post-war development of industrial capacity that would ensure a full-employment economy.

Rehabilitation

The economic development had a large bearing on New Zealand's approach to the most pressing problem in the immediate aftermath of the war — the repatriation of the men and women serving overseas and their reintegration into the economy. Following the First World War, a short-term boom had been followed by a financial downturn, and this had caused great hardship to many returning soldiers, forcing a number to walk off land they had taken up and making jobs for others more difficult to find. Facing a similar rehabilitation task following the Second World War, the government was determined to avoid a repetition of earlier mistakes. A Rehabilitation Department established in 1943 set about developing a comprehensive scheme.

Many men returned to positions that had, by law, been held for them during their absence overseas. Others found jobs in manufacturing enterprises that had expanded during the war, taking the place of former directed workers, especially women. Loans helped men start small businesses or purchase tools; many were assisted to undertake training courses, some overseas. The older student became a feature at universities and training colleges. Others, those with farming experience, tried their luck in ballots for 'rehab farms', carved out of land acquired for this purpose by the government, some of it compulsorily. Some used government rehab loans to buy existing properties, or took over family farms. Land sales were carefully controlled to prevent speculation, as had occurred after the previous war. Overall, the Second World War rehabilitation effort was a major success story.

If the desire for adventure had motivated many to enlist in the services early in the war, most returned having had a surfeit of it. To be sure, some found it hard to settle down to domestic routines after years of varied and sometimes dramatic activity. Many who had held positions of significant authority in the services found the relatively junior and humdrum civilian jobs they now occupied unsatisfying. But most picked up the traces of civilian life and looked to make up for lost time with their families. Housing shortages caused problems at first, but rehab loans helped overcome these. In the decade and a half after the end of the war New Zealand, like other former belligerents, experienced a baby boom that would have a huge demographic impact on the country.

Political legacy

Full employment for males and social security constituted the twin pillars of post-war life for the wartime generation, which dominated New Zealand politics until the 1980s. Labour soldiered on after the war until 1949, when it lost office to Sidney Holland's National Party, which promised a reduction in the regulation of economic activity. But, far from rejecting the basic thrust of its predecessor's approach, National embraced it. During the next 30 years it would dominate the Treasury benches, exploiting the fundamentally conservative instincts of the wartime generation.

The war had greatly reinforced the political influence of the New Zealand Returned Services' Association, not least by replenishing its membership. It proved an effective lobbyist not only on behalf of its members but also on defence and other national issues, especially with a Cabinet that usually included a number of ministers with wartime service. Only in the 1980s did the RSA's political influence decline, as its Second World War members began to pass away.

Social legacy

Despite the prominent part played by women in the war effort, the impact of the war on their status was at first rather limited. Society's view of a woman's role had not fundamentally altered. For married women it still centred on childrearing and nurturing a working husband. Those who had entered the workforce in great numbers as a temporary measure were driven by social pressures to vacate their jobs once the emergency was over. On the other hand, the war had pushed 50,000 women into the workforce who would probably not have otherwise joined it. The war had also undermined previously rigid societal attitudes, and their reimposition at the end of the war could not be as complete. Many women had become more confident in their ability to cope with varied challenges, even if they happily settled down to bring up families once peace came.[191] The long-term consequences of the war would be considerable.

Maori emerged from the war with greatly improved self-esteem and confidence. In part this rested on pride in the exploits of 28 (Maori) Battalion. But it also derived from satisfaction over the way in which Maori in New Zealand had risen to the challenge of not only sustaining the battalion but also contributing to the war effort at home. The Maori war effort lost nothing in comparison to that of the Pakeha population. Almost one in three of every Maori had been directly involved, either in the services or in essential production. The Maori War Effort Organisation, the organiser and co-ordinator of this effort, represented an important Maori initiative to meet a particular problem, and this initiative was dependent on Maori resources, for the government provided no financial backing.[192]

In 1939 most Maori lived in rural areas, and in the northern part of the country. Contact between Maori and Pakeha was limited. By the end of the war twice as many Maori lived in urban areas than had at its outset. In 1945, they did not go home to the country, as expected, and this had important consequences for race relations.

Prejudice and discrimination against Maori continued in many areas after the war. Maori seeking accommodation continued to experience humiliating difficulties in some cities and towns, exacerbated by a general shortage of housing. Nonetheless, the war had created a climate conducive to change in the years that followed it. Maori and Pakeha had fought and worked side by side for years. They had associated in ways that would have been unlikely but for the abnormal conditions. Moreover, many Pakeha soldiers returned from overseas service with an immense admiration for their Maori compatriots in 2NZEF and the other services; the long-term importance of this in influencing attitudes should not be underestimated.

Cultural legacy

In addition to its long-lasting political and social impact, the war left a significant cultural legacy. This took many forms, ranging from the enrichment of the New Zealand vocabulary to the production of a significant body of literary and artistic work reflecting on the experiences of New Zealanders. The latter aspect had not been overlooked during the war, and official war artists and photographers like Peter McIntyre and George Kaye provided a lasting record of New Zealand's war. This was supplemented by the efforts of others, both during and after the war. Participants like artist Austin Deans (a POW in Europe), poet John Male, novelist Dan Davin (a divisional intelligence officer) and cartoonist Sid Scales (POW of the Japanese), to name but a few, enriched New Zealand's culture with their imaginative interpretations.[193] Over the last 50 years a steady stream of personal accounts by participants have appeared, some of them of considerable literary merit, some continually reprinted.[194]

There were changes to the landscape, too, as New Zealanders erected memorials to their war efforts. Unlike the situation following the First World War, these showed a distinctly utilitarian approach. Halls and other community facilities replaced monuments as the basis of recognition, though First World War memorials were often adjusted to include the names of war dead of the later conflict.

Another memorial was provided in the extensive history of the war initiated by the government in 1944 and produced by a dedicated team in the War History Branch of the Department of Internal Affairs. Former 2NZEF officer Major-General Howard Kippenberger oversaw this effort until his untimely death in 1957. By the time the project was finally completed in 1986, 48 large volumes had been published, along with many shorter publications. Together they provide a comprehensive record of New Zealand's involvement, unmatched in their detail by those of any other participants.

Reflections on New Zealand's participation

The determination to produce a lasting record reflected a strong sense of satisfaction among New Zealanders over their involvement in the war. At no time in the half-century that has elapsed since the war's end has anyone seriously challenged New Zealand's decision to participate. Now, as then, the defeat of Adolf Hitler and his regime, and of the Japanese, is seen as a 'just war'. Not least of the reasons for this remarkable consensus is acceptance that German and Japanese aggression precipitated the conflict. Hitler's determination to have a war, so apparent in the late 1930s, was confirmed by historical assessment, initially as a result of the documentation produced in the trial of the major German war criminals at Nuremberg in 1945–46. The consensus rests, too, on recognition that Hitler's aggressive conduct left the Western democracies no other choice but to fight or accept German domination of the

European continent, with all the long-term dangers that that would involve as European resources were developed to create an even more powerful military machine. Japan, of course, precipitated war against the Western democracies, even if there is more willingness now, 60 years later, to recognise that mounting American economic pressure had backed it into a corner from which war seemed to offer the only way out.

As the full scope and destruction of the Holocaust became apparent after the war, revelations of barbarous German behaviour reinforced New Zealand attitudes. Corpse-strewn images of liberated Belsen-Bergen and other concentration camps evoked horror in early 1945, soon heightened by emerging evidence of a Nazi programme of mass murder in other camps in eastern Europe, especially Auschwitz. Evidence of Japanese mistreatment of Allied POWs aroused similar feelings of horror. Most New Zealanders took pride in the fact that they had helped to put down such evil. As one who served with distinction in the navy put it: 'We looked on it as something that had to be done to protect the rights, the welfare and the dignity of the human race.'[195]

Critical assessment of New Zealand's role in the war has focused not on the involvement itself, but on the nature of that involvement. One strand of such criticism has addressed the performance of New Zealand troops. This revisionist approach during the 1980s highlighted disciplinary and other problems allegedly not covered in the official war histories — the difference between the myth and the reality.[196] But in fact the problems and mistakes highlighted in this approach had never been suppressed. Moreover, when set against the very high regard that the New Zealanders earned among both their opponents and those who controlled their fortunes on the Allied side, such aspects assume less importance than was accorded them in this revisionist approach.

Another strand of criticism has focused on New Zealand strategy during the war. Bound up with the issue of independence, it relates in particular to New Zealand's relationship with Britain. According to this argument,

New Zealand subordinated its interests to those of Britain, and the shape of its war effort was designed to gain 'brownie points' in London rather than to secure New Zealand's interests. There have been suggestions that New Zealand did too much, that its determination to meet every British request led to it over-committing itself both on the battlefield and on the home front.[197] This approach mistakes co-operative predilection and realistic appreciation of New Zealand's place in the scheme of things for subservient demeanour.

Associated with this argument has been another. This holds that New Zealand fought not in its own but rather in Britain's war, because New Zealand's main effort was made in the European and Mediterranean theatres whereas New Zealand's strategic interests lay in the Pacific. This is sometimes connected with the proposition that Britain let down Australia and New Zealand by not making forces available in 1941–42 in Singapore and in the South Pacific, which it was morally obliged to do as a quid pro quo for the antipodean contributions to the war in Europe. This argument briefly gained prominence in Australia in the early 1990s, but it has never been favoured in New Zealand. Nevertheless it is sometimes advanced by those critical of New Zealand's apparent willingness to conform to British imperatives — a criticism that often has its basis in poor understanding of strategy and the compromises and accommodations required to conduct coalition warfare, and indeed of New Zealand's circumstances at the time.

War aims achieved

New Zealand's war from 1939 to 1945 was fought to ensure that the British Commonwealth of Nations was not defeated. This was its primary war aim. Given that the Commonwealth could not be decisively defeated in the Pacific, it is not surprising that New Zealand's main effort took place elsewhere. In a global war, New Zealand assumed its share of the burden of defending the system on which it depended. After American entry to the war had finally removed the possibility of the ultimate defeat of that system, New Zealand continued to base its war effort upon supporting the collective strategy of defeating the more dangerous German enemy first before dealing with Japan. It was a strategy that used New Zealand's limited resources to the best effect in the common cause.

Although New Zealand entered the war believing that the door to compromise with Germany should be kept open and that an imposed peace would merely provide the genesis of new conflict, such an approach had not proved possible. At no time in the period of German triumph in 1940–41 did any significant body of opinion emerge within the country to argue that the British Commonwealth should seek peace with Hitler. Most took their lead from the implacable opposition to such a course expressed by Winston Churchill. Nor was there protest in New Zealand, which had not been consulted, when Churchill and Roosevelt finally excluded the possibility of any compromise by enunciating the Allied objective as unconditional surrender of all the enemy powers — foreshadowing a very different outcome to that of the First World War. This despite the fact that such an approach was likely to prolong the war by inducing the enemy to fight on to the bitter end.

Creating the United Nations

New Zealand's secondary war aim, which assumed increasing importance as the prospect of ultimate victory brightened, was to see established a better international system. This was not merely a matter of establishing a new world body to replace the discredited League of Nations. Peace would depend also on attacking the root causes of conflict — economic inequality and oppression.

New Zealand had agreed in September 1944 to participate in the United Nations Relief and Rehabilitation Agency, whose task was to alleviate the suffering of the many displaced and deprived people in Europe and Asia — a short-term problem related to the war. In the longer term, overcoming the fundamental social and economic problems leading to inequality would be essential. New Zealand took seriously the expression of the principles of self-determination for all peoples in the Atlantic Charter. This had awkward implications for the British government, anxious to avoid compromising its control of the empire upon which much of Britain's power depended.

To replace the League of Nations, Fraser looked to a universal system that provided an assurance of security to all members, large and small. This condition was only partially met by proposals that emerged from the Great Powers in late 1944. Maintaining peace and security would become the responsibility of an 11-member Security Council, with members pledging forces for enforcement purposes. In New Zealand's view, the proposed voting arrangement in the Security Council undermined this proposed system. The Soviet insistence on unanimity among the five Great Powers that would be permanent members of the council — the so-called 'veto provision' — seemed to introduce a fatal element of uncertainty. Unable to rely on the Security Council, members would be driven to make other arrangements to cover the possibility that support might not be forthcoming. The old alliance system would be revived.

Delegates of the 50 United Nations addressed these issues at a conference in San Francisco from April to June 1945. New Zealand participated fully and vigorously. Fraser arrived with clear goals, but also had a realistic appreciation of his capacity to secure substantial change in the face of Great Power agreement on the main elements of the system. He mounted a valiant campaign against the veto, knowing full well that it was doomed to failure because of the Russian attitude. Nor did he have much success in securing other changes to the Charter. In the end he signed the Charter on behalf of New Zealand on 26 June 1945 in the belief that an imperfect system was better than no system at all.

Onset of the Cold War

New Zealand hoped that, despite the flaws in the Charter, the United Nations peace enforcement system would be effective. But the growing rift between the Soviet Union and its erstwhile Allies soon stultified the system. Understandably perhaps, in light of the damage wrought in the Soviet Union, Stalin sought to create a buffer zone on its western frontier. In countries liberated by the Red Army, he installed puppet governments, not least in Poland. Efforts to incorporate elements of the London-based Polish government-in-exile succeeded. Few in Wellington or elsewhere believed, however, that Moscow would not dominate the new regime.

The Soviet approach caused much anger and unease in the Western democracies. Many feared that Western Europe might suffer the fate of having been liberated from one totalitarian dictatorship only to fall under the sway of another. Old fears of communism resurfaced and began to overshadow wartime goodwill towards Russia. The state of Western Europe exacerbated these fears. The destruction and dislocation provided fertile ground for communist parties, which had gained considerable strength and prestige through their resistance activities, especially in France and Italy.

From the ashes of the Second World War a new conflict began to smoulder — a Cold War between the Soviet Union and the Western democracies led by the United States. The confrontation developed from a series of crises. One occurred in Iran, where Soviet troops were slow to pull out from a wartime occupation; another in Greece, where communist guerrillas embarked on a contest for power with conservative elements. A third crisis took place in Germany, where the Soviet Union

Prime Minister Peter Fraser signs the Charter of the United Nations at San Francisco on 26 June 1945, with other members of the New Zealand delegation looking on. Secretary of External Affairs Alister McIntosh is second from the right at back.

War History Collection, Alexander Turnbull Library, F-160158-½

217

imposed a blockade on the Western Allies' occupation zones in Berlin. The United States rallied the Western democracies. In the Truman Doctrine enunciated in 1947, it promised support in resistance to communist advance. It also combated the Berlin blockade by organising a massive airlift to the beleaguered former German capital, an operation in which New Zealand played a small role by providing three RNZAF aircrews. A programme of economic support, the Marshall Plan, provided the means of restoring the economies of the European states and removing the conditions in which communism flourished.

As this confrontation intensified, fears grew in New Zealand, as elsewhere, of a new world war. Although the Western powers had the atomic bomb, the continued presence of Soviet armies in central Europe raised the spectre of a renewal of their advance westward. Since the huge American forces had been repatriated after 1945, not a lot stood in their way. Far from relying on the United Nations, the Western democracies began to formulate defence plans, the centrepiece of which was the conclusion of the North Atlantic Treaty in 1949, from which emerged NATO.

Within five years of the German capitulation, therefore, New Zealand prepared to play its part in a third world war. Safe in the Pacific for the time being because of the lack of a threat and American naval preponderance, it again agreed to provide forces for a Commonwealth defence effort on the other side of the world. In what would be essentially a re-run of its initial Second World War effort, it would send an infantry division and air and naval forces to Egypt if war broke out with the Soviet Union. Unlike the 1939–45 effort, however, it committed itself in advance of hostilities and on a much faster timetable than that of 1939–40. This time the troops would need to be ready for combat in Egypt within 90 days. Compulsory military training was reintroduced in 1949.

New Zealand's approach remained unaltered even after the Cold War erupted in Asia, when Soviet-equipped North Korean forces invaded South Korea in 1950. Rooted firmly in the final stages of the Second World War, when both Soviet and American forces had entered the peninsula and established separate occupation zones, the Korean War greatly intensified the Cold War. It prompted a vast rearmament programme in the United States. But even as it dragged on the nature of warfare was changing. The nuclear age heralded at Hiroshima had now arrived. Both sides developed hydrogen bombs, vastly more destructive than the bombs dropped on Japan in 1945. By the mid-1950s a 'balance of terror', as Churchill termed it, made the great powers wary of direct confrontation. The chances of an all-out third world war along the lines of the second faded.

The onset of the Cold War benefited both former enemies, giving impetus to their rehabilitation. The prospect of a post-war peace settlement with Germany quickly faded, and a partition occured in 1949. In the territories occupied by the Western Allies, the German Federal Republic was formed, with its capital in Bonn. The Russians responded by creating the German Democratic Republic in their zone. The GFR emerged as a thriving, democratic state, contrasting sharply with the weak 1919 Weimar Republic that had succumbed in the early 1930s. The undemocratic East German regime also made economic progress but relied heavily on police control. In 1961 the construction by the East Germans of a wall around the Western zone of Berlin cemented the division. This would remain a symbol of the Cold War until 1989, when the East German regime, at last robbed of the backing of a faltering Soviet government, proved unable to resist popular demand for reunification. The destruction of the Berlin Wall marked the end of the Cold War, to be followed shortly by the demise of the Soviet Union itself in 1991.

In the Pacific the United States dominated the peace settlement with Japan. The rapid demilitarisation of Japan and the co-operative stance adopted by its people during the Occupation had rapidly impelled Americans towards a magnanimous peace. The onset of the Cold War strengthened this impulse towards a soft peace, especially as communism made huge gains in Asia. In the Chinese Civil War, which resumed in earnest after 1945, Mao Tse-tung's communist forces finally prevailed, leaving nationalist forces under Generalissimo Chiang Kai-shek clinging to a tenuous foothold on recently reclaimed Taiwan. The advent of the People's Republic of China in 1949, and its rapid conclusion of an alliance with Moscow, alarmed many in Washington and elsewhere. In this new situation, retaining Japan, with its immense productive capacity, in the Western camp seemed imperative to American policymakers. A harsh peace regime worked against this goal by arousing resentment. When Chinese troops intervened in Korea in late 1950, the sense of urgency in Washington became acute. American wishes prevailed. The settlement concluded at a conference in San Francisco in September 1951 restored Japan to full sovereignty early the following year.

Subsequent events have borne out the wisdom of this American approach. At the time, however, Australia and New Zealand firmly resisted it. Both saw telling lessons in the phoenix-like rise of Germany in just two decades after defeat in 1918, and feared that Japan might emulate it. They wanted Japan to be so constrained that it would never again be in a position to embark on an aggressive course. Complete demilitarisation and strict control of its capacity to recreate strategic weapons seemed the safest course. Only very reluctantly did they come round to accepting a completely freed Japan.

Decolonisation

Against the backdrop of the Cold War, and often influenced by it, another fundamental change with roots in the Second World War was taking place. Decolonisation profoundly altered the shape of the international system. Especially after American entry to the war, much had been made of the concept of self-determination for all peoples, extending beyond those countries in enemy hands. The British, as possessors of the world's largest empire, naturally found this unsettling. They agreed to proclaim the need for colonial territories to be administered for the good of their inhabitants, but they jibbed at proposals to bring all such territories within the scope of a UN trusteeship system. In the end they got their way; colonial powers, including those administering former German colonies as mandates of the now defunct League of Nations, did not have to include their territories. Even so, in signing the UN Charter, all members of the United Nations, including Britain, accepted an obligation to prepare the inhabitants of colonial territories for self-government or independence.

New Zealand strongly supported the trusteeship approach and made its 'most constructive contribution' to the UN Charter in this area.[198] Fraser actively participated in the discussions at San Francisco that fleshed out the concept, chairing the Trusteeship Committee. Afterwards, he ensured that New Zealand immediately offered to place its League mandate, Western Samoa, within the new system — the first member to take such a step.

If the trusteeship system provided a beacon for decolonisation, the effects of the war were its flame. The major colonial powers — Britain, France and Holland — had emerged from the struggle exhausted and financially stretched. Especially in the Pacific, their prestige had been badly dented by the rapid conquest of their territories by the Japanese and the humiliating treatment meted out to the former colonial overlords. Moreover, late in the war, the Japanese had encouraged indigenous nationalists who resisted attempts by the colonial powers to retake the reins of power, especially in Indo-China and the Dutch East Indies. Even in Africa, the needs of the war effort had brought changes in economic infrastructure that made the emergence of nationalist movements more likely.

The British government saw the writing on the wall. In 1947 it granted independence to India — the 'jewel in the crown' of the British Empire — whose abundant manpower and industrial capacity had buttressed the whole imperial system. Within a year Burma and Ceylon had also been set free. In South-East Asia the British fought a campaign against communist insurgents — mainly Chinese — in Malaya before granting that territory independence in 1957. By this time the winds of change were beginning to sweep through Africa. Ghana's independence in that year began a process that brought most of Africa to freedom within two decades, though not without bloody strife in some areas.

Searching for security

As the international framework changed, so too did New Zealand's stance in the world. In one sense, the war had reinforced its previous approach; its already immensely strong relationship with Britain had been tightened still further. New Zealanders took pride in the fact that they had stood shoulder to shoulder with Britain in the darkest days of the war and had played their part to their best endeavour in ensuring the eventual victory. They greatly admired Britain's capacity to overcome tragic reverses and to keep the goal in sight even when all seemed lost.

This admiration was reciprocated in Britain, where respect for the fighting qualities of New Zealand servicemen was universal. New Zealand's wholehearted support, both military and non-military, had replenished the fund of goodwill that existed from the previous conflict. New Zealanders' willingness to make sacrifices even after the war to help the British people recover from their ordeal reinforced British gratitude; though, as ever, self-interest buttressed sentiment, for New Zealand's wellbeing depended on Britain getting back on its feet economically. Food rationing continued until 1948, and a voluntary 'Aid to Britain' campaign supplemented the flow of produce. New Zealand also provided financial assistance.

Despite this tightening of New Zealand's ties with Britain, the war had changed New Zealand's status within the international system. It had been forced to grapple more directly with diplomatic problems than previously, it had seen the dangers of relying on traditional arrangements, and it had been pushed into unfamiliar situations and interactions with foreign powers. All encouraged a more assertive and focused approach. New Zealand emerged from the war with a new confidence in its ability to pursue and defend its own interests.

The means of doing so had been provided by the creation of the rudiments of a diplomatic service. New Zealand had started the war with one overseas post, in London, and one officer charged with advising the government on external affairs. It ended the war with additional posts in Washington and Moscow, as well as Canada and Australia, served by a properly constituted but understaffed department in Wellington. In finally cutting constitutional ties to Britain by belatedly adopting, in 1947, the operative sections of the 1931 Statute of Westminster, New Zealand gave formal expression to its changed status. While in theory New Zealand became an independent state by this action, in reality it had long been exercising the rights and duties of independent statehood. The step was of little more than symbolic importance.

For New Zealand, security remained a key concern after 1945. Thanks to Allied success in the Battle of the Atlantic, the war had brought no fundamental disruption of New Zealand's trading patterns, and no incentive existed to change them. Meat and dairy products continued to be sent to Britain under bulk-purchase arrangements for nine years after the end of the war. With wool also in high demand, New Zealand farmers enjoyed the benefits of assured markets. Not until the 1970s did New Zealand's dependence on the UK market begin to wane, and this was a result of British, not New Zealand, initiative. When Britain joined the European Economic Community, New Zealand's access to the British market became problematical. Trading on the goodwill in Britain resulting from the New Zealand war effort — and of course kinship ties — New Zealand secured concessions that eased its way while it sought alternative markets.

Despite its continuing close ties with Britain, New Zealand had no illusions about British capacity to provide security to the antipodean Dominions in all circumstances. The fall of Singapore had shaken the century-old faith in British power. Britain's ability to protect its empire in the east had long been a matter of doubt, and in a sense the Pacific War had been a contest to determine which of Japan and the United States would emerge as the dominant power in the region. Its outcome therefore could not fail to have far-reaching implications for Pacific-located New Zealand. Relief that the Americans prevailed was matched by recognition that henceforth it would be American power that would dominate the Pacific and that New Zealand must adjust to this new international fact of life, one potentially at odds with its still strong ties with Britain. The Pacific conflict, in which New Zealand's participation had been relatively limited, thus became of more long-term significance to it than that in Europe and the Middle East, where New Zealand had concentrated its effort, even though such concentration had been strictly in accordance with overall Allied strategy.

New Zealand (and Australia) did not at first look entirely to replace British power as a key element in their security. They wanted to buttress British power by securing a commitment of support from the United States, to remove the vulnerability imposed by declining British capacity. But their wartime alliance with the United States had ended on the day Japan surrendered, and Washington rebuffed overtures for some form of security arrangement from the two South Pacific states. Only when Washington became convinced of the need for an early peace settlement with Japan did an opening occur. In return for Australian and New Zealand agreement to a soft peace with Japan, the United States agreed to join them in a tripartite security arrangement. The Pacific Security (or ANZUS) Treaty was signed at San Francisco on 1 September 1951, a week before the Japanese peace treaty. It provided what Ambassador Sir Carl Berendsen, who signed for New Zealand, had earlier applauded as the 'greatest gift that the most powerful country in the world can offer to a small and comparatively helpless group of people'.[199] Even so New Zealand subsequently played down the significance of the new alliance. Although continuing to co-operate closely with Britain in defence matters in South-East Asia well into the 1970s, it had nonetheless taken a step of fundamental importance in its foreign policy.

The Second World War was the decisive event of the twentieth century for New Zealand. The roots of this war lay in the earlier conflict, the sacrifice and suffering of which seemed to have gone for naught as the peace was lost. While New Zealand's effort in the First World War had been substantial, that demanded by the Second World War was even more extensive, one that involved the whole community with varying degrees of enthusiasm for nearly six years. New Zealand's war confirmed its credentials as a small but effective ally, and its reputation has never stood higher than it did in 1945. The nature of that war not only gave further impetus to New Zealanders' developing sense of national identity but also greatly increased their confidence in their role in the world. The latter was important because the country was to face many new challenges arising from the war, which had set in motion forces that would in due course transform the international system as the great formal empires that had characterised the pre-war order disappeared. For New Zealanders the struggle had revealed, more directly than in the previous conflict, the depths of barbarity to which even ostensibly civilised states could descend. They recognised too the dangers now presented by the fearsome new weapons that had brought it to an end. To lose this peace, they knew, would be to court death and destruction on a scale that would dwarf that of 1939–45. In the next half-century the key issue for New Zealanders, as for all other peoples, was ensuring that the Second World War really was the war to end all wars — at least those between the Great Powers.

Notes

Chapter 1

[1] *Documents Relating to New Zealand's Participation in the Second World War*, I, p. 6, n.1.

[2] For a fuller discussion of New Zealand's declaration of war see FLW Wood, *The New Zealand People at War: Political and External Affairs*, chap. 1.

[3] David Lange, *Nuclear Free: The New Zealand Way*, p. 108.

[4] Sgt LH (Shorty) Lovegrove, *Cavalry! You Mean Horses?*, p. 8.

[5] Jack Rae, *Kiwi Spitfire Ace*, p. 2.

[6] Bruce S Bennett, *New Zealand's Moral Foreign Policy 1935–1939: The Promotion of Collective Security through the League of Nations*, p. 30.

[7] Wood, p. 11.

[8] Berendsen to Savage, 14 Oct 1938, quoted in IC McGibbon, *Blue-water Rationale: The Naval Defence of New Zealand 1914–1942*, p. 394.

[9] For a fuller discussion of New Zealand defence policy between the wars see WD McIntyre, *New Zealand Prepares for War: Defence Policy 1919–39* and McGibbon, *Blue-water Rationale*. On the Singapore Base generally see WD McIntyre, *The Rise and Fall of the Singapore Naval Base*.

[10] John Crawford, 'Introduction', in John Crawford (ed.), *Kia Kaha: New Zealand in the Second World War*, p. 1.

[11] Bennett, p. 25.

[12] Ibid., p. 4.

[13] Ibid., p. 17.

[14] Wood, p. 107.

Chapter 2

[15] 'Death of a Dreadnought', *Auckland Star*, 22 August 1964, p. 9.

[16] Anon, *Achilles*, p. 14.

[17] S.D. Waters, *Royal New Zealand Navy*, p. 48.

[18] 'Death of a Dreadnought', *Auckland Star*, 22 August 1964, p. 9.

[19] On the treatment of pacifists, see Nancy Taylor, *The New Zealand People at War: The Home Front* and David Grant, *Out in the Cold: Pacifists and Conscientious Objectors in New Zealand during World War II*.

[20] On the development of the New Zealand naval forces, see McGibbon, *Blue-water Rationale* and McIntyre, *New Zealand Prepares for War*.

[21] For a fuller description of New Zealand's wartime naval activities, see Waters, *Royal New Zealand Navy*.

[22] On the development of the RNZAF, see JMS Ross, *Royal New Zealand Air Force*.

[23] The fullest description of the activities of New Zealand airmen in the RAF is provided by HL Thompson, *New Zealanders in the Royal Air Force*, 3 vols. These may be supplemented by the biographies of four New Zealand officers in the RAF written by Vincent Orange, the details of which are provided in the Bibliography. There are a host of personal accounts by New Zealanders of their service in the RAF, including, for example, Air Vice Marshal CE Kay (one of the RNZAF pilots sent to the United Kingdom to ferry out the Wellingtons in 1939), *The Restless Sky: The Autobiography of an Airman*, and Jack Rae, *Kiwi Spitfire Ace*.

[24] A fuller description of this episode can be found in Laurie Barber, 'The New Zealand Colonels' "Revolt", 1938', *New Zealand Law Journal* (1977), and his entry on the same topic in Ian McGibbon (ed.), *The Oxford Companion to New Zealand Military History*, pp. 179–80.

[25] *Documents Relating to New Zealand's Participation in the Second World War*, Vol. I, p. 34.

[26] Lovegrove, p. 9.

[27] Pat Kane, *A Soldier's Story: A Mediterranean Odyssey*, pp. 4–5.

[28] On the Maori Battalion, see JF Cody, *28 (Maori) Battalion*. A more recent treatment, by a Maori, is to be found in Wira Gardiner, *Te Mura o te Ahi: The Story of the Maori Battalion*.

[29] Frank Rennie, *Regular Soldier: A Life in the New Zealand Army*, p. 28.

[30] On Fraser, see Michael Bassett with Michael King, *Tomorrow Comes the Song: A Life of Peter Fraser*, and Margaret Clark (ed.), *Peter Fraser, Master Politician*, especially the chapter by Ian Wards, 'Peter Fraser — Warrior Prime Minister'.

[31] McGibbon, *Blue-water Rationale*, pp. 350–2.

[32] For more detailed treatment of Freyberg's life and career see Paul Freyberg, *Bernard Freyberg VC: Soldier of Two Nations*; Laurie Barber and John Tonkin-Covell, *Freyberg: Churchill's Salamander*; WG Stevens, *Freyberg VC: The Man 1939–45*; Ian McGibbon, 'Bernard Cyril Freyberg', in *Dictionary of New Zealand Biography*, Vol. 5, pp. 177–9.

[33] Alan Stephens, *The Royal Australian Air Force*, p. 60.

Chapter 3

[34] Kain's story is told in Michael Burns, *Cobber Kain*.

[35] Quoted in Burns, p. 96.

36 Charles Gardner, *A.A.S.F.*, p. 189.

37 Kay, *The Restless Sky*, pp. 182–3.

38 Colin Gray, *Spitfire Patrol*, p. 22.

39 Len Richardson, 'Robert Semple', *Dictionary of New Zealand Biography*, Vol. 3, p. 467.

40 On the treatment of conscientious objectors, see JE Cookson, 'Appeal boards and conscientious objectors', in Crawford (ed.), *Kia Kaha*, pp. 173–98; Grant, *Out in the Cold*. For a personal account see Walter Lawry, *We Said "No!" to War*.

41 Grant, pp. 125, 178–9.

42 Megan Hutching (ed.), *Inside Stories: New Zealand Prisoners of War Remember*, pp. 50–1.

43 McGibbon, *Blue-water Rationale*, pp. 347–8.

44 See Gray, *Spitfire Patrol*, and Alan Deere, *Nine Lives*.

45 More details on Park can be obtained from Vincent Orange, *A Biography of Air Chief Marshal Sir Keith Park*.

46 Gray, pp. 59–60.

Chapter 4

47 *Documents Relating to New Zealand's Participation in the Second World War*, III, p. 208.

48 Quoted in Dan Davin, 'Lieutenant-General Lord Freyberg', in Field Marshal Sir Michael Carver (ed.), *The War Lords: Military Commanders of the Twentieth Century*, p. 584.

49 W.M. (41) 21st Conclusions, Minute 2, 27 Feb 1941, Public Record Office, Cabinet Office records, CAB65/21.

50 Sir Carl Berendsen, 'Reminiscences of an Ambassador', Vol. 4, ch. 7, p. 4.

51 'Mr Fraser's Questionnaire to the United Kingdom Chiefs of Staff on the Campaign in Greece and Crete', in WG McClymont, *To Greece*, app. III.

52 Berendsen, Vol. 4, p. 7–04.

53 Megan Hutching (ed.), *'A Unique Sort of Battle': New Zealanders remember Crete*, pp. 146–7.

54 Sergeant Richard Kean, quoted in Richard Campbell Begg and Peter H Liddle (eds.), *For Five Shillings a Day: Experiencing war, 1939–45*, p. 133.

55 Hutching, *'A Unique Sort of Battle'*, pp. 119–20.

56 Letter to Sir Apirana Ngata, quoted in Monty Soutar (ed.), *28 Maori Battalion, 23rd National Reunion*, pp. 36–7.

57 Capt P Tureia to Ngata, quoted in Soutar, p. 37.

58 Allan Yeoman, *The Long Road to Freedom*, pp. 57–8.

59 The best source on New Zealand's involvement in Crete is still Dan Davin's excellent official history, *Crete*. Aspects of the campaign have also been covered in Barber and Tonkin-Covell, *Freyberg: Churchill's Salamander* and Glyn Harper, *Kippenberger: An Inspired New Zealand Commander*. For personal recollections of New Zealand soldiers and seamen see Hutching, *'A Unique Sort of Battle'*.

60 The most authoritative source on New Zealand POWs is WW Mason, *Prisoners of War* in the official history series. There are numerous accounts by POWs of their experiences and escapes, including James Hargest, *Farewell Campo 12*, and WB Thomas, *Dare to be Free*. Personal recollections are provided in Megan Hutching (ed.), *Inside Stories*.

61 His story is told in James Caffin, *Partisan*.

Chapter 5

62 MRD Foot (ed.), *The Oxford Companion to World War II*, p. 1010.

63 McGibbon, *Blue-water Rationale*, p. 358.

64 *Documents Relating to New Zealand's Participation in the Second World War 1939–45*, III, pp. 18–19.

65 P Cosgrave, *Churchill at War, Vol. I: Alone 1939–40*, p. 330.

66 See HR Dean, *The Royal New Zealand Air Force in South-East Asia 1941–42*.

67 On coastwatchers, see DOW Hall, *Coastwatchers*.

68 TEY Seddon, *The Book of the Guard*, foreword.

69 Ibid.

70 Lieutenant John Hickley RN, quoted in Begg and Liddle, p. 249.

71 'F/O Geoff Fisken DFC', *New Zealand Fighter Pilots Association Journal*, no. 28 (2000), p. 15.

72 See Peter Elphick and Michael Smith, *Odd Man Out*.

73 On New Zealand POWs in Japanese hands, see Mason, *Prisoners of War*; DOW Hall, *Prisoners of Japan*; Hutching, *Inside Stories*.

74 Flight Lieutenant RD Millar, 'Narrative of Personal Experiences of War Experiences in the Far East', p. 12.

Chapter 6

75 Interview transcript, at www.danford.net/bargh.htm.

76 Begg and Liddle, pp. 255–6.

77 Rear Admiral Edwin T Layton, *'And I Was There': Pearl Harbor and Midway — Breaking the Secrets*, pp. 418–19.

78 See John Tonkin-Covell, 'The Collectors, Naval, Army and Air Intelligence in the New Zealand Armed Forces During the Second World War', unpublished PhD thesis, University of Waikato, 2000, pp. 96–106.

79 George C Kenney, *General Kenney Reports: A Personal History of the Pacific War*, p. 21.

80 Rennie, pp. 33–4.

81 Keith and Nona Morris, *Franklin Remembers: The war years 1939–1945*, p. 24.

82 No official history of the home defence effort was produced. The most detailed description of it is to be found in Peter Cooke, *Defending New Zealand: Ramparts on the Sea 1840–1950s*, 2 vols.

83 Eve Ebett, *When the Boys Were Away: New Zealand Women in World War II*, p. 140.

84 Wood, p. 233.

85 See Gavin Long, *Greece, Crete and Syria*, pp. 549–50.

86 See W David McIntyre, 'New Zealand, Japan, and the Twenty-Year Last Contest of Empires, 1931–1951', in Roger Peren (ed.), *Japan and New Zealand: 150 Years*, pp. 100–1.

Chapter 7

87 WE Murphy, *The Relief of Tobruk*, p. 420.

88 Sebastian Cox, ' "The Difference between White and Black": Churchill, Imperial Politics and Intelligence before the 1941 Crusader Offensive', *Intelligence and National Security*, Vol. 9, no. 3 (1994), p. 433.

89 Heinz Werner Schmidt, *With Rommel in the Desert*, p. 118.

90 WE Murphy, *Divisional Artillery*, p. 272.

91 Quoted in Major-General Sir Howard Kippenberger, *Infantry Brigadier*, pp. 110–11.

92 Major-General WG Stevens, *Problems of 2 NZEF*, p. 168.

93 See Ian McGibbon, *Kiwi Sappers: The Corps of Royal New Zealand Engineers' Century of Service*, pp. 82–8.

94 On the activities of New Zealanders in Greece, see MB McGlynn, *Special Service in Greece*. For an account by one of them, see Arthur Edmonds, *With Greek Guerrillas*.

95 The best sources on New Zealanders in the LRDG in North Africa are DOW Hall, *Long Range Desert Group in Libya* and Brendan O'Carroll, *The Kiwi Scorpions: The Story of the New Zealanders in the Long Range Desert Group*.

96 Lovegrove, p. 43.

97 Leonard Thornton, in Begg and Liddle (eds.), *For Five Shillings a Day: Experiencing War 1939–45*, p. 105.

98 See RIMH (ed.), *Germany and the Second World War, Vol. VI: The Global War*, p. 714.

99 JL Scoullar, *Battle for Egypt: The Summer of 1942*, p. 127.

100 © 2000, Richard Campbell Begg and Peter H Liddle, (eds.), *For Five Shillings A Day: Experiencing war 1939–45*, HarperCollins, London, p. 98.

101 Harper, p. 163.

102 Kippenberger, p. 180.

103 Kane, p. 21.

104 Lovegrove, p. 30.

105 Ibid., p. 29.

106 John MacGibbon (ed.), *Struan's War*, p. 78.

107 Ibid., p. 76.

108 Sally Mathieson (ed.), *Bill Gentry's War 1939–1945*, p. 160.

109 Thornton, in Begg and Liddle, p. 176.

110 For a detailed description of the battle, see Ronald Walker, *Alam Halfa to Alamein*.

111 Roger Smith, *Up the Blue: A Kiwi Private's View of the Second World War*, p. 48.

112 MacGibbon, p. 129.

113 Harper, p. 231.

114 BH Liddell-Hart (ed.), *The Rommel Papers*, p. 240.

115 Schmidt, p. 163.

Chapter 8

116 Michael Smith, *The Emperor's Codes: The Breaking of Japan's Secret Ciphers*, p. 175.

117 Ebett, pp. 150–1.

118 The most detailed accounts of the wartime US presence in New Zealand are Harry Bioletti, *The Yanks are Coming: The American Invasion of New Zealand 1942–1944* and Denys Bevan, *United States Forces in New Zealand 1942–1945*.

119 Eric Bergerud, *Touched With Fire: The Land War in the South Pacific*, p. 497.

120 The fullest treatment of this incident is to be found in Mike Nicolaidi, *The Featherston Chronicles: A Legacy of War*.

[121] On Barrowclough, see John Crawford, 'A campaign on two fronts: Barrowclough in the Pacific', in Crawford, *Kia Kaha*, and JAB Crawford, 'Harold Eric Barrowclough', in *Dictionary of New Zealand Biography*, Vol. 5, pp. 37–9.

[122] Colin R Larsen, *Pacific Commandos, New Zealanders and Fijians in Action: A History of Southern Independent Commando and First Commando Fiji Guerrillas*, p. 138.

[123] Larsen, p. 122.

[124] On this aspect, see Ross Galbreith, 'Dr Marsden and Admiral Halsey', in Crawford, *Kia Kaha*.

[125] Squadron Leader Bob Spurdle, *The Blue Arena*, p. 134.

[126] Ibid., pp. 144, 146.

[127] Ibid., p. 152.

[128] Ian McGibbon (ed.), *Undiplomatic Dialogue: Letters between Carl Berendsen and Alister McIntosh 1943–52*, pp. 23–4.

[129] McIntosh to Berendsen, 16 June 1943, in McGibbon, *Undiplomatic Dialogue*, pp. 29–30.

[130] Keith Mulligan, *Kittyhawks and Coconuts*, pp. 129–30.

[131] McGibbon, *Undiplomatic Dialogue*, p. 108.

Chapter 9

[132] Fay Main, 'WAACS WW2 Fort Dorset 10th Heavy Regiment', unpublished typescript.

[133] There is no scholarly account of the women's services in the Second World War. The best sources are Bathia Mackenzie (compiler), *The WAAF Book, A Scrapbook of Wartime Memories*; Iris Latham (compiler), *The WAAC Story: The Story of the New Zealand Women's Auxiliary Army Corps*; Grant Howard, *Happy in the Service: An Illustrated History of the Women's Royal New Zealand Naval Service 1942–1977*.

[134] Main, 'WAACS WW2 Fort Dorset 10th Heavy Regiment'.

[135] Marguerite Scott, 'Reminiscences of Service in the Wrens, 1942–1945', Alexander Turnbull Library, Wellington.

[136] Judith Fyfe (ed.), *War Stories our Mothers Never Told Us*, pp. 124–5.

[137] Quoted in Ebett, *When the Boys Were Away*, pp. 52–3.

[138] Fyfe, p. 38.

[139] New Zealand's wartime economy has been exhaustively examined in JVT Baker, *War Economy*.

[140] Ebett, p. 150.

[141] McGibbon, *Undiplomatic Dialogue*, p. 10.

[142] For more detailed coverage of the furlough affair, see John McLeod, *Myth and Reality: The New Zealand Soldier in World War II*, chap. 10.

Chapter 10

[143] Kane, pp. 70–4.

[144] On the Dodecanese operation see RL Kay, *Long Range Desert Group in the Mediterranean*, and Brendan O'Carroll, *The Kiwi Scorpions*.

[145] The most authoritative source on New Zealand's involvement in Italy remains the official history: NC Phillips, *Italy, Volume I: The Sangro to Cassino*, and RL Kay, *Italy, Volume II: From Cassino to Trieste*.

146 Kane, p. 68.

147 Lovegrove, p. 78.

148 Kippenberger, p. 324.

149 Kane, p. 79.

150 Kippenberger, pp. 344–5

151 Ibid., p. 347.

152 Ibid., p. 353.

153 Smith, *Up the Blue*, p. 193.

154 Soutar, p. 44.

155 Smith, pp. 228–9.

156 Alex Danchev and Daniel Todman (eds.), *War Diaries 1939–1945: Field Marshal Lord Alanbrooke*, p. 536.

157 Danchev and Todman, p. 559.

158 John Crawford, *North from Taranto: New Zealand and the Liberation of Italy 1943–45*, p. 58.

159 Kane, p. 132.

160 Geoffrey Cox, *The Road to Trieste*, p. 10.

161 Alex Danchev, 'Great Britain: The Indirect Strategy', in David Reynolds, Warren F Kimball and AO Chubarian (eds.), *Allies at War: The Soviet, American, and British Experience, 1939–1945*, p. 12.

Chapter 11

162 Wing Commander HL Thompson, *New Zealanders with the Royal Air Force*, Vol. 2, p. 36; Clay Blair, *Hitler's U-Boat War: The Hunted 1942–1945*, p. 397.

163 Martin Middlebrook, *Convoy: The Battle for Convoys SC.122 and HX.229*, pp. 247–8.

164 John Holm, *No Place to Linger: Saga of a Wartime Atlantic Kiwi*, pp. 105, 115–16, 120, 165.

165 See David Stevens, *U-boat Far from Home: The epic voyage of U 862 to Australia and New Zealand*.

166 Denis Glover, *Hot Water Sailor*, pp. 144–5.

167 Christina Goulter, 'RAF's Coastal Command anti-shipping campaign', in Crawford, *Kia Kaha*, pp. 90–1.

168 Vincent Orange, 'New Zealand airmen over Europe and the Mediterranean, in Crawford, *Kia Kaha*, p. 67.

169 Thompson, Vol. I, p. 198.

170 Ibid., Vol. II, p. 144.

171 Quoted in ibid., Vol. II, p. 145.

172 Denis Glover, *Hot Water Sailor*, p. 171.

173 Denis Glover, *D Day*, pp. 10–11.

174 Group Captain Desmond Scott, *Typhoon Pilot*, p. 112.

175 Ibid., p. 122.

176 Cox, *The Road to Trieste*, p. 177.

177 Ibid., p. 2.

178 Ibid., p. 190.

Chapter 12

[179] Bryan Cox, 'January 15th 1945, The RNZAF's Blackest Day', *New Zealand Fighter Pilots Association Journal*, no. 24 (1999), p. 7.

[180] Mulligan, p. 169.

[181] Hutching, *Inside Stories*, p. 267.

[182] On Z Special Unit, see FA Wigzell, *New Zealand Involvement 'Z' Special Unit: Special Operations Australia AIB*.

[183] Lewis Martin, 'Memoirs', unpublished typescript, p. 113.

[184] On New Zealand's atomic effort see Owen Wilkes, 'New Zealand and the atom bomb', in Crawford, *Kia Kaha*.

[185] Fyfe, p. 127.

[186] The Jayforce experience is traced in Laurie Brocklebank, *Jayforce: New Zealand and the Military Occupation of Japan 1945–48*.

[187] See Ian McGibbon, 'New Zealand Perceptions of Japan, 1945–1965', in Peren, *Japan and New Zealand*, pp. 123–43.

Chapter 13

[188] Stéphane Audoin-Rouzeau and Annette Becker, *1914–1918 Understanding the Great War*, pp. 22–3.

[189] Nancy Taylor, *The Home Front*, Vol. II, pp. 1285–6.

[190] Ibid., p. 1286.

[191] The most important sources on women in the Second World War are Taylor, *The Home Front*; Deborah Montgomerie, *The Women's War: New Zealand Women 1939–45*; and Eve Ebett, *When the Boys Were Away: New Zealand Women in World War II*. Personal recollections are provided in Lauris Edmonds (ed.), *Women in Wartime: New Zealand Women Tell their Story* and Judith Fyfe (ed.), *War Stories our Mothers Never Told Us*.

[192] On the MWEO, see Claudia Orange, 'An Exercise in Maori Autonomy: The Rise and Demise of the Maori War Effort Organisation', *NZ Journal of History*, Vol. 21, no.1, 1987, and Claudia Orange, 'The price of citizenship? The Maori war effort', in Crawford, *Kia Kaha*.

[193] On this aspect, see Brian O'Brien, 'War literature', in McGibbon, *Oxford Companion to New Zealand Military History*.

[194] See, for example, Jim Henderson, *Gunner Inglorious*; John Mulgan, *Report on Experience*; Geoffrey Cox, *A Tale of Two Battles*.

[195] Holm, p. 166.

[196] See McLeod, *Myth and Reality*.

[197] For an expression of this viewpoint see James Belich, *Paradise Reforged: A History of the New Zealanders from the 1880s to the Year 2000*.

[198] Malcolm Templeton (ed.), *An Eye, an Ear and a Voice: 50 years in New Zealand's external relations 1943–1993*, p. 23.

[199] McGibbon, *Undiplomatic Dialogue*, p. 205.

Bibliography

Primary Sources

Documents
Cabinet Office records, Public Record Office, London.

Published documents
Appendices to the Journals of the House of Representatives, 1948.

Documents Relating to New Zealand's Participation in the Second World War 1939–45, 3 vols, War History Branch, Dept. of Internal Affairs, Wellington, 1949–63.

KAY, Robin (ed.), *Documents on New Zealand External Relations, Volume I, The Australian-New Zealand Agreement 1944*, Historical Publications Branch, Dept. of Internal Affairs, Wellington, 1972.

Newspaper
Auckland Star, 1964.

Secondary Sources

Books

ANON, *Achilles*, Wellington, HMS *Achilles*, nd [1946].

AUDOIN-ROUZEAU, Stéphane, and Annette Becker, *1914–1918: Understanding the Great War*, New York, 2002.

BAKER, J.V.T., *War Economy*, Historical Publications Branch, Dept. of Internal Affairs, Wellington, 1965.

BARBER, Laurie, and John Tonkin-Covell, *Freyberg: Churchill's Salamander*, Century Hutchinson, Auckland, 1989.

BARBER, Laurie, and Ken Henshall, *The Last War of Empires: Japan and the Pacific War*, Bateman, Auckland, 1999.

BASSETT, Michael, with Michael King, *Tomorrow Comes the Song: A Life of Peter Fraser*, Penguin, Auckland, 2000.

BEEVOR, Anthony, *Crete, The Battle and the Resistance*, John Murray, London, 1991.

BEGG, Richard Campbell, and Peter H. Liddle (eds.), *For Five Shillings a Day: Experiencing war, 1939–45*, HarperCollins, London, 2000.

BELICH, James, *Paradise Reforged: A History of the New Zealanders from the 1880s to the Year 2000*, Allen Lane/Penguin Press, Auckland, 2001.

BENNETT, Bruce S., *New Zealand's Moral Foreign Policy 1935–1939: The Promotion of Collective Security Through the League of Nations*, New Zealand Institute of International Affairs, Wellington, 1988.

BERGERUD, Eric, *Touched With Fire: The Land War in the South Pacific*, Viking, New York, 1996.

BEVAN, Denys, *United States Forces in New Zealand 1942–1945*, Macpherson Publishing, Alexandra, 1992.

BIOLETTI, Harry, *The Yanks are Coming: The American Invasion of New Zealand 1942–1944*, Century Hutchinson, Auckland, 1989.

BLAIR, Clay, *Hitler's U-Boat War: The Hunted 1942–1945*, Random House, New York, 1998.

BLYTHE, John, *Soldiering On: A Soldier's War in North Africa and Italy*, Hutchinson, Auckland, 1989.

BROCKLEBANK, Laurie, *Jayforce: New Zealand and the Military Occupation of Japan 1945–48*, Oxford University Press, Auckland, 1997.

BURNS, Michael, *Cobber Kain*, Random Century, Auckland, 1992.

BURROWS, J.T., *Pathway Among Men*, Whitcombe and Tombs, Christchurch, 1974.

CAFFIN, James, *Partisan*, Collins, Auckland, 1945.

CALVOCORESSI, Peter, Guy Wint and John Pritchard, *Total War: The Causes and Courses of the Second World War*, Allen Lane/Penguin Press, Harmondsworth, 1972.

CARVER, Field Marshal Sir Michael, *The War Lords: Military Commanders of the Twentieth Century*, Weidenfeld and Nicolson, London, 1976.

CLARK, Margaret (ed.), *Peter Fraser, Master Politician*, Dunmore Press, Palmerston North, 1998.

CODY, J.F., *28 (Maori) Battalion*, War History Branch, Dept. of Internal Affairs, Wellington, 1956.

COOKE, Peter, *Defending New Zealand: Ramparts on the Sea 1840–1950s,* Defence of New Zealand Study Group, Wellington, 2000.

COSGRAVE, Patrick, *Churchill at War, Vol I: Alone 1939–40*, Robinson, London, 1974.

COX, Bryan, *Pacific Scrapbook 1943–1947*, McGraw Hill, Sydney, 1997.

— *Too Young to Die: The story of a New Zealand fighter pilot in the Pacific war*, Century Hutchinson, Auckland, 1987.

COX, Geoffrey, *A Tale of Two Battles: A Personal Memoir of Crete and the Western Desert 1941*, William Kimber & Co., London, 1987.

— *The Road to Trieste*, Heinemann, London, 1947.

CRAWFORD, John (ed.), *Kia Kaha: New Zealand and the Second World War*, Oxford University Press, Auckland, 2000.

CRAWFORD, John, *Atlantic Kiwis: New Zealand and the Battle of the Atlantic*, New Zealand Defence Force, Wellington, 1993.

— *New Zealand's Pacific Frontline: Guadalcanal-Solomon Islands Campaign 1942–45*, New Zealand Defence Force, Wellington, 1992.

— *North from Taranto: New Zealand and the Liberation of Italy 1943–45*, New Zealand Defence Force, Wellington, 1994.

DANCHEV, Alex, and Daniel Todman (eds.), *War Diaries 1939–1945: Field Marshal Lord Alanbrooke*, Phoenix Press, London, 2002.

Bibliography

DAVIN, Dan, *Crete*, War History Branch, Dept. of Internal Affairs, Wellington, 1953.

DEAN, H.R., *The Royal New Zealand Air Force in South-East Asia 1941–42*, War History Branch, Dept. of Internal Affairs, Wellington, 1952.

DEAR, I.C.B. (ed.), *The Oxford Companion to World War II,* Oxford University Press, Oxford, 2001.

DEERE, Alan, *Nine Lives*, Hodder, London, 1959.

DORMAN, T.E., *The Green War*, T.E. Dorman, Christchurch, 1997.

EBETT, Eve, *When the Boys were Away: New Zealand Women in World War II*, Reed, Wellington, 1984.

EDMONDS, Arthur, *With Greek Guerrillas*, A. Edmonds, Putaruru, 1998.

EDMONDS, Lauris (ed.) with Carolyn Milward, *Women in Wartime: New Zealand Women Tell Their Story*, Government Printing Office Publishing, Wellington, 1986.

ELPHICK, Peter, and Michael Smith, *Odd Man Out: The Story of the Singapore Traitor*, Hodder and Stoughton, London, 1993.

FREYBERG, Paul, *Bernard Freyberg, VC: Soldier of Two Nations*, Hodder & Stoughton, London, 1991.

FYFE, Judith (ed.), *War Stories our Mothers Never Told Us*, Penguin Books, Auckland, 1995.

GARDEN, R.J.P., *Survival in Malaya January to October 1942*, R.J.P. Garden, Dunedin, 1992.

GARDINER, Wira, *Te Mura o te Ahi: The Story of the Maori Battalion*, Reed, Auckland, 1992.

GARDNER, Charles, *A.A.S.F.*, Hutchinson, London, 1940.

GILLESPIE, O.A., *The Pacific*, War History Branch, Dept. of Internal Affairs, Wellington, 1952.

GLOVER, Denis, *D Day*, Caxton Press, Christchurch, 1944.

— *Hot Water Sailor*, Reed, Wellington, 1962.

GOOD, Lindsay, *Mussolini, Bella Maria & Tojo: A Kiwi soldier's memoir of World War II, through New Zealand, Italy and Japan*, Steele Roberts, Wellington, 2003.

GOULTER, Christina J.M., *A Forgotten Offensive: Royal Air Force Coastal Command's Anti-shipping Campaign, 1940–1945*, Frank Cass, London, 1995.

GRANT, David, *Out in the Cold: Pacifists and Conscientious Objectors in New Zealand during World War II*, Reed Methuen, Auckland, 1986.

GRAY, Colin, *Spitfire Patrol*, Hutchinson, Auckland, 1990.

HALL, D.O.W., *Coastwatchers*, War History Branch, Dept. of Internal Affairs, Wellington, 1951.

— *Long Range Desert Group in Libya, 1940–41*, War History Branch, Dept. of Internal Affairs, Wellington, 1949.

— *Prisoners of Japan*, War History Branch, Dept. of Internal Affairs, Wellington, 1949.

— *Women at War*, War History Branch, Dept. of Internal Affairs, Wellington, 1948.

HARGEST, James, *Farewell Campo 12*, M. Joseph, London, 1945.

HARPER, Glyn, *Kippenberger: An Inspired New Zealand Commander*, HarperCollins, Auckland, 1997.

HENDERSON, Jim, *Gunner Inglorious*, Tombs, Wellington, 1945.

HOLM, John, *No Place to Linger: Saga of a Wartime Atlantic Kiwi*, Holmwork Publishers, Wellington, 1985.

HOULTON, Johnnie, *Spitfire Strikes: A New Zealand Fighter Pilot's Story*, Murray, London, 1995.

HOWARD, Grant, *Happy in the Service: An Illustrated History of the Women's Royal New Zealand Naval Service 1942–1977*, Word Publishers for the New Zealand Ex-Wren's Association, Auckland, 1985.

HUTCHING, Megan (ed.), *'A Unique Sort of Battle': New Zealanders Remember Crete*, HarperCollins in association with the History Group, Ministry for Culture and Heritage, Auckland, 2001.

— *Inside Stories: New Zealand POWs Remember the Second World War*, HarperCollins in association with the History Group, Ministry for Culture and Heritage, Auckland, 2002.

JACOBS, Susan, *Fighting with the Enemy: New Zealand POWs and the Italian Resistance*, Penguin, Auckland, 2003.

KANE, Pat, *A Soldier's Story: A Mediterranean Odyssey*, Quality Publications, Wellington, 1995.

KAY, Air Vice-Marshal C.E., *The Restless Sky: The Autobiography of an Airman*, Harrap, London, 1964.

KAY, Robin, *Italy, Volume II: From Cassino to Trieste*, Historical Publications Branch, Dept. of Internal Affairs, Wellington, 1967.

— *Long Range Desert Group in the Mediterranean*, War History Branch, Dept. of Internal Affairs, Wellington, 1950.

KEEGAN, John, *The Second World War*, Hutchinson, Harmondsworth, 1990.

KENNEY, George C., *General Kenney Reports: A Personal History of the Pacific War*, Duell, Sloan and Pearce, New York, 1949.

KERSHAW, Ian, *Hitler, Vol. I: 1889–1936: Hubris, Vol. II: 1936–1945: Nemesis*, Longman, London, 1998, 2000.

KING, J. Norby, *Green Kiwi versus German Eagle: The Journal of a New Zealand Spitfire Pilot*, J.N. King, Papamoa, 1991.

KIPPENBERGER, Major-General Sir Howard, *Infantry Brigadier*, Oxford University Press, 1949.

LANGE, David, *Nuclear Free: The New Zealand Way*, Penguin, Auckland, 1990.

LARSEN., Colin R., *Pacific Commando: New Zealanders and Fijians in Action, A History of Southern Independent Commando and First Commando Fiji Guerrillas*, A.H. & A.W. Reed, Wellington, 1946.

LATHAM, Iris (compiler), *The WAAC Story: The Story of the New Zealand Women's Auxiliary Army Corps*, I. Latham, Wellington, 1986.

LAWRY, Walter, with Allan Handyside and Jack Rogers, *We Said 'No!' to War*, published for W. Lawry by Wordspinners Unlimited, Dunedin, 1994.

LAYTON, Rear Admiral Edwin T., *'And I Was There': Pearl Harbor and Midway — Breaking the Secrets*, Morrow, New York, 1985.

LIDDELL-HART, B.H. (ed.), *The Rommel Papers*, Collins, London, 1953.

LISSINGTON, M.P., *New Zealand and Japan 1900–1941*, Govt. Printer, Wellington, 1972.

— *New Zealand and the United States 1840–1944*, Govt. Printer., Wellington, 1972.

LONG, Gavin, *Greece, Crete and Syria*, Australian War Memorial, Canberra, 1953.

LOVEGROVE MM, Sgt L.H. (Shorty), *Cavalry! You Mean Horses?*, Glendorran, Nelson, 1994.

McCLYMONT, W.G., *To Greece*, War History Branch, Dept. of Internal Affairs, Wellington, 1959.

MacGIBBON, John (ed.), *Struan's War*, Ngaio Press, Wellington, 2001.

McGIBBON, Ian, *Blue-water Rationale: The Naval Defence of New Zealand 1914–1942*, Govt. Printer, Wellington, 1981.

— *Kiwi Sappers: The Corps of Royal New Zealand Engineers' Century of Service*, Reed, in association with the Corps of Royal New Zealand Engineers, Auckland, 2002.

McGIBBON, Ian (ed.), *The Oxford Companion to New Zealand Military History*, Oxford University Press, Auckland, 2000.

— *Undiplomatic Dialogue: Letters between Carl Berendsen and Alister McIntosh 1943–52*, Auckland University Press in association with the Ministry of Foreign Affairs and Trade and the Historical Branch, Dept. of Internal Affairs, Auckland, 1993.

McGLYNN, M.B., *Special Service in Greece*, War History Branch, Dept. of Internal Affairs, Wellington, 1953.

McINTYRE, W. David, *New Zealand Prepares for War: Defence Policy 1919–39*, University of Canterbury Press with assistance from Historical Branch, Dept. of Internal Affairs and the Ministry of Defence, Christchurch, 1988.

— *The Rise and Fall of the Singapore Naval Base*, Macmillan, London, 1979.

McLEOD, John, *Myth and Reality: The New Zealand Soldier in World War II*, Reed Methuen, Auckland, 1986.

MACKENZIE, Bathia (compiler), *The WAAF Book: A Scrapbook of Wartime Memories*, Whitcoulls, Christchurch, 1982.

McKINNON, Malcolm, *Independence and Foreign Policy: New Zealand in the World since 1935*, Auckland University Press, Auckland, 1993.

MASON, W.W. *Prisoners of War*, War History Branch, Dept. of Internal Affairs, Wellington, 1954.

MATHIESON, Sally (ed.), *Bill Gentry's War 1939–45*, Dunmore Press, Palmerston North, 1996.

MIDDLEBROOK, Martin, *Convoy: The Battle for Convoys SC.122 and HX.229*, Allen Lane, London, 1976.

— *The Battle of Hamburg: Allied Bomber Forces against a German City in 1943*, Scribner, New York, 1981.

MONTGOMERIE, Deborah, *The Women's War: New Zealand Women 1939–45*, Auckland University Press, Auckland, 2001.

MORRIS, Keith and Nona, *Franklin Remembers: The war years 1939–1945*, Franklin Historical Society, Pukekohe, 1992.

MULGAN, John, *Report on Experience*, Oxford University Press, London, 1947.

MULLIGAN, Keith, *Kittyhawks and Coconuts*, New Zealand Wings, Paraparaumu, 1995.

MURPHY, W.E., *2nd New Zealand Divisional Artillery*, Historical Publications Branch, Dept. of Internal Affairs, Wellington, 1966.

— *The Relief of Tobruk*, War History Branch, Dept. of Internal Affairs, Wellington, 1961.

NICOLAIDI, Mike, *The Featherston Chronicles: A Legacy of War*, HarperCollins, Auckland, 1999.

O'CARROLL, Brendan, *The Kiwi Scorpions: The Story of the New Zealanders in the Long Range Desert Group*, Token Pub., Devon, 2000.

— *Bearded Brigands*, Ngaio Press, Wellington, 2002.

ORANGE, Claudia (ed.), *The Dictionary of New Zealand Biography*, Vols. 4 and 5, Auckland University Press, Auckland, 1998, 2000.

ORANGE, Vincent, *A Biography of Air Chief Marshal Sir Keith Park GCB, KBE, MC, DFC, DCL*, Methuen, London, 1984.

— *Coningham: A Biography of Air Marshal Sir Arthur Coningham KCB, KBE, DSO, MC, DFC, AFC*, Methuen, London, 1990.

— *Ensor's Endeavour: A Biography of Wing Commander Mick Ensor DSO & Bar, DFC & Bar, AFC, RNZAF & RAF*, Methuen, London, 1994.

— *The Road to Biggin Hill: A Life of Wing Commander Johnny Checketts DSO, DFC, American Silver Star, Polish Cross of Valour, RNZAF*, Mallinson Rendel, Wellington, 1987.

PEREN, Roger (ed.), *Japan and New Zealand: 150 Years*, New Zealand Centre for Japanese Studies, Massey University, on behalf of the Ministry of Foreign Affairs, Tokyo, in association with the Historical Branch, Dept. of Internal Affairs, Palmerston North, 1999.

PHILLIPS, N.C., *Italy, Vol. I: The Sangro to Cassino*, War History Branch, Dept. of Internal Affairs, Wellington, 1957.

POWELL, Paul, *Green Sailor, Green Sea*, P. Powell, Dunedin, nd.

RAE, Jack, *Kiwi Spitfire Ace*, Grub Street, London, 2001.

RENNIE, Frank, *Regular Soldier: A Life in the New Zealand Army*, Endeavour Press, Auckland, 1986.

RESEARCH INSTITUTE FOR MILITARY HISTORY (ed.), *Germany and the Second World War, Vol. II The Mediterranean, South-east Europe, and North Africa 1939–1941, Vol. VI The Global War*, Clarendon Press, Oxford, 1995, 2001.

REYNOLDS, David, Warren F. Kimball and A.O. Chubarian (eds.), *Allies at War: The Soviet, American, and British Experience, 1939–1945*, St. Martin's Press, New York, 1994.

ROSS, Squadron-Leader J.M.S., *Royal New Zealand Air Force*, War History Branch, Dept. of Internal Affairs, Wellington, 1955.

SANDERS, James, *Venturer Courageous: Group Captain Leonard Trent V.C., D.F.C.*, Hutchinson, Auckland, 1983.

SCHMIDT, Heinz Werner, *With Rommel in the Desert*, Harrap, London, 1951.

SCOTT, Group Captain Desmond, *Typhoon Pilot*, Secker & Warburg, London, 1982.

SCOULLAR, J.L., *Battle for Egypt: The Summer of 1942*, War History Branch, Dept. of Internal Affairs, Wellington, 1955.

SEDDON, Captain T.E.Y. *et al, The Book of the Guard*, T.E.Y. Seddon, Wellington, 1944.

SIMPSON, Tony, *The Battle for Crete, 1941*, Hodder and Stoughton, London, 1981.

SMITH, Michael, *The Emperor's Codes: The Breaking of Japan's Secret Ciphers*, Penguin, Harmondsworth, 2002.

SMITH, Roger, *Up the Blue: A Kiwi Private's View of the Second World War*, Ngaio Press, Wellington, 2000.

SOUTAR, Monty, *28 Maori Battalion, 23rd National Reunion*, Maori Battalion Reunion Committee, Palmerston North, 2002.

SPURDLE, Squadron Leader Bob, *The Blue Arena*, William Kimber, London, 1986.

STEPHENS, Alan, *The Royal Australian Air Force*, Oxford University Press, Canberra, 2001.

STEVENS, David, *U-boat Far from Home: The epic voyage of U 862 to Australia and New Zealand*, Allen & Unwin, St Leonards NSW, 1997.

STEVENS, Major-General W.G., *Bardia to Enfidaville*, War History Branch, Dept. of Internal Affairs, Wellington, 1962.

— *Freyberg, V.C.: The Man 1939–45*, Reed, Auckland, 1965.

— *Problems of 2 NZEF*, War History Branch, Dept. of Internal Affairs, Wellington, 1958.

TAYLOR, Nan, *The New Zealand People at War: The Home Front*, Historical Publications Branch, Dept. of Internal Affairs & Govt. Printer, Wellington, 1986.

TEMPLETON Malcolm (ed.), *An Eye, an Ear and a Voice: 50 Years in New Zealand's External Relations 1943–1993*, Ministry of Foreign Affairs and Trade, Wellington, 1993.

THOMAS, W.B., *Dare to be Free*, Pan Books, London, 1951.

THOMPSON, Wing-Commander H.L., *New Zealanders with the Royal Air Force*, 3 vols, War History Branch, Dept. of Internal Affairs, Wellington, 1953–59.

VERCOE, Tony, *Yesterday's Drums*, Steele Roberts, Wellington, 2001.

WALKER, Ronald, *Alam Halfa and Alamein*, Historical Publications Branch, Dept. of Internal Affairs, Wellington, 1967.

WATERS, S.D., *German Raiders in the Pacific*, War History Branch, Dept. of Internal Affairs, Wellington, 1949.

— *Royal New Zealand Navy*, War History Branch, Dept. of Internal Affairs, Wellington, 1956.

WIGZELL, F.A., *New Zealand Involvement 'Z' Special Unit: Special Operations Australia AIB*, F.A. Wigzell, Auckland, 1995.

WILLIAMS, Tony, *Anzacs: Stories from New Zealanders at War*, Hodder Moa Beckett, Auckland, 2000.

WOOD, F.L.W., *The New Zealand People at War: Political and External Affairs*, Historical Publications Branch, Dept. of Internal Affairs in association with Reed, Wellington, 1958.

YEOMAN, Allan, *The Long Road to Freedom*, Random Century, Auckland, 1991.

Bibliography

Articles

BARBER, Laurie, 'The New Zealand Colonels' "Revolt", 1938', *New Zealand Law Journal*, 6 December 1977.

BELL, Christopher M., 'The "Singapore Strategy" and the Deterrence of Japan: Winston Churchill, the Admiralty and the Dispatch of Force Z', *English Historical Review*, Vol. 116, no. 467, 2001.

COX, Bryan, 'January 15th 1945, The RNZAF's Blackest Day', *New Zealand Fighter Pilots Association Journal*, no. 24, 1999.

COX, Sebastian, '"The Difference between White and Black": Churchill, Imperial Politics, and Intelligence before the 1941 Crusader Offensive', *Intelligence and National Security*, Vol. 9, no. 3, 1994.

— 'F/O Geoff Fisken DFC', *New Zealand Fighter Pilots Association Journal*, no. 28, 2000.

HARPER, Glyn, 'Threat perception and politics: the deployment of Australian and New Zealand ground forces in the Second World War', *Journal of the Australian War Memorial*, no. 20, 1992.

LAWLOR, Sheila, 'Greece, March 1941: The Politics of British Military Intervention', *Historical Journal*, Vol. 25, no. 4, 1982.

McGIBBON, Ian, 'New Zealand and Germany at War', in James Bade (ed.), *In the Shadow of War, The German Connection with New Zealand in the Twentieth Century,* Auckland, 1998.

ORANGE, Claudia, 'An Exercise in Maori Autonomy: The Rise and Demise of the Maori War Effort Organisation', *New Zealand Journal of History*, Vol. 21, no. 1, 1987.

TARLING, Nicholas, 'The Wars of British Succession', *New Zealand Journal of History*, Vol. 15, no. 1, 1981.

Theses

TONKIN-COVELL, John, 'The Collectors, Naval, Army and Air Intelligence in the New Zealand Armed Forces During the Second World War', PhD thesis, University of Waikato, 2000.

Unpublished typescripts

BERENDSEN, Sir Carl, 'Reminiscences of an Ambassador', 5 vols, nd, Victoria University of Wellington Library.

MAIN, Fay, 'WAACS WW2 Fort Dorset 10th Heavy Regiment', unpublished typescript (copy in possession of the author).

MARTIN, Lewis, 'Memoirs', Alexander Turnbull Library, Wellington.

MILLAR, Flight Lieutenant R.D., 'Narrative of Personal Experiences of War Experiences in the Far East', New Zealand Defence Force Library, Wellington.

SCOTT, Marguerite, 'Reminiscences of Service in the Wrens, 1942–1945', Alexander Turnbull Library, Wellington.

Websites

www.danford.net/bargh.htm
www.nzhistory.net

Index